People *of the* West Desert

The Bishop family

Three generations of a family on the Gosiute Reservation in Ibapah, Utah—Molly McCurdie, son George, and grandson Kurt Bishop. When Molly died in 1994, the tribe lost a link to its past. McCurdie was the last Gosiute who knew how to weave willows and work leather into cradleboards for infants and string beads into symbols from the past. The Gosiutes were among the first of the diverse people of the West Desert.

People *of the* West Desert

Finding Common Ground

Craig Denton

Utah State University Press
Logan, Utah   1999

Utah State University Press
Logan, Utah 84322-7800

Typography by WolfPack

*Publication of this book was supported by a subvention from
the George S. and Dolores Doré Eccles Foundation.*

Library of Congress Cataloging-in-Publication Data

Denton, Craig, 1947-
    People of the West Desert : finding common ground / Craig
Denton.
        p. cm.
    Includes bibliographical references.
    ISBN 0-87421-262-6 (pbk.)
    ISBN 0-87421-263-4 (cloth)
    1. Community life—Utah. 2. Community life—Nevada. 3. Community
life—Utah—Pictorial works. 4. Community life—Nevada—Pictorial
works. 5. Desert people—Utah. 6. Desert people—Nevada. 7. Desert
people—Utah—Pictorial works. 8. Desert people—Nevada—Pictorial
works. I. Title.
    HN79.U82 W473 1999
    307'.09792—ddc21
                            98-58065
                              CIP

To my brothers, Tom and Rob
In spirit and place

Contents

Acknowledgments

I would like to express my deepest gratitude to the following:

The George S. and Dolores Doré Eccles Foundation, whose generous, ongoing financial support made this documentary possible.

Julianne H. Newton, University of Texas, and an anonymous reader for their close reading of the manuscript and gentle criticisms. I've been happy to incorporate several of their thoughtful suggestions for improvement into this final presentation.

Carole Gallagher, who found while pursuing a parallel track that kindred spirit and will in people of the West Desert and shared it with me.

Thomas Carter, University of Utah, for introducing me to new western history.

John Alley and Utah State University Press, who provided guidance, enthusiasm, and foresight.

Members of the Visual Communication Conference, who provided comment and insight on earlier segments: specifically, Robert Tiemens, University of Utah; Paul Messaris, University of Pennsylvania; Derek Bousé, Albion College; and the late Brian Stonehill, Pomona College.

The faculty of the Department of Communication, University of Utah, for their longtime support of diversity and eclecticism in their vision of communication.

All the people of the West Desert I've been privileged to meet. Their grace, warmth, and willingness to share made my work a pleasure.

Thanks to all. You helped make this book the best contribution it can be.

Introduction

The genesis of this documentary lies in the waning lunatic days of the Cold War. Wiser heads had prevailed. The MX missile-basing scheme, whereby nuclear warheads would run in circles on railroad cars in Utah's western deserts and act as a nuclear sponge, was relegated to the dustbin with other Rube Goldberg plans from the Department of Defense. Still, I was anxious that some people had been willing to sacrifice such a large land mass, partially because it was perceived as lifeless and therefore worthless, but mostly because it was unknown.

I decided to assemble a landscape documentary of that land, the relict area of Lake Bonneville, so that people would have some visual experience with the place, should it again be placed on the public works chopping block. While I was working on that project from 1983 to 1987, I began meeting denizens of the area from eastern Nevada to western Utah that has come to be known as the West Desert. They were tough, resolute, yet gracious people who mirrored the dry iceberg landscape, where the greater substance is below the surface. Initially astonished that anyone lived and made a living in the raw place, I came to realize that the culture is equally diverse and rich. I then decided to undertake a second photographic documentary, telling the stories of the people who live in the West Desert.

The more I listened to these people's stories, the more two ideas struck me. First, their ways of life and their self-definitions are fundamentally shaped by the landscape that surrounds them. Second, they feel their life-styles face extinction due to government policies and public crusades forged in the political caldrons of the urbanized Wasatch Front in Utah and also in Reno-Carson City and Las Vegas in Nevada, all only 150–250 miles distant but light years away.

Many people of the West Desert would cast themselves as descendants of Jeffersonian agrarianism. They believe their close-to-the-land, neo-frontier life-styles represent what is good in the American character. They would see their work as the storehouse of American democracy and themselves as guardians at the gate. Since we are approaching another turn of the century and because it's approximately 100 years since the official closing of the frontier, I decided I would organize the documentary around "the state of democracy on the last frontier at the millenium."

I also was interested in how community is formed and maintained in the West Desert. Given the sparse population, I wondered whether small numbers would be a help or hindrance to community formation. I thought the documentary should look at the notion of community on what's left of the American frontier. Is it as independent as Thomas Jefferson envisioned, or is it marked more by interdependence and dependence? Moreover, is the West Desert a microcosm of the American commonwealth or is it an historical artifact?

"West Desert" in this work is both place and metaphor. In one sense it is an ethno- and geocentric term coined by urban Utahns to describe the Great Basin area of Utah, cradled by the peaks of the Wasatch Range on the east and the Deep Creek Mountains and Snake Range in Nevada in the west. In another sense "West Desert" applies to the entire Great Basin, that land mass that lies between the western edge of the Rocky Mountains and the eastern flank of the Sierra Nevadas. It is the basin and range province, the largest land mass in the continental United States, a parsimonious topography that prevents any of its meager water resources from reaching the sea. It is the high desert, where winters are cold and summers are hot. It is the quintessential West. For the most part, the stories that are told take place in that third of Utah and small strip of Nevada that was Lake Bonneville 10,000 years ago: On atomistic ranches, farms, and religious enclaves, and in small towns of 50 to 200 people with names that most urban Great Basinites have never heard—Callao, Trout Creek, Ibapah, and Eskdale in Utah, and the epicenter in Baker, Nevada. On the perimeter are larger small towns like Delta and Milford, Utah, products of the railroad; Dugway, Utah, an army post town; Ely, Nevada, and Eureka, Utah, once company towns for mining conglomerates, now with uncertain futures; West Wendover, Nevada, a neon reminder of the get-rich-quick lure of the West; and Wendover, Utah, a remnant of the past whose fortunes ended with the dropping of an atomic bomb in Japan.

"West Desert" also is metaphorical. It refers to a geography of the soul, where people share a kindred spirit and future. The land is their shared cultural resource and the gritty cement that binds them together. For instance, one group that tells its story on these pages, the Walker River Paiutes, lies outside the ethnocentric "West Desert" borders that Utahns perceive. Its reservation is nestled close to the eastern flank of the Sierra Nevadas. But the Walker River Paiutes are included for two reasons. First, the tribe allows broad access to Anglos, unlike some other tribes in the West Desert. Second, the tribe is part of that West Desert that is a metaphorical place. Native Americans resonate with those other people who choose to live in a harsh, unforgiving environment, where plentitude is a descriptor only when one considers space and scale, where the sea is a wistful dream, where rainfall is measured in single digits.

Because the West Desert is in a sense metaphorical and in the hope that its communities will retain some of their out-of-the way privacy, I have not included a map that would circumscribe the region, pinpoint the towns, and provide AAA-like directions to those communities. Locations can be determined easily enough from the text and a standard road map, but those who do not already know the way should have to put at least that much effort into finding it. The metaphor, though, is wide open and free to roam.

You also should conceive of these people of the West Desert as archetypes. While everyone you will meet on these pages is a distinct, complex personality, they represent the roles that people play in the West Desert. Native Americans, ranchers, hard-rock miners, back-to-the-land utopians, migrant workers, social activists, land managers, and boom-or-bust dreamers living shy of the edge of success. Their individual stories change as you are reading this, but as some move on to new opportunities in their lives, others move in to occupy their social and environmental niches.

Some of the people whom I interviewed and photographed are not present in this book. That's simply because the economics of publishing force considerations of space. What they revealed to me was equally valuable, but rather than roll several people into one archetype, I opted to focus on individuals.

Very rarely did anyone turn down my request to be interviewed and photographed. One miner, who has a valid permit to use hydraulics to separate flakes of gold on his claim, a man who used to provide tours of his operation for Boy Scouts, opted out, having become media shy, fearing exposure would target him by Earth First!ers.

My attempts to incorporate polygamists into this document have been rebuffed too. Attracted to the isolation of the West Desert, often putting down roots in Snake Valley, an 80-mile-long basin that begins where fractional inches of water mark the boundary between the Great Salt Lake Desert and arable land and stretches to the communities of Callao, Trout Creek, and Baker, they reason they have nothing to gain from public exposure and a lot to lose. They are probably right, and I've honored their wishes. This is more troublesome to me than losing access to one miner, however, when another could fill his archetypal place, because polygamists are not in these pages to tell their stories from their points of view. Their voice is missing. Yet polygamy might be the most fundamental change happening in the West Desert. Some residents see it as a community cataclysm, becoming the most important factor in the social politics of the region. Still, you will only see polygamists indirectly, through the eyes of others, and most often, those appraisals will be negative.

If there is one thing that still astounds me about these people of the West Desert, it is the openness and hospitality they extended to me. With no reason to trust an academic from the Wasatch Front, they nevertheless were generous with their time and spirit for this project. I have made some new friends through this work, and that is the most important result for me. While I sometimes disagree with philosophies that lead to certain life-styles in the West Desert, I have learned to be more tolerant, usually because of the effusive good will of the people with whom I disagree. Process ultimately is more important than product.

The people you will meet on these pages have been honest and willing to speak as multidimensional people. An occasional few were only interested in furthering public relations. Those rarities who simply mouthed the party line, seeing their role as spin doctor for their particular interest, whether it be ranching, mining, or tourism, play minor roles in this documentary. Instead, the vast majority of participants have been willing to be self-critical.

This introspection and revelation have been critically important to this project, because from its inception I've tried to conceive of this documentary as a vehicle for finding common ground. Too often in the wrenching debate over the antagonisms between the Old and New West, the public discourse has exacerbated our problems. The media, lacking time to develop a story or honestly trying to apply clarity in limited space, have tended to allow the most strident voices to set the agenda. Issues have become defined by the ends of the continuum. Sometimes, those media voices have conflicts of interest. As lobbyists, they have vested interests in maintaining a sharp edge, if not outright conflict.

While these people of the West Desert have identifiable self-interests and are archetypes, they *are* complex. They will not speak to you as spokespersons. Often times, they will upset your preconceptions of how they should speak. That's fitting, because the space that separates us is not as great as we would sometimes think. There is more we have in common than separates us. That tender seed of cooperation that we are beginning to glimpse in the West, of forming new coalitions to actually get things done, of trying to move beyond public postures, can be seen in this book.

This documentary also upsets some other tenets of traditional journalistic objectivity. Instead of acting as an outside observer, listening to both sides, carefully balancing point with counterpoint within the same story, I've attempted to function as a conduit. I've tried to allow each person or group to speak for themselves with minimal third-person, authorial intervention. While I hope I have not become a shill for self-promoters, I have not purposely deflated a person or group's beliefs by coyly interjecting and juxtaposing a fact or countervailing opinion that would call a belief or position into question. Instead, I hope that objectivity, breadth, depth—and understanding—will be present in the collection of all stories, when all voices are heard. I have faith that you will be able to sort things out for yourself.

To help broaden interpretation beyond my limited perceptions and knowledge, I adopted a methodology that elicited the skills of the people in telling their own stories. Besides oral interviews, I spent several sessions with respondents whenever possible. After the initial photographic shoot, I would print work photographs from all my negatives that I felt best captured the story, applying my background in developing narratives and picture editing. Then, I would take these prints back to the people and ask them to comment on them. I'd ask their feelings as they saw themselves performing a ritualistic act. I'd ask them to point out detail that was important or distracting. I asked them to select those pictures that they felt were the most comprehensive, accurate documents or identify those pictures that could promote misunderstanding without adding proper context. If there was universal agreement regarding a picture, I followed those wishes. If there was not a shared perspective, which usually was the case, even among seemingly monolithic cultures, I reserved the right to make final choices of images used.

Of course, visiting groups two or three times takes a lot of time. That luxury of time is something that traditional journalists crave but usually lack. I've tried to give this project enough time to develop those complexities and trust between the participants, to explore the long, knotted thread of community that reveals itself only over time. A great elapsed period between the beginning of the documentary and the publishing of this book also means that people's lives and conditions have changed sometimes dramatically. I've tried to keep the stories up-to-date in the text. If that was not possible, I've tried to signal where their lives and beliefs might lead, sometimes carrying on the systaltic beat of life in an epilogue.

An explaination of my documentary method may be useful here. The verb form of "document" means "to provide evidence," and over time, a documentary has been defined as a reliable record of something that happened. In this definition document as evidence is equated with veracity. That's an awesome responsibility for a documentarian—truth-telling—and to meet that heady goal, would-be chroniclers have been advised to adopt the pose of unseen observer, usually described as a fly on the wall. Presumably, veracity can be achieved if the documentarian cloaks himself in anonymity.

This approach pairs with the old notion of photography as a mechanical process. Nurtured by George Eastman's slogan, "You press the button, we do the rest," people were led to believe that photography is simply an extension of the scientific method of investigation. A camera is a machine, a product of physics and engineering, faithfully recording images that are frozen in time with the assistance of another branch of science, chemistry. A photographer need only transport the machine and aim it at the factual world.

But any photographer, let alone a documentary photographer, will tell you that photography is a process and a photograph represents a set of choices, some intended and some unintended, some born of careful planning and some the result of quick reaction. A photograph can be a later construction, too, when in a moment of serendipity, a photographer finds a picture in a forgotten frame that revealed itself in photo editing.

Inevitably, a documentary image is a record of two beings—the self and the other. A photographer trying to record literal truth must necessarily fail in that quixotic quest because of what physicists call the "uncertainty principle." Just as we cannot know the speed and location of a particle at any moment in time, we cannot observe without affecting the thing or process being observed. The documentarian is present within the frame that reveals a dynamic, interpersonal process that we call a documentary image. A documentary photographer only can fix the relationship between himself and the subject, not the subject alone.

People in the 1990s are media-savvy. In a sense, interacting with the mediated camera has empowered people in front of a lens. They are aware of the telescoping power of the selective eye that records. They have seen how it sometimes fails to tell the whole story, and they are wary. They know they have the ability to manipulate the camera too, just as it attempts to objectify them. People of the West Desert are no different. They have been interviewed time and again by journalists who are attracted to what the mass communicators feel is exotic from their cultural perspective. Because of that experience and a general knowledge of how the media work, people of the West Desert know well how to tell their stories, to reveal what is real to them, and I have understood that part that I play in the process. In a documentary, when people have informed consent as they have had in this work, there is an inevitable complicity in storytelling between the documentarian and the "document." The key for the documentarian is not to orchestrate the story according to a previsualized narrative. The documentarian never can suggest, only query. The story must emerge from the partnership that is forged between the participants in the documentary process.

Similarly, in oral interviews people share their self-perceptions. A journalist worries about that, questioning whether those self-perceptions square with reality or the historical record. For instance, westerners like to proclaim their fierce independence, but ample evidence shows that the West has been dependent upon the federal government and eastern money for development. A journalist might be tempted to deflate that seemingly wrong self-perception, but that would be missing the point. Self-perceptions, whether real or the product of mythologizing, motivate people in their lives, so they are documentary truths when people choose to reveal themselves.

In the end a documentary is a negotiation. It records the interpersonal relationship between observer and the observed. The documentarian knows that to ask others to reveal themselves, he needs to be willing to reveal himself, and his biases, to establish the trust necessary for real communication. The veracity reflected in a document is as much a mirroring of what people reveal to each other in the documentary encounter as it is an antiseptic record of human action outside the schema of the documentarian.

Perhaps the reader is that fly on the wall, that voyeur, that the documentarian cannot be. After all, the reader is separated in time and space from the event pictured in a document. But the documentarian is aware of his audience too as he puts together the documentary. If nothing else, the documentarian knows that people are interested in people and that people always like a good story. Documentarians also have sensitive antennae. In putting together a narrative, they are aware of parallels, the points of convergence either in the news or common lives. So, I've made choices in this documentary, ones that I hope forge a connection between people of the West Desert, you, the reader, and the things that matter in our lives.

You also should note a tension in the images as I attempt to display a common ground in documentary photography. A documentary photographer can take three different approaches, although those lines inevitably will be blurred by the contexts of publication. Usually, an image is classified as a documentary photograph, a photo-journalistic image, or an artifact of visual sociology, due to the intention of the photographer.

The larger term, "documentary photograph," is simply a photograph that says, "This is the way it is, or was." It might also have an edge of advocacy about it. Ultimately, it will make a statement about a generalized condition—say, the changing West—although that claim must come through a series of photographs because few images can tell complete stories. If a documentary photograph were not accompanied by text or if its context were not implicit in its detail, then it could be an art photograph. If not enough space is available for presentation, then documentary photographs become less reliable or persuasive.

Photojournalistic images are tailored for publication in newspapers and magazines. They get much of their meaning from those contexts. Because they often are used to anchor pages and to arrest skimming readers, they are composed with strong graphic elements or hook the reader with emotive content. They are less successful in telling complete stories because they usually are solitary and therefore lack supporting documents. Also, photojournalistic images magnify, and magnification usually means that something has been eliminated to better focus attention. These images sometimes rely upon stereotypes to speed communication off the page. News photographs are immediate too. Yet they can have continuing interest after that moment. When they do, they become documentary images, if the context is supplied.

Images of visual sociology are involved with complexity. Makers of these images are interested in revealing cultural patterns and social structures. Details in these images become even more important, and more numerous, than in documentary photographs. These images tend to be analytic and investigative. They also can be visually dry, eschewing the emotive and graphic for precision, science, and the need to catalogue visual data for the future. They are descriptive, and that detailed description usually must be revealed and verified in written text of significant depth to make sure the viewer sees what needs to be seen. Images of visual sociology must establish reliability and maintain their temporal quality. They are less "timeless" than classic, memorable documentary images.

You will see all three types of images in this work. In fact, the range of styles, from the boldly graphic to the intricately plain, might make you wonder if they were taken by the same person or if there were too few images from which to choose. But I have not tried to make personal photographic style or genre the subject of this book. Just as I made choices when I took pictures, I made choices in selection. Breadth of style, and knowledge that the same content captured from particular perspectives could say different things in different contexts, motivated my picture-taking. I tried to cast a wide net.

Any photographer, documentary or art, hopes to capture the imagination of the viewer, perhaps with a riveting photograph that welds composition and emotion in one stunning moment. Those kinds of pictures go into annuals and retrospectives. Like most of life, however, the peaks are far apart. In between the summits are the real grist of life. If you look closely, there is more real substance, and perhaps even wonder, in life that is steady. Certainly, that's where the real stories are.

So, I've included a few of those images that will catch your eye, but there are more of those captured with wider angles that necessarily include more complexity. When in doubt, I've opted for detail and expanse over magnification and closely cropped view. Ultimately, I've envisioned this documentary as a record for the future. Because I can't know what will be singularly important one hundred years from now, I've tried to include detail and perspectives that might become important. There must be a little bit of everything.

Tule Valley hardpan

Vegetation on ephemeral desert lake beds, called playas, varies according to depth of the water table and soil salinity. Greasewood can tolerate higher salt content in its tissues and tap into water thirty feet below the surface.

South of Granite Creek Canyon

Vegetation zones in the West Desert interweave. The mouth of Granite Creek Canyon at 6,300 feet in the Deep Creek Mountains is classical piñon-juniper woodland. Yet cottonwoods outline the streambed.

Granite Peak and Milford Needle

Sagebrush and rabbitbrush populate the higher basins from 4,500 to 5,500 feet, preferring approximately seven inches of moisture. Yet sagebrush can be seen on south-facing slopes at 10,000 feet. Mountain mahogany is typical West Desert brush, and scrub oak is a colonizer from the Rocky Mountains.

Looking north in the Deep Creeks

Rising to over 12,000 feet. the Deep Creek Mountains are one of the wetter ranges in the West Desert and one of the few to include six different life zones from mountain base to peaks. The range has typical Great Basin conifers, as well as such recent colonizers from the Rocky Mountains as white fir and subalpine fir.

I

The Land

Alpine tundra
Above the tree line of the subalpine lies the alpine zone, although not all ranges in
the Great Basin have one. Alpine tundra plants need cirques to shelter them,
granitic soils to hold water, and abundant summer sun.

Red Cedar Creek

West Desert streams harbor the last pure strains of Bonneville cutthroat trout. One of seven continually flowing streams in the Deep Creek Mountains, Red Cedar Creek is the center of debate over hydropower projects and wilderness water rights.

Hogup Cave
As Lake Bonneville rose and fell over the eons, wave action carved corrosion caves out of the rock ledges. Desert Archaic Indians occupied Hogup Cave on the edge of the Great Salt Lake Desert beginning in 6400 B.C.

That spot on earth where people of the West Desert took hold and which they call home, the place they feel first and speak of second as "the land," is not what you'd call a hospitable site. Nor has it always looked the same. At one moment in geologic deep time, billions of years ago, the West Desert was part of one gigantic continent. Then it split apart, the seas rushing in over the land. Always on the move, the West Desert alternated residences, sometimes homesteading in the Northern Hemisphere and sometimes in the Southern. All the while rocks folded under each other, as massive crustal plates waged wars of supremacy, determining who would remain on top.

Not too long ago in geologic time, about 40 million years ago, the West Desert was vomited from the earth's bowels. Land formed from volcanic dust falling to earth, after first having strained heavenward. Pyroclastic flows of mud, ash, and then magma made for a bleak landscape.

It was only when the earth started cooling in the Ice Age that the West Desert became habitable for human beings. While the land is still active, the crust underneath constantly being stretched to capacity and sometimes renting along faults, one slide of a block slipping against another in tiny tremors we call earthquakes, this place called the West Desert is relatively peaceful now. But its cataclysmic past, its severe demeanor, and its rocky core are the bedrock against which personalities are formed.

The land is both sculptor and foil for people of the West Desert. If you ask them what's most important in their lives, outside of their families, they will tell you "the land." Like Antaeus in Greek mythology, they draw their strength and character from their place. Taken from it, they risk losing their vitality. As it is hard, they are hard. As its topography bends and changes, so do they.

The land of the West Desert is a stern mother. Never overabundant nor profligate, never doting and certainly never spooning up Eden, it teaches precise lessons. It can provide physical sustenance, but in small portions. It is more generous in its tutoring of spirit and will.

Ultimately, however, this land of the West Desert has never been enough to sustain a people. Place may shape character, but water is the medium that courses through veins. Together, land and water are a fecund and sometimes volatile mixture. Together, they give life to the desert.

1

Etching the Landscape
The Yin and Yang of Water and People

"I come to you on prevailing westerlies as cruel promise," this writer overheard water whispering to life, "and just when you would hold me, I disappear as melancholic vapor. I am co-architect of the landscape, temptress, and stern calculator of being. You may yearn for more, yet I am all you have. I make you what you are."

Water. The Paiutes call it "pah," and it must become the first chapter in any story of people of the West Desert. All life in the Great Basin, where this chronicle takes place, must strike a balance with its offering. Of all life in the West Desert, however, only *Homo sapiens* covet and try to control the lifeblood.

There is so little water in the high desert of the Great Basin because the land mass lies within the rain shadow of the Sierra Nevadas and Cascade Range to the west. In winter when a large low-pressure area forms in the ocean near the Aleutian Islands, winds bring water-bearing clouds to the continent. As the clouds climb the western cordillera, that air condenses and releases its moisture on the windward side of the 14,000-foot peaks, leaving the clouds dry as they pass over Nevada and Utah. In summer a subtropical high pressure moves north in the Pacific and routes any moisture-bearing clouds north of the Great Basin.

The basin and range system accounts for wide variances of precipitation in the West Desert. Mountain ranges like the Deep Creeks and Snake at 12,000 to 13,000 feet can wring some moisture from the relatively dry clouds,

and the Great Basin itself can be a storm generator in spring, moving moisture from snowmelt, so that peaks of the Wasatch Range can grab 30 to 40 inches of precipitation yearly. Wendover, on the other hand, near the level bottom of a desert playa and with no tall surrounding mountains pumping the clouds, receives only 4 to 5 inches of rain a year. Sixty percent of moisture in the West Desert falls as snow.

This creates a multitude of microclimates in the West Desert that stimulate biodiversity. Biogeographers identify six life zones that are a product of precipitation, temperature, soils, and symbiotic relationships between plants and animals. Starting at the lowest elevations on desert playas, they have been labeled Lower Sonoran, then Upper Sonoran, Transition, Canadian, Hudsonian, and Alpine. Others prefer to differentiate according to vegetation zones. Either way, elevation and angle to the sun are the mediators that make change sudden and dynamic.

Water flows downhill, of course, and that movement molds the surface and subsurface landscape of the Great Basin. When rain and snow reach the West Desert, the moisture first falls on mountain tops of limestone, granite, or dolomite. Then, it begins either dribbling down mountainsides formed by uplift from the stretching and cracking of the tectonic plate under the Great Basin, or percolating through the rock, dissolving the minerals that bar its way. North-facing slopes hold the surface water longer, while

Chimney Rock

Chimney Rock is part of the Basin, a once heavily grazed area that was purchased and transferred to federal control by the George S. and Dolores Doré Eccles Foundation and the Nature Conservancy for inclusion in the BLM Deep Creek Wilderness Area. It possesses transition and montane forests.

Stella Lake

Stella Lake is one of the few high mountain lakes in the West Desert. It is formed by subsurface runoff from Wheeler Peak in the Snake Range. It occupies a depression where Transition, Subalpine, and Alpine zones meet.

Bristlecone pine

The subalpine zone is the last vegetative link in the Great Basin with the forests of the Ice Age. Bristlecone pines find little competition on cool, dry ridges at 9,000 to 11,000 feet. The oldest trees are over four thousand years old.

Carved aspen

Aspens can be found in the zone above piñons and junipers where soil is moist and there is plentiful sun. Aspens are pioneering trees, spreading primarily by cloning in the Great Basin. They provide needed shade for spruce and fir seedlings, which later will overgrow aspens.

southern slopes yield it quickly. This gives rise to the schizophrenic look of some West Desert mountains, seemingly lush on one facet and parched on the other.

As drips from the melting snowbanks join to form trickles, gravity accelerates the flow, the etching water turning into rivulets and then small streams, the climax stage of moving water in the West Desert. Few streams ever reach flatter ground where they are free to meander. They are redirected by people. Yet up to 80 percent of vertebrates in the Great Basin rely on woodland streamside plant communities. Riparian areas are the arteries of life, and people, too, inevitably cluster and cling to the sides of water in the West Desert.

Monsoonal rains generated by warm, moist air flowing north through Mexico in the summer act roughly on the land. Flash floods disperse soils, creating new habitat. Boulders move begrudgingly, followed by gravel, pebbles, silt, and then fine clays washed onto the lowest elevations. Each of those soils can hold water to varying degrees, providing different opportunities for life to exploit niches. Those flash floods also wash down organic debris to the desert floors, where life begins.

In spring, water's freeze-thaw cycle begins to cleave the ancient rocks, some metamorphic schists in the Grouse Creek area over 2.5 billion years old, subdividing them like a teacher demonstrating fractions. Since most slopes exceed the angle of repose, rocks in the West Desert begin an inexorable passage down the mountain, eventually collecting in the basins as loosely packed sediment, sometimes 10,000 feet deep, with bedrock underneath acting as an impervious liner.

Subsurface water slipping through cracks or leaching through rock is pulled by gravity, too. Great underground rivers collect the flow that is sometimes discharged to the surface as seeps, springs, and lakes. Much of the subsurface water, however, reaches the sedimentary reservoirs at the lowest basins. Occasionally, dry, cracked playas can become wet when these reservoirs overfill. Wet, discharge playas have salt build up around their edges as water evaporates. Dry, recharge playas are rarely salty because the water leaks through fissures in the bedrock below the sedimentary reservoirs, carrying away the salt and other dissolved minerals.

Water in the West Desert flows between sedimentary reservoirs in one basin to the next as it seeks a lower level. Subsurface water underground only a short time is cooler and less saline. Regional water moves lower in the earth. It is heated by magma below the bedrock. Then it moves upward when it reaches a fault, bubbling up in geysers or hot springs.

The West Desert is drying out and has been since the pluvial period, a cool era that slowed down evaporation, allowing those underground reservoirs to fill. During the Wisconsin era in the last Ice Age, the basin and range consisted largely of deep lakes and island mountain ranges capped with snow and glaciers. Only small bands of bristlecone and limber pine eked out an existence between frozen and liquid water. But with the Hypsithermal, beginning from 7,500 to 4,500 years ago, increasingly higher mean temperatures began evaporating and shrinking Ice Age lakes like Lake Bonneville, with Great Salt Lake its saline remnant.

Accelerating the dessication of the West Desert is that rain shadow effect. Once cooling clouds release their moisture as they pass over the Sierras and Cascades, that air heats up more quickly on the other side of the slope. The leeward side, the Great Basin, has proportionately warmer air, and surface moisture therefore evaporates quickly. Moreover, as the clouds dissipate, the land receives more direct rays from the sun, leading to extreme summer temperatures. The relatively high number of sunny days in the West Desert, coupled with downslope winds in the evening, upslope winds in the morning, and vicious blows that periodically streak across the Great Basin from high to low pressures, create a rapid drying effect. More water is lost in the Great Basin in annual evaporation than it receives in precipitation. No water leaves the Great Basin, except by evaporation, transpiration, or in the public works schemes of human beings.

The drying out of the West Desert is an arbiter that forces strict discipline. Annual plants in areas of low precipitation have adapted by growing, flowering, and producing seeds in only a few weeks during the wetter spring. Perennials can exist during the harsh summer and winter months as roots or bulbs below the ground, where they store water. Or they send tap roots deep, sometimes 60 feet or more into the water table. Because leaves require much moisture in the transpiration process, some plants produce relatively few, smaller leaves, shed them during dry seasons or eliminate the need for leaves altogether by photosynthesizing in stem surfaces.

Cacti preserve water by opening their stomates to obtain carbon dioxide only at night when the air is cool and less dehydrating. Other plants have evolved in wetter saline areas by tolerating a high salt content in their tissues that would kill most plants. Some plants living on dry playas can survive debilitating dehydration and loss of osmotic pressure.

Animal adaptations to the high desert are no less ingenious. Some insects can absorb water from the air when humidity tops 80 percent. Birds prosper by flying great distances to available water, and with reptiles, are able to excrete uric acid and urates in dry clumps, preserving water that mammals waste as urine. Light coloration in birds and mammals reflects light and heat, and feathers and hair provide a layer of insulation preventing water loss. Small mammals are especially vulnerable due to their relatively large surface areas, so they remain dormant during the hot days and only move during the cool nights, or they can go into estivation during the most severe summer months.

When moisture becomes momentarily plentiful on normally dry playas, the pulse of life quickens. Phytoplankton and algae are the first to race life's course. Those seeds from annuals that might have lain dormant for several years, their genetic natures giving them patience, waiting for just the right mix of water and warmth through lengthening days, explode into activity. Eggs from fairy and tadpole shrimp and freshwater clams begin cellular division and differentiation into adults, mating before evaporation makes the water too salty again.

Humans can study the dynamics of water conservation in the desert and still fail to apply the lessons. Hubris and biocentrism combine into a powerful force that sometimes parallels but often diverges from natural adaptation to desert water management. The delusion started early on. The first cartographers of the Great Basin, drawing somewhat from thirdhand reports of mountain men, though mostly from rumor and hope, penciled in a great river, the Buenaventura, that flowed west from Great Salt Lake to the Pacific Ocean. In the middle of the 19th century, land developers trying to jump-start the settlement of the West decreed that "rain follows the plow," and many would-be farmers trailed the mantra west into dry oblivion.

That which the land steals from the clouds possesses ultimate value in the high desert. Water has become the eternal object of struggles between peoples of the West Desert, with the landscape a mute victim of the combat. Humans attempt to control natural law with water law. Water flows downhill still another way—to money. That channelization molds the cultural landscape of the West Desert. In fact, the political cuts and twists of that watercourse are more tortuous than the arroyos carved on the surface.

The legal doctrine of prior appropriation is the glue that keeps water in its place, ironically the only compound on earth that water seemingly can't dissolve. It begins with the presumption that water is primarily for human use, an outgrowth of developmental ecclesiasticism that maintains that all land and life was created and ordained by God for human benefit. In water regulation practice it translates into the catchphrases, "First in time, first in rights" and "The right to divert shall never be denied." If great-grandpappy had water rights and didn't sell them, those rights are honored in a court of law before those of another's grandpappy. The offspring of great-grandpappy can do with those rights what they wish, even if it means diverting them away from a better contemporary use.

But water in the West must be put to beneficial use, hence another popular decree, "Use it or lose it." Water in springs, streams, or lakes has no rights. Under some circumstances plants and animals have legal standing, but water can't argue for itself, to be left alone. Instream flows are not beneficial use, no matter that land and its dependent riparian life are benefitted by water remaining in the creek. That is a gift that can be given to plants and animals only if a human decides to purchase it from a senior rights holder and dedicate it to that use. Even then, that gift and use might be challenged in court because it is not beneficial—to humans.

This makes water law sound simplistic, if not bizarre, when it really is Byzantine. There is the companion political struggle of ownership of water versus regulation of water. Individual entities might own water rights, but political subdivisions like states, counties, and cities lay claim to regulating those rights, and by extension, the water. Even political subdivisions might argue over who has the right to regulate.

For instance, the federal government reserves water rights on land it owns in the West for public use. That might be for national defense, national forests and parks, wilderness, or Indian reservations for which the United States government has a trust responsibility. When Anglos decided at the turn of the century that the best way to assimilate Native Americans into American culture would be to turn them into Jefferson's yeoman farmers, the federal government had to carve out water for them to raise crops. At the same time Washington began selling land to whites that used to be part of Indian reservations, usually the best bottomland nearest the local water source. Creating a conflict of interest was the Bureau of Reclamation, created in 1902 to dam western rivers and develop water, typically for Anglo farmers. When it came time for the federal government to honor an agreement and release those reserved water rights for Native American use, western states said "not so fast." We have the right to regulate water use within our state boundaries, and we are not going to take away water from Anglo farmers and give it to Indians, who might want to use it for a non-beneficial use like developing a fishery.

Water regulation and development come with great economic costs. Typically, governments subsidize water development, since no one person, nor even most corporate entities, can afford to build dams and delivery systems. Moreover, water development usually is on a grand scale so costs can be spread to a variety of beneficiaries.

Then it's argued that the public is served and should pay for it with taxes. When possible, the new dams are designed to generate hydropower, the watts sold to distant cities, sometimes below cost, so that urban populations will vote for rural water development. When the development is for a relative few—ranchers, farmers, or miners—the general public often has to chip in, because even though those extractive industry users might obligate themselves with hefty loans, the populace still needs to help pay for the project.

Development projects sometimes have a conservation benefit. Better use of the water, by constructing concrete ditches that prevent seepage loss or installing sprinkler or drip irrigation systems after leveling the land to retard runoff, means new water is created without having to build another dam. But the question arises of who should use that new water. Should it go to a new party, or can the previous user claim it and "spread" it to new projects, even though it was subsidized by the public?

Extracting groundwater is a kind of mining of time. Those deep sedimentary reservoirs in the Great Basin originally were filled with runoff in the last Ice Age. Digging wells into those aquifers provides relatively cheap water. Proponents maintain that it's acceptable to drain those reservoirs, using more water each year than is replenished because less expensive water allows for a rapid expansion of population. That creates economic growth and wealth, which later can be used to afford pumping and distributing water from distant sources, perhaps from another basin. A city like Las Vegas, drawing down its groundwater and reaching maximum allotment of its share of the Colorado River, might begin to covet water rights in rural counties to the north, in the West Desert.

The environmental price tags of water development are equally great. Drought is frequent in the West Desert. Because they have the rights, water users can dewater streams in low-water years or channel them to prevent meandering, killing plants, insects, fish, and other aquatic species. With no feed and cover, migratory waterfowl must fly on, often when they are desperately in need of nourishment, losing one-third of their body weight in migration.

Drawing groundwater lowers the water table. When it gets too low, plants die as their roots no longer reach it, creating more surface erosion or a habitat for exotic and noxious weeds that thrive on damaged land—plants that are less nutritious for game or livestock. When water no longer flows in arroyos, even in wet periods, they deepen. Flash floods are more damaging then because there are no longer streamside plants to hold the soil. It's all washed away, and downstream areas become silted in.

Selenium, a natural element, is a legacy of the volcanic past of the West Desert that came to rest in concentrated silts and mud left by pluvial lakes like Lake Bonneville. Those muds became shale under pressure and heat. The Great Basin's scant rainfall slowly leaches out the poisonous selenium in amounts small enough not to harm fish and waterfowl. But when irrigation projects accelerate the leaching, and when that runoff works its way into desert marshes, the habitat becomes toxic.

There now are cries for environmental reform. The National Environmental Policy Act allows new players at the negotiating table. Water developers must provide environmental assessments at the least, and full-blown environmental impact statements when environmentalists can successfully argue the massive scope of a proposal. Cost-benefit analyses, user fees, cost-sharing reforms, and mitigation become part of the new vocabulary of water regulation.

Time may have come for water policy reform in the West. After all, water laws and precedence have led to the gross anomaly where the two driest states in the nation, Nevada and Utah, the primary tenants of the Great Basin, also lead the nation in per capita water consumption. But water policy reform comes with great social costs. Water law, rightly or wrongly, sustains western culture. Unraveling the law means undoing the social fabric. While admitting new players in water policy-making reflects the fact that times are changing, that rural western culture is not monolithic, that people of the West Desert are now a diverse lot, it challenges historical self-perceptions of old stakeholders and broadens the perspective of newcomers, who used to think that water simply materialized in a faucet.

The course of water in the West Desert is resolute, and the region's people are much like that: determined and directed. Reflecting water's dramatic etching of the surrounding landscape, their personalities are chiseled. Like the rocks under them, some of the oldest on the North American continent, they are granitic and have endured. Eventually, however, water will dissolve all bonds.

I asked the land what it would prefer its people do with its water.

"A fair share for everything," it replied. "Enough to build a common ground."

The dinner table
Residents of Eskdale eat all meals in the community dining hall, with nuclear families sharing long tables and serving themselves family style. When visitors have dietary restrictions, the cooks prepare special meals for those guests. The Aaronic Order eschews coffee, tea, alcohol, and pork, with fresh vegetables the primary staple.

Work meeting
At weekly work meetings, the only mandatory meeting, Home Farm residents talk about community problems and divy up the work responsibilities. Shifts for the washing machine are agreed upon, as well as cooking schedules. Typically, people self-select themselves for the necessary community chores.

II

Communities of the West Desert

Buck Douglass working at Eskdale

Since the family farm runs a debit, Buck Douglass must support the homestead and
his family by picking up work wherever he can. He commutes to Great Basin
National Park, where he is carpentry foreman. His engineering and construction
prowess is a legend in Snake Valley, so he often is hired to work at places like
Eskdale, where he lays a concrete slab.

Arrow Drive

Homes on the reservation have a look of regularity that is a product of HUD financing and regulation. Otherwise, streets resemble a typical low- or middle-income, desert subdivision. The xeriscaping, a harbinger for the New West, isn't always by choice. Elveda Martinez relates the story of when a visitor dropped by her house and remarked that she had planted some shrubs. "Those are my trees," I said. "They've been growing for years."

Crosses

While the Walker River tribe has lost many of its people to alcohol-related traffic accidents off the reservation, the physical and emotional carnage seldom has hit home. When two teenagers died in front of tribal headquarters, Monty Williams, the tribe's drug and alcohol abuse counselor, sensed that for the first time the tribe was coming out of self-denial. He organized an alcohol-awareness intervention and healing ceremony, the Cry Dance, for the tribe.

1

Native American Communities
First in Time, Last in Line

Approximately 20 miles from the borders of Indian reservations, bone-white sentinels often loom on hairpin curves of two-lane roads. Sometimes solitary, sometimes clustered in twisted heraldries of five or eight, crosses mark the spots where Indians have fallen in the 20th century. In March 1995 two plaintive crucifixes, jabbed into the gravel macadam 100 yards from tribal headquarters, penetrated the heart of the Walker River Paiutes.

"This has been the craziest thing that's ever happened in this community," Elveda Martinez said. "It's like a love story-tragedy."

One tribal member, drunk, ran head on into another car, whose occupants were a teenage couple anticipating their marriage in two weeks. She died instantly. He lasted a few weeks. The older woman in the other car had multiple injuries, but would survive, at least in body.

Martinez, water resources officer for the tribe, didn't want to begin my tour of the reservation in Schurz, Nevada, that way, but there was no avoiding it. So, while she showed me the tribe's work with water development, an undercurrent of blood and pain coursed below us.

It was the eighth year of drought, and the tribe was building concrete ditches to conserve what little water they received from the Sierra Nevadas to the west. Although the reservation is over 324,000 acres, and although the tribe owns the oldest water rights in the area, it

is entitled to only 26.5 cubic feet per second (cfs) for 180 days from the Walker River, enough to coax alfalfa from 400 acres of the alkaline soil for 200 Walker River Paiute farmers, 25 percent of the tribe. Still, upstream and downstream water users complain that the Indians are getting too much.

"We're always getting blamed for using all the water," Martinez said, "because we're the Indians on the end of the trail. But they don't talk about the people in Mason Valley irrigating 85,000 acres plus irrigating for I don't know how many months, and digging wells and tapping into the underground water. We always get blamed for everything. It's not fair."

Water hadn't flowed in the Walker River through Schurz for many years. The tribe retained its share and the river's last swallow upstream in Weber Reservoir. Downstream, cottonwoods were being cut for firewood, and they are not growing back. But the land still remembered water, as cattails filled the bottom of the riverbed, finding some subsurface trickle.

Fifteen miles downstream Walker Lake was choking with salt, and a cutthroat fishery that once produced 15-pound fish was dying. Only fish born in the lake can survive; hatchery fish go belly up from toxic shock once they enter the gray-green water. "Save Walker Lake," a group of fisher enthusiasts, wants to move water from an abandoned copper mine into the lake, but the tribe would have to live with the consequences of the heavy metal-laden water running through the reservation.

Meanwhile, towering Mt. Grant next to Walker Lake has all the water the lake needs to thrive again, but the mountain and its water belong to the U.S. Army's Hawthorne Army Depot nestled at its foot. Mt. Grant, a holy mountain for the Walker River Paiutes, was taken from them when the reservation was whittled down in size during the homesteading movement in the early 1900s. If the tribe regained control, it would restore that alpine water to the brackish lake.

The Walker River Paiutes have more interest in the health of the lake than any other community in the area. A branch of the Northern Paiutes, they are known as the "Agai Diccutta," or trout eaters. Fish was a staple in their diets until only recently. When they lost the lake, the tribe was denied access to its dietary heritage.

Many of the tribe's current problems can be traced to 1906. That's when the federal government bent to contrived charges that Indians weren't using reservations to full economic benefit and carved up Indian lands into allotments, opening the rest to Anglo homesteading and development.

"It was pretty much all the land around Walker Lake," Martinez said. "Because way back then it was major mining. In the history books you read about how the miners actually lined up elbow-to-elbow all around the reservation for that twelve o'clock time when they says, 'Go in and get what you want.'

"When the miners all came in, they really didn't find the major gold deposits that they thought were there. Yet they winded up taking the reservation and cutting it down, for of course, it's always been greed and money. What's really crazy, we can't find any reason why Walker Lake shouldn't have reverted back to the reservation."

Now, the tribe has a new problem with the federal government. Since 1949 navy fliers from nearby Fallon Naval Air Station have been illegally bombing 5,600 acres of reservation land. After years of complaints, the navy finally swept the surface of ordnance, picking up 1.5 million pieces of unexploded bombs and shells. But the land still is uninhabitable.

"A lot of the bombs are down fifty feet probably," Martinez said. "They drop a lot of 500 pounders. They usually do those on the weekends, for some reason, because you're at home and the house is rattling."

The tribe can't afford lawyers to sue the navy, so it is working with the local brass on its own. The Walker River Paiutes want a land swap and $8.4 million for the bombed acreage, funds that would be used to dig two new range wells to replace the ones that were destroyed. The local navy officials are sympathetic, but agreements tend to unwind in Washington.

Like all Indian tribes the Walker River Paiutes have complaints about another federal agency, the Bureau of Indian Affairs. For years they've charged that administration is top-heavy. They've argued that the BIA should cut administrators and move that money down to local agents and works on the ground, yet when BIA funds finally were cut, the money stream reversed course.

Raymond Hoferer, Walker River tribal chairman in 1995, said, "Now, the money's going back to the feds, and the tribes haven't received any of that funding that they, in essence, initiated to save. Now, they're reduced in staffing levels and we're still not realizing anything."

Relations with state government are worse.

"A combination of state governments," Hoferer said, drawing out the "s" like a hiss, "and their influence on Washington policy. Different senators from different states. They have their anti-Indian forces."

Indians see the states' rights movement as a particular menace and are opposed to block grants to the states.

"Probably the greatest threat that we have is intrusion on our sovereignty," Hoferer said. "Congress diminishing our sovereign authority by using states as a middleman in determining our funding when it should be a government-to-government, us directly to Washington. The thrust of legislation now is allowing states to basically determine our funding levels, whether it be social services, welfare, what have you."

Hoferer worries about a new land grab at the millenium. Legislation has been introduced that would survey those 20-acre Indian allotments granted in 1906. If they have become fractionated to a level of 2 percent, Republican sponsors want the federal government to buy out those individual parcels, sell them back to the tribes, or give them to the states.

"Again, it's all part of government policy," Hoferer said. "We've had several: extermination, assimilation, the Dawes Act, allotments, which was basically designed to fractionate our lands. It's still ongoing. This think tank of theirs is always thinking."

The closer government gets to the people, it seems, the worse that government is for Indians. The Walker River Paiutes' immediate problems are with Mineral County, Nevada. Due to shrinking population, the county is losing money, and as coffers drop, racism rises proportionately.

The current focus of the antagonism is the reservation school. The main school building is condemned, and Schurz kids have to be taught in portables scavenged from the old town of Babbitt. Schurz people have been pressing the Mineral County School District for a new school. Just prior to the recent bond election, advertisements placed in the Hawthorne newspaper opposed the bond, saying there should be no money for Indians. The bond election failed.

The county doesn't want to fund a new school for Schurz because it would be on reservation land. The county argues it receives no property taxes from the tribe, but it tends to dismiss the in-lieu money it gets for classified federal land. In turn, the tribe has filed a civil rights suit against Mineral County, charging unequal educational opportunities.

The school issue is only the most recent sign of the ongoing problem.

"It's basically what I call the 'frontier mentality,'" Hoferer said, "where Indians have their place and basically we [Anglos] never should have given them their land in the first place. And, they're all on welfare. And, they're all sucking up federal funds. That's the concept of people in Mineral County."

There is a social pathology that makes Indian reservations and reservation towns like Schurz different from other small towns in the West Desert. Like the problems with Anglo governments, it's a pathology whose roots are embedded in the past, but whose cancers adapt to the times. It's what happens when a community is severed from its cultural heritage. To fight the disease, that community has to rediscover its past.

Diabetes afflicts 35–40 percent of all Walker River Paiutes, and the incidence is largely due to a historical change in the tribe's diet. Piñon pine nuts, for instance, have been a food staple for Paiutes for centuries. The seeds are rich in proteins and carbohydrates, and Paiutes made them into anything from bread to mush to soup. They could be stored for winter, too, and that fat-laden supplement helped Indians make it through the brutal winter months in the Great Basin when game hibernates.

Paiutes, through genetic evolution, developed an ability to put on a great deal of fat during the bountiful summer eating periods. During the lean winter months, they could work off the fat as food supplies became low. The problem is that the Paiutes now practice a "meat and potatoes" regime. They are still genetically predisposed to put on weight easily, but it doesn't come off. Paiutes tend to be obese, and diabetes is a disease that prospers in that culture. With it come circulatory and kidney problems and a higher level of blindness. Hypertension, a fellow traveler of poverty and cultural dislocation, aggravates the condition.

Alcoholism, though, is the most noticeable Indian health problem, and tribes wrestle with it, even when they cloak the demon in community self-denial.

"Has the tribe ever talked about not selling beer on the reservation?" I asked Elveda Martinez.

"No," Martinez replied. "The last time they talked about it was the time they decided *to* sell it. That was in 1980. Now, because of this terrible accident affecting all these families, they might reconsider it, but I doubt it. You know, it's like people are going to drink. They always have. One of the reasons that they did start selling it was because we thought it would keep people off the highways. Because we've lost people on the highways, too, on every highway from Schurz to Fallon to Yerington to Hawthorne because of alcohol."

Welding

Most jobs the tribe can offer its people are blue-collar ones, working directly for the tribe or created by requiring contractors to hire Indians first through the Tribal Employment Rights Office. Ironically, the tribe finds that its best-educated members are usually the ones who can't find employment on the reservation and who must move on, taking their resources with them.

Tribal Court

Joseph Van Walraven, Tribal Court Judge, lightly says being on the bench "is the only time I can pontificate and rant and rave and no one can talk back to me. I don't even get that in my own family." Then, more reflectively, he adds, "And, every once in awhile I can turn a person around."

Alcohol-related charges are the most common ones in the Walker River Tribal Court—DUI, domestic abuse, traffic offenses. In effect, it's a misdemeanor court. The Walker River Paiutes have their own tribal law code, yet there is evidence of Anglo colonialism in its administration. The tribe pays an Anglo lawyer in private practice in Reno to hold two sessions a month. The prosecutor is another Anglo attorney from Carson City. Most Paiutes, though, can't afford an attorney.

"It's like an unequal justice system," Elveda Martinez said. "If they do bring in their own attorney, they usually win, but, then they wind up paying more for their attorney than if they woulda' paid the fine."

The judge and prosecutor show up approximately one-half hour before the court session begins and try to familiarize themselves with the cases by wading through a long spreadsheet containing the record of previous offenses and guilt, as well as bargains that have been made. The same names appear over and over.

Like Anglo society, Native American culture is not monolithic. There are social divisions, class consciousness, and stories of brilliant success and numbing, cyclical failure.

The reservation school and its students are a good example. The tribe encourages its bright young people to go to college, hoping they will return and serve the tribe. In 1992 they had over 60 kids in college, ranging from Harvard and Stanford to local universities and community colleges.

There are, however, signs of problems among young people. Trash talk. Surliness. And, unlike the perplexing hieroglyphics in urban communities whose semiology is known only to gangs, the graffiti in Schurz have a hard-edged, demeaning tone. "Fuck," "Suck my cock," and an homage to the rapper Ice T.

If some Walker River Paiute children are becoming disillusioned, it's not hard to understand the source. While the student population is climbing—the K–8 Schurz School has 136 kids now and must plan for 250 within five years—there really is no school, only separate cells of surplus barracks. Moreover, the tribe has a difficult time finding Indian teachers to serve as role models for Schurz students, and when they can find a good one, she faces severe discipline problems.

Raymond Hoferer recognizes the signs but has faith in the tribe's children.

"I believe they are a little disheartened over the school issue," Hoferer said. "I think that has a negative effect on their self-esteem. 'Why don't we have the same facilities that non-Indians do?' When they go to other schools, they look at it and say, 'Wow! This is nice.' Here they have to eat their lunch outside. When they leave here, that's aggravated when they go to a high school. They still have that ingrained, 'Are we as good?'"

"Do they respect authority as much as they used to?" I asked.

Hoferer paused before speaking. "Uh . . . I think so, I think so. It depends upon how you approach them. I've never had a problem. I also see a resurgence in their cultural attitude. What they are losing from being in this non-Indian school system and what it's doing to them, at the same time, they're searching, too, to find something to grasp onto."

Ben Leva, director of the tribe's Senior Center, isn't so sure about the direction of the tribe's children.

"What about the kids?" I asked. "Are they any different than when you were a kid?"

"Yeah, big change," Leva laughed.

"You're smiling. How are they different?" I asked.

"In our day Dad used to take us out behind the barn if we didn't mind. Well, we can't do that now and kids know it. So, they more or less try to run their parents, also their teachers at school."

"So, discipline is a problem," I said.

"One big problem," Leva replied in drawn out words.

Too often, Native Americans are set up to fail when they are expected to adapt to an Anglo society without any allowance for cultural difference. That happened with one of the tribe's business ventures, a truck stop. Initially, they hired non-Indian managers. Those managers scheduled Indians rather than Anglos to work on weekends. Families are exceptionally important in Native American culture, and Indians save weekends for families and visiting other Indian bands.

Then, the Anglo managers hired people simply because they were available. Charlie Em, the tribe's other unofficial public relations person besides Martinez, put it this way:

"The people who wanted to work were already working. The people that got hired were people that stayed home a lot and took care of their kids. So, they really didn't know how to work. No one ever taught them how to work. Because if you're not working already, you must not want to work. Because there's jobs available."

Elveda Martinez added, "People that had worked, like Charlie's mom who works for Indian Health Services, she'd go up and work on weekends and she knows how to talk, say 'Hi. Hello. How ya doing? Whatcha want?' Be friendly. Whereas, for these other people it was really hard for them."

There is resentment on the reservation, just like in Anglo communities, between achievers and nonachievers. It crops up in rents for tribal housing, much of which is financed through HUD. According to HUD regulations renters must pay 30 percent of their monthly income. If they are under- or unemployed, they pay next to nothing.

"So, if you're making good money," Martinez said, "you might be paying four or five hundred dollars a month to live here, and your neighbor's not paying nothing. It's real unfair, and it causes bad feelings."

"How does the dissension come out?" I asked.

"In meetings. Shunning. People being mean to each other. People making fun of you because you work and try to do good," Martinez said.

When it faced cultural annihilation in the late 1880s, the Native American community became attracted to a spiritual purification movement called the Ghost Dance. Led by the Paiute prophet Wovoka, Indians believed that if they prayed hard enough, eschewed alcohol, did not mourn, and danced in great circles, the old world would resurrect. Dead kinsfolk would reunite with the living, buffalo would return, and the white man would disappear.

While that desperate attempt to regain control of Indian culture led to the tragedy at Wounded Knee, that spirit is alive in the Walker River descendants of Wovoka. Posters of the great mystic adorn walls in tribal buildings. But in this latter-day regeneration movement, there is a critical difference. His disciples are pragmatists. Instead of dancing in circles, they use the tools of modern political warfare.

"Personally, I feel that the religious influence Wovoka had on this reservation is starting to come back," tribal chairman Raymond Hoferer said. "Recently, we had that funeral ceremony, which is similar to some of the ceremonies that were performed during the Ghost Dance period. What I saw there was a resurgence of youth, people of my generation starting to look for those teachings. Some of the rebirth of his thoughts, and I believe that's going to be a nation-wide movement at some point."

Just as in the larger U.S. society, baby boomers are assuming power in the Native American community.

"It's like a phasing in of the baby boomers versus the old school," Hoferer said.

"Is there any kind of tension between those generations as one takes over?" I asked.

"Not really," Hoferer continued. "I think there might be concern with our generation and our thoughts of being progressive, the type of aggressive attitudes that we take in terms of trying to get things done in a more expeditious manner. Whereas, before, it was kinda like, 'Well, it'll get here when it gets here.' Our position has basically been, 'We want it now.'"

Hoferer and others like him no longer will be the white man's Indian. They want control—political, economic, and social—over their destiny. They don't want to be defined paternalistically by an Anglo society, those definitions changing on the whim of political winds. For Hoferer and his tribe, the American Dream no longer means striving for what Anglo culture dangles like a carrot to the good Indian.

"I would differentiate between an American Dream and a Native American Dream," Hoferer said. "The American Dream is your basic house and two-car garage, surburban setting, housewife, and two kids, making fifty, sixty, seventy-five thousand a year. In my own opinion the Native American Dream is when we are culturally intact. One where we're spiritually intact. Where our children are spiritually intact. Where we develop our social relationships with the elders in a traditional way. We're economically comfortable, where we can provide what we need to for our kids, and at the same time maintain that cultural integrity."

To build that Native American Dream, the Walker River Paiutes are becoming more aggressive. Partly because they lack the funds to file legal suits, and partly because the tribal council believes that sovereign nations should meet face-to-face, the tribe spends more time in Washington, D.C., with congressmen and department undersecretaries rather than dealing with their local Nevada staffers.

"Do you feel they respect you more as the leader of a sovereign nation when you go back to Washington, rather than when they come here?" I asked.

"I get that feeling, I really do," Hoferer replied.

"They sometimes forget that, don't they?" I said.

"They sure do," Hoferer said with direct affirmation. "Even in D.C. it's hard to have them recognize Indian tribes as sovereign nations. They still have this concept of manifest destiny and that the tribes have been defeated."

"So, you think the aggressive strategy is working out better?" I offered.

"Well, it has to. It's the only strategy we have left," Hoferer replied.

The Walker River tribe is efficient at block voting in Mineral County elections, with everyone on the reservation registered to vote, mustering an 80–100 percent turnout when needed. Their concerted efforts in a recent election ousted a county clerk and district attorney. The tribe also is demanding seats on county commissions.

They've filed suit for 10,000 more acre-feet of water, their Boulder, Colorado, attorney charging the tribe a fairy-tale hourly rate. They are pressing the county for Title V funds for Indian children. They are seeking Title XII monies from the Elementary and Secondary Education Act for a new school, although that

act, as well as Bureau of Indian Affairs support, are ongoing targets for deep cuts by Congress.

Companies wanting to do business with the tribe must comply with its Tribal Employment Rights Office. Tribal members must be the first hired. Funds from TERO fees are used for the tribe's adult training programs.

Nationally, the Walker River Paiutes are taking the lead in environmental affairs. In 1995 the tribe chaired the National Indian Environmental Council. All this activism comes with a political price, however. The hair on the necks of government officials at all levels is bristling.

Raymond Hoferer interjected, "A friend of mine said, 'Any publicity is good publicity,' whether you raise the hair on their neck or whether they accept you for what your position is. You're still gaining their attention. Whereas before it was, 'You'll get it when I have time to get it to you.'"

It would be a mistake to suggest, however, that the tribe is trying to secure its future by demanding things from outsiders. The power of the tribe ultimately lies with the people, and both Hoferer and Martinez point out that community involvement is broad and deep in the Walker River Paiutes, even if tribal members often disagree. Attendance at community meetings reaches well over 50 percent. According to Ben Leva, the Senior Center director, the tribe's seniors program is the envy of western Nevada, other Indian tribes included. Walker River seniors aren't charged for their weekly outings, and the tribe pays their power and gas bills. Certain housing is designated as "handicap homes," and seniors are first on the list for that.

Although elders are the first priority in the community, children are not far behind. Besides exploring all available options to build a new school, the tribe uses any opportunity to create leadership programs for its children. It identifies and places its brightest in outside programs like the Council of Energy Resource Tribes, and while federal summer jobs programs are being cut, the tribe tries to scrape together some funds in its budget to meet that need.

Free health care is an entitlement for Walker River Paiutes at the tribe's health clinic. Although the clinic lost its status as a hospital,

Lobbying in Carson City
Realizing their vulnerability and need to employ sophisticated lobbying tactics in the state, western Nevada Indian tribes have begun holding a "Tribal Reservation Night" in Carson City, the state capital, when the legislature is in session. In 1995 they rented a hotel banquet room and catered a buffet to serve over 100 people. Five legislators and their spouses showed up.

Podiatrist
The Walker River Health Clinic has a family practitioner and a dentist who commute to Schurz daily. The tribe contracts with an ENT on a quarterly basis and an allergist monthly. The podiatrist and optometrist visit more regularly due to the high incidence of diabetes in the tribe and its related circulatory and eyesight problems. A nurse is the single Native American care provider at the clinic.

once serving all Indians in Nevada and large parts of California under the Indian Health Service, and now having to contract out much of the tribe's specialized health care, the tribe has picked up some of the slack, purchasing an EKG machine and defibrillators. On top of seeking funds for that new school, the tribe wants to identify $1.5 million in community block grant funds for a new health clinic.

Next on the docket for Raymond Hoferer and the tribal council is reorganizing the tribe's three businesses—a feed lot, a convenience store, and the boarded up truck stop—making them profitable by cutting staff and marketing more of what sells to tourists, like Indian crafts. This time, the truck stop will be under tribal management. While hoping to win back truckers, the tribe also plans to install an RV park and slot machines for tourists, the latter a bone that sticks in the tribe's craw because it means placing itself under the control of the Nevada Gaming Control Board, giving up one claim to sovereignty.

Hidden in the desolate, hardscrabble corners of the reservation looms a kind of prophetic Sophie's choice for the Walker River Paiutes. Recent exploratory work revealed that some gold and silver lie underneath the arid soil, the ghost of 1906 reappearing. How the tribe decides to handle any fortune will test its sense of community. Now, the tribe is in control, not the antagonistic other.

Negotiations with the navy have jumped to a new level of complexity because the tribe believes some of the precious ores are buried under the bomb-pocked and possibly bomb-laced land. Then, there is a patented mining claim, another vestige from 1906, within the reservation. If the owner finds a vein, he is entitled to follow it under the Mining Law of 1872, even if it moves through reservation land. So, if the tribe doesn't move quickly to develop any gold and silver resources, it could lose them.

Kennecott Copper Corporation has a gold mining operation close to the area, and the tribe could enter a partnership with the mining giant, granting Kennecott the right to mine the ore in exchange for royalties. But neither Hoferer nor the tribal council would enter into such a venture without the consent of the people, since to extract that gold, the tribe would have to rain cyanide onto its land.

"How do we integrate our cultural values into a mining operation?" Hoferer said. "There is a sincere feeling throughout our tribe that we shouldn't be disturbing the mother earth and we shouldn't be digging, making these big holes.

"On the other hand, we have social needs and economic needs and educational needs. Basically, we act as a state or municipal government and we have to provide those services. If we don't have money to provide those services, then . . ."

It's a touchy subject and Hoferer maintains there would have to be a referendum. Nor does he envision a short-term, get-rich approach. "It's not something that all the sudden we're going to embark on and all the sudden we get a bunch of money and, 'You're on your own and that's it. End of story.' That would be self-destruction."

"Would people be able to handle money?" I asked.

"This is all tribal land," Hoferer replied. "Whatever we get from the mine isn't going to go directly to the individual. It's going to be a matter of developing our nest egg, something for future generations to use if they need to use it, because this is a nonrenewable resource. Once the gold is gone, it's gone.

"It's not going to be a thing where tribal members get a whole bunch of money. Far from it. They will get what we can provide, an annual Christmas stipend. It's not something where everyone gets a million dollars and goes nuts. Forget about that. It's not going to happen."

Ultimately, the strength of the Walker River Paiutes lies in its relationship to the land. The land grounds the tribe and is the medium that links people to each other and their ancestors. Even though the tribe's dance with the land has shifted from hunting, gathering, and peripatetic tracings of life's seasons to sinking roots in the last vestige of ancestral territory, reverance for the earth is no less important. Listen to Elveda Martinez:

Passing note in school

The tribe was thrilled when Marlo Steel returned to the reservation to teach the seventh and eighth graders, as she would be a Native American role model for the youngsters. But the first-year teacher was discouraged when her bright energy was met with a lack of respect from some of the students.

"It's like when we're fighting with the navy, they have no understanding of the importance of land to Indian people. It might not look like much. It might look like desert and dry lake. But it's still ours. It belongs to us that live here. Even though that piece out there might not be mine, it's still a part of our reservation. And the future.

"It's all we have. It's some kind of belonging."

2

The First Anglo Settlers
Dugouts on the Land

Thomas Jefferson and his bulldogs, the land promoters, spoke to the first wave of pioneers. "You are the chosen and shall turn the desert into a garden." That refrain still echoes inside many people of the West Desert. To them it is sacred prophecy.

The reality of the West Desert, though, is that the land can only support a marginal life-style. That's one reason why Anglos, when they began their inexorable march across the continent, largely leapfrogged the Great Basin. It became the space that others left behind.

Earlier Desert Archaic Indians had lived on the edge between bare sustenance and oblivion. The lives of Paiutes, Gosiutes, and Shoshones in the middle 1800s relied on a similar, spare materialism. Quickly, West Desert ranchers and miners discovered that lesson—that existence

doesn't allow much margin for error. Not content with just scraping together a life, however, whites began a new orogeny. To prosper on the land, they had to extract its lifeblood.

While Native Americans' life-styles had rendered the landscape less pristine, Anglos grappled with the land with a faith and fervor born in the Protestant ethic. At a rate unseen in geologic deep time, whites began to whittle away the West. In their relentless energy they have carved themselves from the land. A pervasive myth was born, one that begins to intertwine with self-perception and self-actualization, forming a kind of cultural DNA, an Old West that perpetuates itself. Those first Anglo communities balance on the thin divide between cooperation and autocratic independence.

Cattle Ranching
A Tale of Two Aristocracies

"I look at farming and ranching as being the vestige of the aristocracy," said Ron Webber, a rancher in Ibapah, Utah. "It's not that you live an aristocratic life-style, because you don't. The cash flows are low. Most businesses, you can be borrowing and amortizing and still take away a salary. Farms and ranches, especially out here in

the West, you're paying off a mortgage and there's nothing left to go on.

"And, you're fighting. Any time you have equipment, you are fighting a losing battle, because entropy is going to overwhelm you in the end."

"That's the law of disorder?" I asked.

"Yeah. The gradual disintegration and dissolution of all things. So, you don't live an aristocratic life-style, but in order to have that life-style you can only gain it in one of two ways. One is, under the current market conditions, you either inherit it or you have a better-than-average income so that you can purchase it."

In Ron and Dorothy Webber's case, they purchased it 16 years ago and support it with two income streams, Dorothy's as a counselor for Intermountain Health Care and Ron's as a structural engineer. While he used to own an engineering firm in Salt Lake City with eight engineers and equivalent support staff, working on such large-scale projects as the old Salt Palace, he decided he wanted to do something else with his life, so he downsized the business to one employee and now runs it with telecommunication and UPS from a trailer on his ranch.

It always had been in the back of Webber's mind to have a place, but it was only a vague itch. The impetus came when Webber lost his climbing partner in an accident in New Zealand and he had some time on his hands. He first looked in Castle Valley near Moab. It was a long drive and you couldn't really do anything with the 5 to 15-acre plots. He didn't want a ranchette.

"I looked in the ranch ads. There was a terse, two-line ad that said, 'Ranch, Ibapah, Utah, and the phone number.'" Ron and Dorothy had been backpacking in the Deep Creek Mountains for years. They always had gazed down on Deep Creek Valley on the west side and thought it looked like a moonscape. "Nevertheless, I called them, and one thing led to another. But if my climbing partner hadn't been killed . . ." and Webber's voice trailed off into a world of other possibilities.

The Webber spread is small. Three hundred acres with 75 head of cattle. Two hundred acres planted in alfalfa, eyeing an eventual operation with 150 head. That could sustain the Webbers without supporting income, especially since they are childless.

The Webber ranch doesn't look like others in the West Desert. The surrounding yard is lush green grass watered by Rainbirds, rather than broken farm implements interspersed with tenacious weeds. They've turned an old root cellar into a guest house. Its warm wood motif exudes a gentrification in the outback. Indian rugs grace the ranch house's interior walls. Plush, upscale furniture and an occasional modern-looking lamp reveal people who have feet in two different worlds. Their hearts, however, are firmly planted in Ibapah.

Born in 1935, ranching came late to Ron Webber. Originally an English major, Webber earned a bachelor's degree in civil engineering from the University of Wisconsin, Madison, and a master's degree specializing in structural engineering from the University of Utah. He's also completed the course requirements for a Ph.D.

When asked if he only maintains his engineering business for income, Webber replied that he still enjoys the intellectual challenge and "elegance of theory." He disdains the notion of being a gentleman rancher, though, already feeling closer to the Ibapah community than Salt Lake City. Although Ron spends three seasons on the ranch and Dorothy joins him on weekends, they would like to wean themselves from the Wasatch Front and become full-time ranchers.

"I like being isolated. And, I am isolated," Webber said, with the ranch at the end of the road in Deep Creek Valley, close to the Gosiute Reservation. "And, I am particularly isolated because I don't go anywhere. I live a very monkish existence out here. It's a very ascetic existence, and I kind of revel in it."

Many would describe Webber as an intimidating, extreme man. Stallion-like in the hard-to-break ranching community, his chiseled physique of broad shoulders and narrow waist mirror an athleticism that has made him a successful ultra-runner, recently finishing a race from the South to the North Rim of Grand Canyon—and back. His crisp white hair and beard contrast sharply against his brown, leathery skin. He normally averts his light blue eyes when talking, probably knowing that they are shocking when he trains them on you, using them sparingly for emphasis. An occasional broad smile is counterpoint to his more common, pensive demeanor. Ultimately, however, it's his intelligence and penetrating insights that are more intimidating than his physical exterior.

Webber is a man of absolutes and no compromises. He bristled when I used the phrase "the myth of the Jeffersonian yeoman farmer." To him it is history and not myth. Moreover, history is sacrosanct. Since it must be pure fact, there cannot be multiple interpretations. A staunch conservative who would like to absorb his winters writing political tracts, he is widely read, spending nights reading the *National Review*, *American Spectator*, *St. Croix Review*, *Reason*, *Atlantic Monthly*, *Fortune*, *PC World*, and *The Wall Street Journal*. Inevitably, our discussion turned to the politics of ranching.

"This is a ticklish subject," I said, "but what about the subsidies that wind up going to ranchers?"

"There's nothing ticklish about that," Webber quickly replied. "It's ridiculous."

Webber disliked the congressional refinancing of mortgage debts of troubled farms in the 1980s. He felt that political movement was influenced by overly sentimental movies like *The River* and *Country*. He pointed to the fact that many of the troubled farmers were third and fourth generation farmers. The farm had been paid off. So they had borrowed on land speculation. That, Webber felt, was a slap in the face to people like him, who paid their bills and managed wisely.

"But I'll take every one [subsidy] I can get," he continued. "They've been helpful. We'd still be here without the subsidies. We'd still have everything that we've got, although I must say that the subsidies have done our pipelines. They were incentivized," meaning that the Webbers put in $15,000 of the total price of $25,000.

"What's the incentive to the government?" I asked. "Is it making the land more productive and getting more taxes?"

"Well, no, it's not taxation based. The purpose of it is to increase the efficient use of water, primarily. And, in this case it has made use of that water."

Webber would like to pull away from some repetitive ranch chores to devote more time to building his cattle herds. He said he'll hire a Mexican to do his irrigating. "He'll work hard for not much money. I'll be helping out in two ways," Webber said. While a revisionist historian of the West might say there's a hint of traditional western exploitation of new immigrants in that statement, Webber firmly believes that people have to start at the bottom and work themselves up the ladder. That's the core of human progress and social strength.

"That's still the American Dream and that's still the thing that brings people to this country," Webber said. "People don't come to this country because they're looking for an egalitarian society. They come here for one reason only—because there is opportunity to better your life by working hard."

"Would it be safe to say, fair to say, that you've achieved the American Dream?" I asked.

"Oh, absolutely," Webber replied without his usually slow, careful consideration of the question. "We haven't arrived. We'll never arrive. I guess the glory is in the journey. We're not wealthy people, although I guess we are by some measurements. We'd probably be wealthy people if we had invested in the '80s stock market!

"This place is a big black hole. It sucks up the green stuff. But it's kind of a philosophical thing. A building thing. It will be worth something when we have it put together. That's another reason why I'm such a staunch conservative, believe in individual versus collective rights, is that I didn't start out with any special help. My mother and father each had an eighth grade education. My father was kind of a tough case. My parents were divorced. If they'd had a poverty level when I was growing up, we'd have been there, but we didn't know we were poor as kids. And I never thought of myself as being poor. We lived on a nice working class street in a kind of a nice working class rented house. We put paper in our shoes when the soles wore out. We replaced the cardboard, and finally we'd have to go down and get a new pair of shoes," Webber said matter-of-factly, as if to draw no special distinction from the experience.

"I wonder whether or not it's possible to transplant [the yeoman farmer] to the cities. Probably, we haven't done a very good job of it. But is it impossible?" I asked. "The self-reliance and the individual responsibility?"

**Ron Webber
fixing sprinkler head**
Ranchers have to be jacks-of-all-trades, with engineering topping the list of skills necessary for keeping a spread alive. Ron Webber easily slips into that role, as he has a master's degree in structural engineering. But ranch engineering is a different challenge for Webber. It's where the "elegance of theory" must meet the Rube Goldberg practicalities of repairing parts.

Webber looking at plans
Webber maintains his structural engineering practice from a trailer on his Ibapah ranch with a computer and fax machine. He subs out his drafting and sends shop drawings back and forth via UPS. With a three-day turnaround, it's approximately the same amount of time as when he staffed an office in Salt Lake City.

"If it isn't," Webber replied, "then, in my opinion, there's no hope. Then, we're just on the downhill slope. And, what we've been seeing happening is just going to continue happening. Because if the majority of the people don't have a sense of self-sufficiency, then they've got to become takers. If more of the population loses their feeling of self-sufficiency, then they embrace some manner of victimhood, which is what we are finding today.

"I've had people tell me that I am [extreme]. I don't think I am. I don't come off intentionally as being more extreme than I really am. I try to be rational and objective." Certainly, Webber's arguments are peppered with an engineer's penchant for hard facts and disdain of emotionalism. "But it's not irrational to respond to extremism by opposite extremism. There's a certain amount of catharsis in that if nothing else."

"I just don't know how constructive it is," I replied.

Webber concluded by saying, "Well, it's only constructive in the sense that that seems to be the way that the battles are fought. So, you always have to counter extremism with extremism. There's no moderation on the other side. By moderating yourself you're letting things slip by."

Dave Eldridge was born to the land in 1942. The second Eldridge to labor ceaselessly for Mt. Moriah Ranch on the Nevada-Utah border, he's proud that his father is pleased with what he's done with his inheritance, although the challenge of carrying on the tradition initially worried him when his parents bought a highway rest stop so he could take over the ranch.

"Dad'll tell stories to other people [about the things that Dave's done with the ranch], and that makes you feel good. To feel that your parents figure you did well with what they handed you. That was always important to me. To keep the ranch going instead of lettin' it fall apart."

Now, Dave and his wife Helen are facing the third generation syndrome with their two daughters, that awkward time when a ranching family has to consider how to divide a spread a second time for children. You don't want to leave a ranch to someone who's basically uninterested, "because they'll lose it, in a flash of fire," Eldridge

said. When the Eldridge's youngest daughter Evvie and her husband Joe expressed an interest in the ranch, they had full-time jobs in Ely. Dave and Helen had a continual soul-searching conversation with themselves:

"How can Evvie learn where to take the cows in the summer when she doesn't have the time to come along when she works in Ely every day? How can she or Joe learn where not to take the cows? How can they learn where cattle tend to hole up, or where the bulls hide? Desire to be a rancher isn't enough. You have to be able to devote a lot of time. Full-time ranching isn't a weekend job."

Evvie and Joe eventually decided to embrace the life, and a pleased Dave and Helen helped them into it by buying a second ranch in McGill, Nevada, approximately 90 miles away. Now, the combined ranches can run from 400 to 500 cattle, and that can support two ranching families. That only postpones the Eldridge decision, however, since their oldest daughter, who doesn't want to ranch, must inherit something of equal value, while protecting Evvie's grubstake. Eldridge would like to buy more land, but there isn't much for sale, with the federal government owning 80 percent of the land in the area and much of the rest belonging to the large Baker Ranch, Dean Baker having three children himself.

The Eldridges are lucky because they have someone to take over. With the third generation, a ranching tradition can fall apart, especially when there are several children. Having become comfortable, one or two children eye the comforts of the city. Not interested in ranching but wanting to parlay their legacy, they force the ranch's sale. Or, if all the children want to continue ranching, the spread can't be split into multiple parcels large enough to support the children and their families in the style in which they have become accustomed, so it must be sold regardless.

Inheritance problems, though, weren't foremost on Dave Eldridge's mind that October morning in 1992. We were heading to Eldridge's Forest Service grazing allotment on Mt. Moriah to round up the cattle and move them to winter range. Because his allotment is within the Mt.

Moriah Wilderness Area, we were working on horseback.

It was the sixth year of drought. Eldridge hoped to find all 34 pairs of cows and calves plus two bulls, although a cattle rancher has to assume a 2 percent livestock loss on the range every year. He had less hope that the calves would be in good shape when we reached the rarified table-top at 11,000 feet. Calves need water to give them energy to graze and to help get the most nutrition out of the grasses they can find.

Eldridge was concerned, too, about the future of his Mt. Moriah allotment in the Humboldt National Forest. Although grazing was written into the wilderness bill, he knew the Forest Service faced pressures to withdraw it. More important, Eldridge had personal misgivings. During a drought cattle cluster around available water. Unless they can be forced to move, they tend to overgraze the limited area where grass grows. Because he has only himself, he can't spend his summer herding on the table-top. So the land can suffer, and the only thing that concerns him almost as much as losing the ranch is damaging the resource with which he's entrusted.

Eldridge can't give up his Mt. Moriah allotment, though, because like most cattle ranches in the West Desert, his is a balanced operation, raising stocker calves. Born on the range, he'll carry those calves over the winter, having to supplement their range feed with hay during a drought, and sell them in the spring when they are 12 to 14 months old and approximately 700 pounds. So Eldridge has to find equilibrium between winter and summer grazing lands. The land can be public or private, but you can't eliminate one factor in the equation, say losing a federal grazing allotment, without the entire operation falling out of balance. Moreover, there is no available private land, even to lease, if the federal allotments are withdrawn. The Eldridges would have to run less cattle.

Eldridge doesn't always use all the animal units per month (AUMs) he's allowed on either his Forest Service or Bureau of Land Management allotments. He runs fewer cattle because he wants to leave some feed on the ground to allow for a worse year in the future.

He sometimes moves his cattle off his allotments sooner than necessary.

As our horses ambled up the trail, Eldridge periodically would break off a dead branch and beat other dead branches with it. He'd been poked more than once, and he was looking out for the greenhorn behind him. He also just had to keep his hands busy. Usually, if he has a rare, idle moment, Eldridge will begin swinging a lariat, calling himself a "ropin' fool." When he was young, he dreamed of being on the rodeo circuit, but, "There's no money in that either," Eldridge said.

I looked forward to reaching the Mt. Moriah tabletop. People had described it as a shangri-la, especially in summer with its wildflowers. When we reached it that dry autumn day, I had a different reaction. Hampton Creek had stopped flowing at the top, and water that supposedly bubbles up in the summer on the tabletop had become small sinks of baked clay. The grass was brown and cropped close to the ground by grazing. Moreover, I wondered how any plant could get its roots started on the tabletop, as the ground consisted largely of 6-inch flat rocks, arranged in regular geometric patterns like scales on a stegosaurus's back. Aspens at that elevation were stumpy, not much taller than 15-20 feet. The douglas firs were short and relatively few, sometimes spreading out along the ground, like englemann spruce.

The dominant conifers on the tableland were bristlecones and limber pines, and they seemed to be in good shape, with relatively more needles to wizened bark than I'd seen in other areas in the West Desert. One bristlecone suggested the tabletop was no place to be in an electrical storm. It was shattered, like someone had placed ten sticks of dynamite inside it, reducing its tough, resinous wood to Tinkertoys. Radiating out like bicycle spokes from the base of the bristlecone were thick cords of disturbance in the soil, anywhere from 20 to 40 feet long. The surface rocks looked like they had been overturned with a spade, instead of a lightning bolt.

The first calves we saw reflected Eldridge's concern. They were scrawny and listless, when usually they are a bit wild after living all their lives on the range with little human contact. We began looking for the rest of the herd,

Dave Eldridge with horse and dog

Running a small cattle ranch with his wife Helen has emotional underpinnings for Dave Eldridge. He takes satisfaction in being a second generation rancher and increasing the productivity of the spread he inherited from his parents.

Committed to protecting and conserving ranch resources in a fragile environment, he's concerned how one man can manage the pressures on the land.

Eldridge feeding calves
When he looked at this image of himself feeding his new calves, Eldridge expressed satisfaction. He likes the fact that he still performs some ranch chores the old-fashioned way. When he finished feeding this bunch, Eldridge moved to the back of the corral and pitched hay to the the bawling runts who were muscled out of the way by the larger calves. They are at risk of pneumonia while being weaned from their mothers, and Eldridge periodically would sprinkle the corral to keep dust out of the calves' lungs.

Pond at Mt. Moriah Ranch
Most ranchers in the West Desert have more land than they can put into cultivation. Water is the merciless arbiter when raising hay. Without irrigation, only one crop is possible. In a good water year and with proper storage facilities like the pond at Mt. Moriah Ranch, ranchers can have three cuttings.

Scavenging

Dave Eldridge is leery of getting rid of broken ranch equipment. Like most ranchers he keeps old derelicts strewn around the ranch for spare parts, chastizing himself for the mess and saying he needs to tidy things up but lamenting the lack of time to do it. Sometimes, suburbanites try to practice the same kind of recycling.

Eldridge herding cattle

Cattle have a homing instinct and sense the change in seasons. In October when Eldridge moves his cattle down the mountain from his summer range allotment in the Mt. Moriah Wilderness Area, he can drive the cows and calves with only himself and a dog. The cattle are so skittish of the canine that they risk impaling themseves on branches if they bolt when the dog nips at their hooves.

taking a wide circular path on the tabletop, heading for meadows or springs where the cattle might bunch up. Periodically, Eldridge would pick up manure and break it in his fingers. By its dryness he could tell how long it had been since the cattle had been in an area. He looked at the excrement to determine what they were eating, as that also could be a clue to their whereabouts. What was most uncanny was Eldridge's ability to see cattle tracks on nothing but rock. From slight indentations in the ground, not even one-quarter of a print, he could tell how many cattle were together and their ages. Eldridge uses those considerable tracking skills in the winter, too, running a hunting guide service. He charges $450 per person for hunting deer or mountain lions, but he offers hunters a discount if they'll agree to only photograph the cougars when treed, rather than killing them.

Eventually, we were able to find only twenty pairs of cattle. Typically, the bulls hid. Eldridge felt the rest had already worked themselves down another canyon, since the cows remember when it's time to leave the mountain.

On the return trip to Mt. Moriah Ranch, Eldridge began to open up a bit more to the stranger wearing academic chaps. When I plumbed him about the political pressures of having a grazing allotment in a wilderness area, he said he considers giving it up, in spite of his attachment to it. He was recalcitrant because he didn't want to appear that he was giving in to the "antis," the name given to those who want to force all cattle off public land. Maintaining that only 3 percent of the total poundage of beef consumed in the United States comes off public land in the West, the "cattle-free" people believe it is not a reasonable cost-benefit, given the damage they feel cattle inflict on the land. That abstract economic equation, however, doesn't figure in what would happen to families like the Eldridges or small towns like Baker, Ibapah, and Callao if ranching were eliminated.

Eldridge is worried about that "hard-core" mind set. "It's almost like a religion to them," Eldridge said. 'They're real fanatic. Maybe some of the ranchers is just as hard the other way, but I don't think so, most of them."

Eldridge acknowledged there used to be a group of ranchers in the past who didn't give a damn how they treated the land. "Back when I was a kid, some of the real successful ranchers were really greedy. By golly, they seemed to me that they were all sheepmen," Eldridge laughed, knowing cattlemen and sheepmen now peacefully coexist, even trading off allotments in winter to give the land a rest from one type of animal grazing. "They'd hire guys to shoot deer just so they'd have one more mouthful of grass out there," disregarding that deer browse, not graze.

"But you don't see that no more. It's very small. The people have died and a lot of people watchin' them—at least I did—they went the same direction in a box just like everybody else's going to go. It doesn't matter. Some of their kids fought over their place," and Eldridge suggested that they simply became more human.

"I guess there may be some [who still abuse the land]," Eldridge continued, "but on the whole I don't think the ranching industry is hurting anybody. If they do, they're not real good ranchers. You've got to take care of what you have, or you're not going to have it." He acknowledged that drought causes problems with extra pressures on the land. "We have to use it a little harder, because you're trying to maintain. But you do the best you can so you don't destroy it for the next year."

Eldridge said in the early days people had to be especially tough to make it, and he guesses that's why they developed such tough, inflexible attitudes. Ranching or mining was the only way to make a living. "They sure as hell didn't have nobody coming out here to go picnicking," Eldridge laughed, referring to tourism, "because they had no grub to come picnic with or a way to get there."

Eldridge also didn't think the idea of leasing BLM land to almost anyone will work either. He has seen what leasing and absentee ownership often means. "If they go to their leasing plan where any Joe Blow can come in here and lease it, we've seen what happens when they do that. He don't care. He just tracks his cows up and he's . . . goodbye. He cares very little about the area." He doesn't worry about the next year. "If it doesn't work for him," Eldridge continued, "he's just gone."

Eldridge finds it somewhat easier to work with the BLM, especially the Utah BLM, than other federal agencies charged with regulating grazing. Utah BLM managers are more consistent in application of policy because there is less changeover in personnel. He guessed that's because of the Mormon culture, which causes some Utah land managers to forego transfers, preferring to remain in the state.

Eldridge has a grazing allotment in Great Basin National Park, too, written into the enabling legislation. I asked him if he supported the creation of the park.

"Personally, I guess it was inevitable for that park to come, but we were against it. It hasn't terribly hurt us, and it probably has done some good for some people. It helped my niece. She got a good job there. But I guess we're selfish. We just figure, 'Well, we know it's beautiful country and we just as soon there wasn't that many people come and tromp over it.'"

Making it a park poses a threat to his family's way of life. "It's going to make it tougher for us because it draws the type of people who don't like livestock grazing. That's one of the reasons why I don't care for it. But if we get enough opposition here like wilderness on Moriah, well they probably will start saying, 'Well, we don't think them cows are compatible.'"

The increased concern over grazing practices somewhat baffles Eldridge. He maintains grass can lose its nutrition if it gets too old. Then, the grass develops a crown and the center dies. Eventually, the dead tufts in the center fall over the tender green grass, and the plant dies. He's interested in experiments in holistic ranching like the Tipton Ranch in central Nevada, but recognizes that kind of grazing is labor-intensive, needs the cooperative support of land management agencies, and is not oriented toward the small rancher.

Eldridge also believes that if a riparian area isn't grazed the grasses eventually become so long they fall over and die, creating a thick mat where nothing else can grow. In the West Desert rose briars would move in on that riparian habitat. If a riparian area is properly grazed, Eldridge maintained, all flora does much better. It becomes a more biologically diverse community. He agreed there are areas that need regeneration, but he doesn't want to lock them up for

long. He also thought that fencing can solve some of the problems, but he wonders where the funding will come from. Should ranchers have to pay for the environmental mitigation that others demand?

Then the conversation turned to the controversy regarding how much ranchers should pay to graze their cattle on public land. The Clinton administration wanted to increase the AUM fee from the then $1.97 to something around $3 to make it more in line with prices paid by ranchers on leased land. Eldridge felt it could be boosted to between $4 and $5 and still make economic sense. He paid a $5 AUM on leased Steptoe Valley land. Beyond $5, private pastureage is more economical. That's because most of the costs are built into the leasing fee for private pastureage. On public land the rancher must maintain the fences himself, haul water to the site or maintain the windmills, and spend time and money watching and rotating the cattle. Given that, Eldridge said the Farm Bureau claims that raising cattle on public land actually costs the rancher approximately $14 per animal unit, though there was a hint in Eldridge's voice that he didn't believe that figure either.

As we neared Baker and the full moon cast sagebrush shadows across the dirt road with knife-edge clarity, Eldridge began talking about the local community, especially those he perceived as the movers and shakers.

"I'm not real much of a joiner and neither is my wife," Eldridge said. "My folks really weren't either. We just kinda go our own way. We're involved a little bit in a few things around Baker, but we probably should be more. We were more involved when the kids were there in school.

"It's a decent enough community," Eldridge continued. "There's nothing wrong with Baker." Refering to the School of the Natural Order, Eldridge said. "We got a lot of people who come from outside who are running it now, who want to or think they're running it. I don't know that they're always right, but if I don't get involved, then I guess I don't have any bitch. They're good people. I'm not saying they're not. It's just that they tend to like to do that. That's their type of entertainment, going to meetings.

We're still the old breed that thinks that we just want to let us run our cows and leave us alone," he laughed. "But it's not gonna happen."

We passed by a small family cemetery etched into a rocky hillside. As we turned silently, I could only guess what was going through Dave's head. Families like the Eldridges have a unique closeness to the land that mobile urbanites can't quite appreciate—the family graveyard. Usually next to the dirt road the family uses daily, they remind the old guard of the West Desert that they are part of the continuum. The family's beginning and final resting place are the same.

Although it's still a fledgling industry, tourism has brought in many of the newer people in the West Desert community, some without a resting place. Eldridge feels the impact of tourism in Snake Valley.

"There are people everywhere on this desert. And on the mountain," Eldridge said. "You go up any dry canyon and you'll run into people. They're just trying to get away from whatever it is that they're trying to get away from. They want to come out here and ruin my life-style," Eldridge laughed.

In spite of the new recreational pressures, Eldridge doesn't think ill of the tourism business. "They're just trying to make a living," Eldridge said. "That's the big thing that everybody [should realize]—especially the antis who want to get rid of us who make a living like me raising these cows—that I'm just trying to make a living. Some way, they've got to be trying to make a living. They lose sight of that. Even some of our government people. They come in and they feel they're going to save the world," and Eldridge's voice began to climb in pitch for the first time. "People just need to sit back and say, 'Wait a minute.' If you're not destroying something, don't hurt that guy. He's not trying to hurt you.

"I don't think everyone can jump in and make a living off tourists," Eldridge continued. "I don't think that would work totally to have a real good base. It would become a lot looser society. It wouldn't have the roots.

"Each time a whole family leaves one of these ranches, most of them had roots that went back one, two, or three generations. Now they're selling to people who don't seem to stay as long.

There isn't any way of preserving that, I guess, because once a family is gone, they're gone."

A group of recreationists in an off-road vehicle passed us in the dim light and Eldridge waved.

"Do you wave at people less now on these roads?" I asked.

He replied the converse was true.

"I believe I wave at people more now, especially the antis, out there on my horse," Eldridge said. "Some of them like to wave to the cowboy, and the others just as soon [wish] you wasn't there. But you might as well be friendly to them. Besides, it blows their mind. They don't know what you're thinking, I guess."

Epilogue

When the Nature Conservancy approached Dave Eldridge about selling his grazing allotment in Great Basin National Park in 1996, Eldridge said he'd be willing. He'd take that money, sell the two ranches, and buy one larger one, probably in central Nevada, where he, Helen, Evvie, and Joe could raise 800–1,000 head and the generations could live together. But he sensed the Nature Conservancy was losing interest when it declined to exercise its option in 1997.

Low cattle prices in 1995 and especially 1996 had buffeted the Mt. Moriah Ranch. But the Eldridges held on without going into debt, by cutting back on planned equipment expenditures, like a pickup truck, and foregoing a profit.

Dave Eldridge felt 1997 was looking better with prices up almost 50 percent. He also had success selling his herd by videotape broadcast over satellite. It saved him time and money he'd have had to spend trucking his cattle to Salina or selling them on the spot without an auction. The satellite auction gave him five cents more per pound.

Eldridge and the Forest Service also worked out a one-year experimental allotment near Eureka in central Nevada so that he wouldn't have to run cattle on his allotment in the Mt. Moriah Wilderness Area. Eldridge got more AUMs, but they came at a higher price. That didn't matter much. He got more emotional satisfaction from leaving the Mt. Moriah land alone.

Sheep Ranching
Salad Bowl of the West Desert

While you can sense a dreamy, tangible link to the Old West when you are momentarily swallowed up in a sheep herd moving slowly to the horizon through its winter range, sheep and sheep ranching are mythic echoes of their former selves. Even the common belief that sheep eat everything to the ground like wooly locusts was a stretcher spread by cattlemen as they jockeyed with sheepmen over grazing rights. Another myth that sheep ranching reveals is that ethnic mixing in the West isn't really a melting pot. Rather, it was and is a salad bowl.

The global market is undercutting the once powerful influence of the U.S. sheep industry, too. U.S. sheep ranching only accounts for 1 percent of the world's annual consumption. China is the world's leading sheep producer, with Australia a close second. While there are 4 million sheep in the United States, Australia slaughtered 24 million sheep a few years ago because of overproduction when wool prices were high. The Aussies offered the meat free to any country that would come and get it, but all declined. It just wasn't worth the transportation costs.

With over 8,000 head Loren Moench is one of the largest sheep ranchers in the West Desert. His Thousand Peaks Ranch at Trout Creek is the site of his winter range and spring shearing operations. Moench runs a sheep replacement operation. Each year he buys replacement yearling ewes. While he used to raise his own replacements, he finds it pays him to have someone else do that. That other sheep rancher typically has more contained land and fewer predators, so he can run his operation with fewer losses.

In 1993 Moench bought 1,404 yearlings from the replacers at $96 a head. A three-year-old ewe is worth approximately $65. Older ones are $35. Yearlings cost more because they have more breeding years. Also, yearling wool is finer and

Moench can get a better price for that. While ewes can breed until they are age seven or eight, Moench begins to get rid of them at age five. After that, they typically don't have the strength to manage the hard winters on the West Desert. In that tough winter of 1993, Moench lost over 100 due to the uncharacteristically deep snows, 3 feet, at one of his winter allotments south of Wendover. He also lost some to predators. Moench grimaced as he reported the $10,000 loss.

"It's like I see these $100 dollar bills flying away."

With over 1,100 head of cattle, Moench also is one of the largest cattle ranchers in Utah. In fact, his cattle business supports his sheep operations. Even though sheep provide wool in addition to meat and hides, cattle ranching in a good year like 1993 can run with an 8–9 percent profit, while sheep only bring in 4–5 percent in the best years.

"Raising cattle is a piece of cake compared to raising sheep," Moench said in somewhat of a hushed tone, looking over his shoulder for any cowboys. "Cowboys don't like to hear that, but it's true. A cowboy puts a calf out on the range and forgets about him for six months. But sheep have to be tended for 24 hours a day. Then, there's the expense of shearing. And, they have to be moved a lot, and gas is expensive."

In the recent past there has been a glut of sheep, leading to low prices for meat and wool. Sheep ranchers lost their federal government price support for wool in 1995, a subsidy provided when wool was a strategic commodity for the armed forces, in a move to cut the federal budget when the armed forces began to rely on other fibers. The average American eats one pound of lamb versus sixty pounds of beef a year, and meager marketing by food brokers hasn't budged that figure.

So, while sheep ranching operations haven't changed much since the halcyon days of the late 1800s and early 1900s, the sheep industry is in decline. Nevertheless, sheep ranchers' employment practices are deeply embroiled in current public discussions of immigration and ethnicity in the West. Except for tourism, which attracts Asians and Europeans to national parks and provides jobs for Hispanic immigrants and resident aliens, sheep ranching has a more distinctly ethnic and foreign tinge than any other industry in the West Desert. But the migrant nature of the business keeps its minorities separate, much like ethnic groups in the West of the late 1800s lived in China or Greek Town, or land development in the 1990s creates *de jure* segregation at the edge of the railroad tracks.

Many of Moench's problems center on hiring alien labor—Peruvian sheepherders and New Zealand sheepshearers. Because it is migrant labor, it is carefully regulated by the U.S. Department of Labor. The agency sets all wages and responsibilities for the contractors and owners. Moench is audited every few years.

Each sheepherder can work for three years in the U.S. as a legal migrant worker. Then he must go back to Peru. Some eventually get green cards and become resident aliens or citizens. By law a shepherd makes $700 a month. Moench picks up the other expenses: room and board, transportation within the United States, and from Peru to the U.S. and back. He once hired Americans, but switched to Peruvians because they worked harder and were more reliable.

The Peruvians usually don't want to go back to their homeland after three years, especially because of civil unrest due to the Shining Path guerrilla movement. In fact, coming to the U.S. to herd sheep is a plum job in Peru, and shepherds sometimes bribe recruiters to get on the list. Typically, the shepherds are recruited from the Peruvian highlands, where most of the sheep are located, also the stronghold of the Shining Path. Guerrillas know who has gone to work in the U.S. They are targeted when they return and robbed.

Moench contracts with a Joseph, Oregon, outfit for sheepshearing. Although the contractor is an American, he mostly hires New Zealanders. The contractor follows the western shearing season in a diesel truck and semitrailer, the shearers tailing behind in their pickups and "caravans." The semitrailer is specially engineered to fold out into a shearing room, the floor extending out on the sides and a yellow canvas awning creating walls.

The truck cradled itself into the corrals at Thousand Peaks Ranch. After herding thousands of sheep into holding pens, Peruvians forced them one-by-one down a long, narrow chute towards the shearing van by beating on the sides of the chute. If a sheep was recalcitrant, a herder would sic a dog over the wall.

Once the sheep reached the inside of the van, a shearer would stand down on a pulley-driven gate, grab one, and begin shearing its belly by either sticking one front leg of the sheep through his legs or sometimes the sheep's head. While the nine New Zealanders in the crew sheared off the wool, two women ran nonstop picking up the pelts and taking them to the back of the trailer where a wool buyer sorted them by quality into three bins for later shipment to woolen mills like Pendleton and Burlington.

Above each shearer was an electric motor run by a generator in the front of the semitrailer that powered the cutting shears. When all the shearers were operating, the din was like listening to nine old-fashioned, low-speed dentists' drills going at once. Several of the shearers wore cotton in their ears, although most did not.

The temperature that mid-April day was perfect for shearing. Although there had been a deep freeze the night before, and the shearers' fingers were noticeably stiff when they began work, the afternoon temperature reached 65 degrees, the optimum. Above that, the heavy air in the trailer would become unbearably hot and choking. That's partly why the shearers start work in the early spring in the southern U.S. and work north.

It took between four and five minutes for a Kiwi to shear one sheep. When done, he would manually click a counter that hung on a wire above his work station. Then he'd let in the next sheep. A shearer would stop only to change or oil blades or take a drink from a gallon water jug.

Herding sheep

One of the tasks of Peruvian sheepherders at shearing time is to separate yearlings from the older ewes. Because the wool of younger sheep is finer, it can fetch a better price. Later, the oldest ewes will be culled from the herd for sale to ranchers in a warmer climate or to slaughterhouses in Mexico, where mutton is more saleable than in the United States.

Tamping wool

After quality sorting by a representative of the wool buyer, freshly sheared, coarse wool is tamped and bundled into burlap sacks. Later, the 500-pound bales will be sold to Pendleton or Burlington mills. Two people run the bundler, in this case a member of the New Zealand shearing crew and a Peruvian shepherd. When questioned, neither of the workers expressed anxiety about sticking their faces into raw wool laced with ticks.

No wasted motion. The kind of operation that would make Frederick Taylor happy. There wasn't even time to stretch one's back.

Many of the older men rode a kind of sling attached to two large, tubular springs on each side. Like a baby's doorframe jumper, the shearers rode the device and let it absorb some of the weight of the sheep and their torsos, as they had to work bent over all day long. Still, none of the shearers could straighten up for over an hour at the end of the day.

A shearer will shear approximately 200 sheep a day. Moench paid the contractor $2.25 a head, from which the shearer got $1.40 a head. The contractor also was responsible for paying workers' compensation premiums.

Sheepshearing is a young man's work, so it was odd to see Bob Michie, 52, in the crew. He shears one-half the year in the United States and England, always winding up at the World Shearing Championships, the other half tending his small sheep ranch in New Zealand. His wife, Barbara, had joined him for two months.

Michie's attracted by the money, trying to save for retirement and to finance a move into the sheep pregnancy scanning business. When he signed up for migrant shearing, he figured he had four good years in his body, but he was now already into his fifth. He'd "chuck it away" if his health suffered.

"But so far my health's reasonably good," Michie said. "I get a bit sore in my back, you know, when not wearing my harness."

I asked him if there are any preferred positions in the shearing line.

"In the stands there is an advantage in being in certain positions," Michie replied. "If you've got two sheep in front of you, which would you take, the one that looks the best or the roughy?" implying that the rough one might take longer to shear. "The man up the end gets what's left."

Yet Michie purposely took the position at the end of the line because "probably pulling sheep and grabbing 'em like this [like the younger shearers] is a bit harder on me now than way on the end where the head of the sheep is here and I can grab it under the jaw and then I can help swing it around, which is probably actu-ally easier on me than pulling them down the chute [by their hindquarters]."

The shearers and herders retreated to their separate trailers at the end of the day. There was little mixing of the Peruvians and New Zealanders, largely because of language differences. Michie and his wife love to talk to Americans, however. When they have wet weather and are holed up for awhile, they find a tavern where they can talk to some of the locals.

Bob Michie mentioned his change in perception regarding Americans after he came to the U.S. to shear. The Michies' earlier experience had been with the stereotyped American tourists who always wanted things their way. "Especially the older tourists in New Zealand," Bob said. "They sort of have a squawky, screechy voice." Barbara added, "And cameras running."

"I always thought the Americans were loudly spoken because I'd met a few tourists in New Zealand. But I got over here and got off the plane and said, 'Where are the Americans? I can't find the Americans!' They're polite and softly spoken. I couldn't get over it."

But both Barbara and Bob felt there are too many policemen in the United States and that gun totin' laws are too liberal. They also didn't support U.S. nuclear politics, becoming angry when the U.S. government tried to bully New Zealand into accepting U.S. warships with nuclear weapons in its harbors, and proud of their country when it refused to knuckle under.

That night after being a guest at their table, I accompanied Bob and Barbara on their walk through the cottonwoods at Thousand Peaks Ranch. The dust had settled, the sheep were bleating softly in the background, and the sky over the Deep Creeks was streaked with burnt orange and charcoal wisps. In spite of its gross difference from their lush green homestead in New Zealand, the Michies love the West Desert, especially its wildness and austerity. For the Michies the word "frontier" is inextricably entwined with "wild West." It has an American tinge for both of them, conjuring up visions of Billy the Kid and Butch Cassidy.

I asked them if they'd heard of the phrase "the American Dream."

Shearing trailer and corral
Sheep ranchers contract with shearing crews staffed primarily by itinerant New Zealanders or Australians. A semi-truck and trailer wheel into the shearing site and cradle into the corrals. Freshly sheared sheep are pushed through chutes to the ground. Inevitably, some will get nicked. If it's bad enough, Peruvian shepherds will paint the cuts with an antiseptic. They also give the sheep a tetanus shot and spray for ticks.

Inside the shearing trailer
Inside the shearing trailer sheep lint floats in the air like cottonwood seeds, and shearers look like they could step into Millet's *The Gleaners* and not look out of place. Loren Moench instructs these shearers to use a wider comb to keep some wool on his ewes. April is unpredictable on the West Desert. It could snow and freeze, and he wants to give his pregnant sheep a bit of extra protection.

Michie getting a hair cut

New Zealand sheep shearer Bob Michie has three daughters. Mary, who recently graduated from college with a degree in tourism, is part of the shearing crew, although she stays with her boyfriend in another caravan. At the end of an 8 to 5 shearing day with one hour for lunch, father and daughter give each other haircuts.

"I've heard it," Bob said, "but I couldn't tell you what it's all about." When I described its scope, they replied that there was much the same thing in New Zealand, just not called that. It might mean getting to fish as much as one wanted, Bob said.

"What is your dream?" I asked.

Barbara replied, "I wish we had time for a dream. As long as you are happy in what you're doing."

Bob said, "You never know what your dream is, you know."

Barbara continued, "You never really know if you're happy or unhappy, do you now?"

Then I asked the Michies where that crossroads was when Bob would give up shearing and go back to full-time ranching.

Bob laughed and said, "Probably when I make megabucks," referring to the dollar slot machines in Nevada. "There's about four million in the jackpot at the moment."

While sharing with Bob the dream of hitting it big in Nevada, Barbara replied with a more tempered and fatalistic "What happens will happen."

Farming
Yeoman at the Millenium

The atmosphere inside the water rights hearing held in 1993 at the West Desert School was tense, charged with a kind of energy that can only be generated by a clash of cultures and the will to live. George and Buck Douglass wouldn't look at their nemesis, Glen Allred, patriarch of Granite Ranch. Two men from the Utah State Engineer's office nervously shuffled through the stack of papers from the court decree that would be sacred writ in that meeting. Only two people openly acknowledged each other's presence, by glaring at each other: Glen Allred and Cecil Garland, the court-appointed river commissioner.

The yearly meeting held to monitor the status of the agreement between the Douglasses and Granite Ranch began with the water engineers going over the minutes of the previous year's meeting. Allred had questioned whether or not the occasional water flowing down Cottonwood Canyon on the east flank of the Deep Creek Mountains should be counted by the Douglasses toward their needs before they could tap into Granite Creek or Red Cedar Creek water. The engineers, after a year's thought, agreed that it should. The Douglasses were quick to agree to this request and said they would install a water meter on Cottonwood Creek. They knew that the flow was so infrequent that measuring its paucity would mean they'd likely be able to tap into Granite Creek water sooner.

Then the subject of measuring water flow out of Red Cedar Creek came up. As river commissioner, Garland was to read the water meters or weirs and determine when Granite Ranch, the concern with senior right, had had its 2,000-acre-feet share, 3.5 acre-feet per acre irrigated according to Utah law, signalling the time to open a head gate allowing the Douglasses to begin getting their water.

The Douglasses charged that too often Allred's water meters on both Red Cedar and Granite Creeks didn't work. Allred admitted that, for a period of approximately two weeks during the irrigation season, the water meter on Red Cedar Creek hadn't functioned, but that a weir was still working during that time, so that it was possible to get a rough reading of how much water was going to the Granite Ranch. Garland countered that the weir leaked and that as much water seemed to be going around the weir and then into the Granite Ranch aqueduct as over it, so that even a rough measurement of water flow wasn't possible. Allred agreed to fix the measuring devices, but the Douglasses had heard that before.

Water is the mother's milk of western politics, an elixir that becomes volatile when it's mixed with two additives: power and survival. The extent of its flow marks the boundaries of influence and empire. For small farmers like the Douglasses, however, it is more fundamental. Water is the key to their longevity on the land. It's the high drama of their lives, albeit a drama that plays out painfully slowly. It began in 1972 when they moved to the West Desert and has not yet reached its climax.

Before George and Veronica Douglass and their three children moved from Salt Lake City to their 160 acres, George had carefully matched their water needs with available rights. The old Falkenberg place had rights to the intermittent runoff from Cottonwood Canyon and a sporadic spring, not enough to raise hay and a family of five. But George figured water conservation and later a well would give them enough to survive.

He first needed to tear out the old, leaking wooden stay pipeline and replace it with concrete. Through a cost-share deal, the Agricultural Stabilization and Conservation Service agreed to furnish the pipe if the Douglasses would provide the labor. Without funds to hire a contractor, George spent three months their first year on the homestead with a pick and shovel and dug a trench a half-mile long, 3 feet deep, to allow more wash and spring water to reach the farmhouse.

When the spring ran dry, they'd haul water out of Granite Creek. For one and a half hours daily, they'd pump creek water into a 500-gallon tank on the back of a small trailer, drive three-quarters of a mile, and dump it into their cistern. That was enough to live on and water a small garden, although not enough to irrigate. The family practiced water conservation like a religious rite.

"We'd use it to flush the toilets and mop the floors and then recycle the water," Veronica Douglass said. "We never had any waste. After we finished washing 10, 20 loads of clothes we'd use the water to put on the cabbages, or water the garden." There also were a lot of baths in the same light brown water.

They devised ingenious ways to tap into what water they had. They put in a pond to store spring runoff, christening it with a diving board. They planted fruit trees along Cottonwood Creek to capture the water that leaked through the pipes. They canned or froze the water they harvested in foodstuffs, keeping a large pantry and four to six freezers full.

In a tradeout for back pay on a mining project that soured, a well driller agreed to dig George Douglass a well. With a 5-horsepower pump, they could draw 100 gallons a minute, enough to make them drought-proof should Cottonwood Creek and the spring dry up. The problem was it takes a lot of electricity to lift that water 200 feet on the Deep Creeks bench, and the Douglasses had little extra income.

In fact the farm has never supported itself. Buck Douglass, George and Veronica's son, earns money from selling eggs and an occasional pig. He tried raising ferrets, but the state passed a law outlawing that. He went into aquaculture, wanting to supply the family with fish protein, having read about the amazing growth rate of talapia, a warm water type of catfish found in South America. But the state wouldn't give him a permit, fearing the fish could escape Buck's closed system aquarium and get into the waterways of the arid lands abutting Great Salt Lake Desert. Buck switched to bluegills, but after the

state raised the permit fee every year, at $50 it was no longer worth it.

Father and son can fix or build anything. Jay Banta, manager of Fish Springs National Wildlife Refuge, attested to Buck's skills. "Buck is the first person I met who is a mechanical genius," Banta said. "If you put the space shuttle in front of him and told him to fix it he'd be able to fix it. He'd just use some scavenged material from around the ranch and fashion it into a new part."

But there's not much money for engineering genius in Snake Valley. In order to farm and live on the land, George and Buck Douglass must become itinerants on it. George is a millwright at an aluminum recycling plant in Wendover, and comes home only on weekends. Buck commutes three hours daily to Great Basin National Park where he is the carpentry foreman. He does his farm chores at night when he returns. Shelly Douglass, Buck's wife, cuts the hair of north Snake Valley women from a stool in the farmyard overlooking 150 square miles of open land below. Their life, as Buck said, is, "Get a load here, get a load there, and scratch your ass where you can."

The itinerancy is especially hard on George Douglass. For him the American Dream is being happy with what you're doing. He has that at Deep Creek Mountain Ranch. "The only thing that I would like would be [to be] able to stay home," George said. After all, next to his family, homesteading the West Desert is George's *raison d'etre*.

Every aspect of the Douglasses' life has had to be measured. Until George landed the millwright job, there never had been any money for extras. Used clothing hung in their closets. The only Christmas presents anyone received were homemade.

They were equally deliberate when they decided to buy a place in the West Desert. George and Veronica, born in 1938 and '42, grew up in Salt Lake City. George finished his biology degree at the University of Utah and worked on a contract with the U.S. Army doing disease surveys in wildlife populations at Dugway Proving Ground. There two streams came together for the Douglasses. They fell in love with the cleansing

Buck Douglass building a road

Buck Douglass is one of the few Anglos allowed on the Gosiute Indian Reservation, where the old Queen of Sheba mine is located. Due to the tribe's trust in him, Goldfields Mining Company hired Douglass to cut a road into the mining claim that they were interested in reopening. Even though he has only one eye, due to a childhood accident, Douglass isn't intimidated by the precariousness of cutting a road on 45 degree slopes at over 9,000 feet.

Buck Douglass irrigating

After a three-hour commute, Buck Douglass returns to Deep Creek Mountain Ranch, where he must begin the farm chores. Water percolates quickly through the granular soil at the base of the Deep Creek Mountains, making raising hay in the high desert even more problematic. When water supplies are halted by upstream users, drought-tolerant weeds gain the upper hand.

Buck Douglass at weir

Water flow from perennial streams like Granite Creek in the Deep Creek Mountains varies even within a day, especially during snow-melt. So measuring flow is critical for Buck Douglass. Moreover, when the flow dips to less than 10 cubic feet per second, and a family's survival hangs in the balance, there is no margin for error. Living in the West Desert is a measured existence.

George and Carter Douglass at home

George Douglass is well known in a region where knowing how to make things work is esteemed. He seldom has a problem finding work in distant towns. Not enjoying living away from home, Douglass would rather be at the homestead with his grandson Carter, but the farm won't support one family, let alone two. The only time he and his wife Veronica return to Salt Lake City is for Johnny Mathis and Yanni concerts.

isolation of the West Desert, and they became friends with similar professionals at Dugway who were part of the back-to-the-land movement in the 1960s.

"They had the same idea of buying a place way out somewhere and becoming self-sufficient," George said. "They'd make a down payment while they were working, and then move out there, borrow some money to buy a tractor. But you can't support yourself farming. Or ranching or anything else, any more."

Simply wanting to go back to the land isn't enough. "You can't do that because you lose the place," George continued, "and that's what happened with these people."

The Douglasses swore they would do it differently. They made up their minds that they'd have the place paid for first. Something she read had left its mark on Veronica. "I'd read *The Grapes of Wrath*," Veronica said, "and I thought someday I'd like to buy a house. But I didn't want to lose it."

Any money Veronica made went into the credit union. When the elder Falkenbergs died and their place became available, the Douglasses made an offer of their $12,000 life savings, even though the asking price was $25,000. Eventually, they settled on $16,000 and the Falkenberg children agreed to float the remaining $4,000, which the Douglasses paid off in 18 months by liquidating all their worldly goods.

The farmhouse was near collapse. All the windows were gone and the house had to be insulated before winter. "The place had been badly vandalized, and people'd hauled stuff off," George said.

"Local people?" I asked.

"Yeah," George said. "The brethren."

While the well helped the water supply, it wasn't the answer. Too often, it ran dry. George thought about trying to drill a second well, and even toyed with Buck's request to let him try water witching. George doesn't believe in dowsing, but he's always been intrigued by Buck's sensitivity to electrical current. While George cannot feel a shock that is less than 40 volts, Buck can feel an electrical current of 6 volts from a battery.

"Why not," George said. "It's a crap shoot anyway."

Then, in 1975 George noticed that water out of Granite Creek belonging to the Granite Ranch, then owned by Loren Moench, wasn't being used because the ditch had completely sanded in. George knew state law allowed anyone to claim water rights unused for five years because Utah mandates that water has to be put to beneficial use. If they could get hold of that water, they'd have a third source, and their problems would be solved.

In 1980 the patient Douglasses filed claim on the unused water. After the state advertised the new claim in the Nephi newspaper and no one responded, the Douglasses began putting in the piping to bring Granite Creek water to the farm. The supplementary water would give them enough to guarantee two cuttings of hay and possibly a third, providing them an $8,000 profit. They even talked about putting in a new hay field. Moreover, the drop in elevation from Granite Creek to the farmhouse would enable them to develop a small hydroelectric plant which they could use to pump water from the well.

"When I went in and filed on that water," George said, "[the clerk] pulled records and saw what was going on here. And he said, 'Are you sure you want to file on this?' and I said, 'Yeah, they haven't used that in five years.' He said, 'Well, that doesn't matter. You'd better be prepared because ultimately this will wind up in court.' And I said, 'Fine.' See, I never bothered with any of these lawyers [at first]. Big mistake. We just waited until that water hadn't been used for five years."

The state took over 18 months to visit the farm and make an inspection. Arguing that the Douglasses' work on their pipeline had caused the ditch to sand in, Loren Moench filed for an extension, a right granted by the legislature to accommodate damage caused by record flooding in 1983. That stymied the Douglasses' plans. When Moench sold Granite Ranch to the Allreds, they built a diversion dam above the Douglasses' head gate, effectively cutting off their water. Granite Ranch took complete control of Granite Creek. The dispute wound up in court.

Douglasses bringing in a well

Well drilling was one of the first skills George Douglass realized he'd need to attain if his family of five were to survive in the desert. He's practiced by drilling two wells on the farm, but occasionally the water table falls below the intake pipe and the wells dry up. If future development in the area led to more drilling, pumping well water a greater height wouldn't be economically feasible for the Douglasses and other farmers and ranchers in Snake Valley.

George Douglass in Wendover

George Douglass has parlayed a bachelor's degree in biology and further study in geological engineering, with long experience in construction, into a job as a millwright in a Wendover plant that recycles aluminum cake. Paying more than any job he's had, it provides some extras. But an obsession with water born from a struggle to find it and keep it spurs him to get his well-drilling license, with which he could work for himself.

In 1996 there still was no resolution. In spite of the court's 1991 stipulation that the Douglasses must have any water from Granite Creek after the Allreds have had their 2,000 acre-feet from all sources combined, the diversion dam prevents that. The Allreds covet any water they can get to generate their own, saleable hydropower, since the arable land on Granite Ranch can't support the families.

"It's been ten years it's been dragging on," George said. "Most of this has been dragging on because of our lawyers."

"We think most of it's because of the state. Reluctance to enforce the law," Buck continued.

The only year the Douglasses got their legal share was when they paid for the river commissioner to read measuring devices. But Cecil Garland eventually gave up in frustration, never getting the assistance he needed from the state.

"If I had the money I've spent on lawyers and legal costs, I could be retired," George said. "This legal battle has taken half of what I've made for the last ten years."

In a moment of frustration, George wondered whether the homesteading move was a good one. After all, he gave up two careers—epidemiology and real property development.

"I damn sure wouldn't start again," George continued. "It may be nice for the kids, but I wouldn't start now. This water thing goes on and on and on. I'm tired of it."

"The thing is," Veronica added, "everything's dying. Things die if you have no water."

Veronica Douglass still saves dirty wash water for the cabbages and fruit trees. While the garden is smaller now, partly because the kids are gone, she dutifully cultivates it, feeding the choicest weeds to the trusting pronghorn that graze the dry stubble left after the family's sole cutting of hay.

That act of grace suggests why the Douglasses will remain on the land. In spite of their draining battle to secure enough water to nurture their roots on the land, where others have failed due to suffocating debt or emotional exhaustion, the Douglasses endure. Pressure is met with toughness, ingenuity, and resoluteness. Prevailing on the land inspires a vision that kindles the Douglass will.

With the help of scholarships and money from Veronica's wealthy mother, who wonders why anyone would want to live in such a god-forsaken place, George and Veronica put Buck and his sister Susie through the private Wasatch Academy. They encouraged Susie to follow her dream of becoming a country western singer, and she is on the brink of stardom penning songs in Nashville. Their youngest daughter Bonnie, a foreign exchange student, left West Desert High School a year early to attend Utah State University. Buck and Shelly just built a solar-powered house.

But the Douglasses' yeoman independence comes across as iconoclasm to many in northern Snake Valley, especially to the dominant polygamist and Mormon cultures. The Douglasses' well-considered outspokenness has won them some respect in the local community, but not many friends. Buck Douglass stated it like an open challenge. "Out here, you have to declare. You can't straddle the fence." In his more openly rebellious years, there was a carved wood sign that hung over the doorway of his home: "Men are not the dreams of gods, but gods are the dreams of men."

That contrarianism isn't just a product of testosterone. When Susie Douglass delivered her valedictorian address at West Desert High School, she gave voice to the family's beliefs.

"Most of the people here were in favor of MX, any kind of development," George related. "'It's gonna bring jobs. The kids won't have to leave the community.' Susie brought it up when she was the valedictorian that these kinds of things already exist. In cities. If that's what you want, go there. We came out here to get away from all that."

"How did that go over?" I asked.

"It didn't go over very big," George replied. "But Ronnie was sitting next to Norma Matheson, and she leaned over to Ronnie and said, 'This is wonderful. It just leads right into what Scott [then Utah's governor] is going to say.'"

The Douglasses still get flyers in their mailboxes informing them of local social events, usually sponsored by the school or local Mormon church, but they really don't feel a part of the community. They were strong supporters

Veronica Douglass dehydrating apricots

There is irony in Veronica Douglass dehydrating apricots, since the Douglass family uses and recycles every drop of water it can find. Offering juicy apricots to the searing West Desert winds of July is a kind of transcendental asceticism that trains the will and sharpens the focus of desert farmers.

Shelly Douglass canning

Shelly Douglass captures some of the water that the 12,000-feet Deep Creek Mountains steal from storm clouds wrung dry after ascending the Cascade Mountains to the west by canning fruits and vegetables. Stocking a pantry and four to six freezers with foodstuffs from a large garden will carry the extended Douglass family through the winter.

of the school when their kids attended, but recent changes in the school culture make them leery.

"I don't want to be part of it. It's a strange place," George said. "These people are mostly related. They all go to church together. Yet they're suing one another for this, that, or the other."

"Cecil Garland once told me that a community is tied together by mutual animosities," I said.

"I think that's a pretty good definition," George replied.

"I guess a lot of it is over water, isn't it?" I said.

"Yeah, water, but most of it is over trivial nonsense," George continued.

One of the reasons why the community eyes the Douglasses with some angst is because they don't preach the party line. Being independent to the Douglasses means keeping a sense of balance, even when you are nominal farmers. George wrote a common carrier article for the *Salt Lake Tribune* arguing that farming in Utah isn't very important to the economy, pointing out that less than 1 percent of the state's gross receipts come from agriculture, and that agriculture is more important to the state of New Jersey.

George wishes his community would be more willing to change. "These farmers and ranchers don't want to change. The cattle business has gone to hell, but they won't consider doing anything else. They were born into it, and they should be able to do that for the rest of their lives. Now, in my short life, I've done a lot of different things. Just because you're born into something . . ." and George's voice trailed onto a well-worn path of incomprehension.

His views on grazing aren't any more palatable to his rural community. "There are two things I'd like to see in my lifetime," George opined. "The failure of Glen Canyon Dam and the other one is elimination of private stock on public land. It will be a full life if that happens."

Ardent environmentalists, the Douglasses were early supporters of maximum acreage of BLM wilderness in the Deep Creek Mountains, as long as it wasn't drawn purposely low on the bench to make their water line from Granite Creek illegal, a challenge from mysterious political quarters they had to address at one time. Their environmental views don't sit well with the community either.

"If they'd just wake up. Come into the modern world," George said. "They're all against wilderness. See, that's going to infringe on the mining."

George Douglass, like many other farmers and ranchers, did some prospecting, even finding a promising body of titanium once, over 5 percent. He thought about putting in a claim on it, until he talked to a Bureau of Mines employee who told him to forget it. Australia has an unlimited supply of titanium that runs 14 percent, and their mining laws allow an open pit.

"How are you going to compete with that?" George asked. "Hey, mining's a thing of the past."

So, while the current public perception may be that Thomas Jefferson's yeoman farmer must be a rock-ribbed conservative, it seems that he can come with liberal stripes too, underscoring the argument that contemporary definitions of conservatism and liberalism differ from the classical philosophies practiced by the nation's founding fathers. Maybe it's just a healthy strain of common sense and a courage to challenge hallowed public beliefs that shape the Douglasses' view of the world. The irony is that this independent thinking, which Jefferson envisioned as the strength of the yeoman farmer and the salvation of a democratic republic, isolates the Douglasses from their community.

Mining
Chipping Away at the Prospector

When I interviewed Jack Shaffer in 1994, it was a dessicating 97 degrees in his mining shack, the first summer in several he had been able to stay in Gold Hill, Utah, as a gall bladder operation and prostate cancer had kept him tethered to his home in Salt Lake City. The delayed exposure to the West Desert sun was sorely evident. The arms below his short-sleeve, white shirt were fried a lobster red. His sunburned lips were blistering, and Shaffer couldn't eat anything but liquids. It hurt to push words past those lips, so they tended to stop there, muffled like he was talking through wadding.

Realizing what he must have looked like, Shaffer, 65, said, "I was trying to make up for lost time of the previous two years when I couldn't work due to health problems. But I've overdone it."

One hundred yards from Shaffer's cabin is Joe Murphy's Airstream trailer. Murphy is one of only three full-time residents in Gold Hill, having lived there for over 30 years after first sheepherding in the area. Well into his 70s, he prospected until just a few years ago, when three heart attacks and a triple bypass finally drained his energy. During his last heart attack, he had to drive himself from Gold Hill to Salt Lake City, approximately four hours. The pain was intense. Murphy would rather live in Gold Hill, though, than close to a hospital.

"When you die, you die by yourself," Murphy said. "And, nobody can help ya. Nobody can do your dying for ya. And, it don't make a damn bit of difference where you die, because you're goin' to die anyway."

Unlike Shaffer, Murphy has gotten rid of all his mining claims, mostly because he can no longer work them. Besides, he thinks the future is dim for the small prospector. Although the Republican changeover of Congress in 1994 stalled changes in the Mining Law of 1872, he believes some of the proposed changes are inevitable. Since the BLM put in new regulations regarding doing assessment work, he said most other prospectors have let claims go too, unless they are patented, when you only have to pay taxes.

"They aren't worth hangin' on to," Murphy said. "The federal government wants to charge a hundred dollars per claim instead of requiring yearly assessment work. [A claim is 20 acres.] But a claim holder still has to do the regular work for the state to hold on to the ground. Tooele County charges ten to fifteen dollars yearly for maintaining the claim, too. But since you can't get anything out of them, what's the use?"

Prospectors only just "look around a bit now," Murphy said. If they find a bit of mineral, they make claims on it, but only in the hope that some big outfit will come in and buy the claim. Murphy believes the BLM will begin raising the assessment fee every year.

"A little more and a little more and a little more. They're using it to drive all these little miners out of it. Now, if you even take a piece of heavy equipment in to do your assessment work with, you have to file an environmental report with the BLM to get a permit to even drive a Cat across a piece of this old desert. They make it so miserable that you can't turn over a shovel-full of dirt without getting a permit."

Murphy also pointed out that if you disturb over two acres of ground, you have to put up a $2 million reclamation bond to cover it. The people doing the hard rock prospecting can't afford all that, especially when it's done more as a hobby than anything else. Murphy also figures that the last people holding the claims are going to be required to fill in the holes.

Describing themselves as "loners" and "misfits," Shaffer and Murphy are all that is left of Gold Hill, their ilk the remnants of small

Joe Murphy

Joe Murphy calms two dogs frightened by one of the frequent, low-level sonic booms that plague the area. A self-described misfit, he lives alone in Gold Hill. He married three women, each time only for their children. Those seven step-children implored him to have triple bypass surgery. Otherwise, he would prefer nature take its course.

prospecting in the West Desert. Large, multinational mining companies might borrow the myth of the luck-and-pluck prospector when they argue against changes in the Mining Law of 1872, but all their prospecting is done by staffers or consultants with graduate degrees.

Gold Hill, established in 1892, has gone through three boom-and-bust periods. After the initial rush for gold and silver petered out, the federal government built the Deep Creek Railroad in 1917 to gain access to the rich deposits of arsenic, which were used to control insects destroying cotton fields in the South during World War I. At its height Gold Hill boasted a population of 3,000 people, most living in tents. There was a mercantile, a school, a pool hall, a movie house, a miners hospital, a Ford garage, a hotel and two boarding houses, a lumberyard, two railroad depots, two brothels, a newspaper, a post office until 1949, and a bowling alley during World War II.

When cheaper sources of arsenic were found overseas, the railroad pulled out and the small miners had no way to get their ores to a smelter. The town languished until World War II, when the nation needed Gold Hill's tungsten for steel and electric filaments. After the war, the town busted again.

During Prohibition, bootleg whisky was distilled in the mine tunnels, wherever there was a trickle of water, and sold in Wendover. It was a relatively safe operation because moonshiners could sit on the surrounding points and see 50 miles for a cloud of dust, which meant the revenuers were coming.

Besides the transportation problems, the geology of Gold Hill has made it difficult to mine. The mining area is scarn-type, meaning the finds are either like pipes or lenses, saucer structures that are flat and not too thick, high-grade, streak ores that go about 300 feet deep. Now the only ore that is worth anything is gold, but you can't find enough of it in one place to make it economically feasible to get out. You really need to find a glory hole, and the old prospectors were uncannily adept at locating those.

The Gold Hill ores also are complex. When Joe Murphy discovered molybdenum, "just about the time the bottom dropped out of the market," the only one of his claims that ever paid

off, he sold it rather than trying to deal with the complexity of rocks that can range from 0.6 to 1.2 billion years old. Now it takes an investment of $10 million to develop the cyanide heap leaching process to get the remaining gold out of low-grade ores.

According to Murphy, more investors were mined in Gold Hill than minerals. Promoting began when a little seam was hit. Then promoters would get the story in a mining newspaper and begin "peddling stock and crap till hell wouldn't have it. Then the promoters would divide that up and wait for another go-around," Murphy said. "Those mine promoters would promote a stock for about ten times what they'd ever get out of these mines."

More recently, Murphy said that another promoter came to Gold Hill and bought a lot of property, expecting to eventually resell the lots for a resort community. It was advertised on TV as a "select community of nothing but doctors and lawyers."

"He was full of bullshit," Murphy said.

Mining has left the Gold Hill water supply undrinkable with salts, arsenic, and other heavy minerals. Joe Murphy drank it for six years, but his hair fell out and most of his teeth rotted away, "getting soft in the middle and loosening up so you can pull them out with a pair of pliers," Murphy said. Now he has to bring in a 50-gallon drum of water monthly from Wendover for drinking. Murphy tries to keep a few fruit trees alive, but most die within four years from the alkalinity of the water. Vegetables can't stand the salts at all. Murphy and Shaffer will only bathe and wash dishes in the community water.

All that's left of Gold Hill's heyday is overburden and mine shafts that Jack Shaffer won't enter because of rotting timbers, snakes, spiders—and now hantavirus from mice droppings. Shaffer has kept a few of his claims, although one by one he's filling them in, worrying that a small boy on a weekend outing might fall into one. He has hopes for his patented claim, although he doubts he'll ever get to work on it because the adjacent claim holder, a mining engineer in Missouri angry that Shaffer managed to get one of the six Hicks claims, won't give him an easement to build a road, even though it would give them both access to their claims and the other claim holder would be legally entitled to any overflow from Shaffer's well.

"The claim is just something that I'll give to my boy someday," Shaffer said.

Still, all summer long Shaffer picks at rocks in mine dumps. Hunched over, he looks for gold, silver, lead, zinc, tourmaline, mica, calcapyrite (copper), and tungsten. In all the years that Shaffer has been splitting leftover rocks, he has never found one with any gold flaking in it. The old miners were like crazed, alchemic vacuums. They found everything and took everything. Why, then, when he doubts he'll ever be able to develop his patented claim, and for 20 years he's never really found anything from breaking apart rocks in overburden piles, does Jack Shaffer hold on?

He's wedded to the process. "It's just the idea I like," Shaffer said. "It's freedom. I'm by myself. I'm a loner, really."

Shaffer hates to see access to land cut off, either by government regulations or by mining companies that buy up all the claims they can and hoard them. Shaffer charges the American Consolidated Mine in Gold Hill is run like that, using claims to inflate company stock, while doing little work on the ground. While he's aggravated he might have to pay $100 for each of his remaining claims, Shaffer likes the idea that American Consolidated will get its comeuppance, having to cough up half a million dollars for its 5,000 claims.

"That's going to cost him some money," Shaffer said. "He's going to have to put up or shut up, because Uncle Sam's not going to take it."

Neither Shaffer nor Murphy is particularly fond of government, especially the Bureau of Land Management, although Shaffer is less strident, due to retiring from Hill Air Force Base.

"That BLM's as crooked and rotten as the IRS, and they've got more power," Murphy said. "They can do anything they please. You got no recourse when it comes to them. They just tell you what it's going to be, and that's it."

Murphy believes that power, once established, acretes more to itself. "It just keeps building up and building up and building up to where they keep passing them laws to keep perpetuating themself. Pretty soon, there's nothing you can do about it."

Murphy's animosity toward the federal government is deep, despite the positive role the federal government had in developing the Gold Hill mining district and town. The Gold Hill community for Murphy exists separately from government and coalesces around expedience. Murphy pointed out that if the water system breaks, "whoever is down below it has to get someone else to help him fix it." Occasionally, though, the outwardly gruff Murphy belies a soft center. When telephones were offered with plans for the MX missile, four residents of Gold Hill needed Murphy's fifth phone in order to qualify for a spur line. Murphy acquiesced, though he didn't want one.

I asked Murphy what kind of an argument they made.

"They said, 'You'd be a shit if you didn't,'" he replied.

Otherwise, residents of Gold Hill, full- or part-time, don't mix too much, understandable for self-described "loners." They maintain a distance, like people in a bus station waiting room. Murphy said he could count on help if he needed it, but would only ask for a neighbor's help "if it was life or death."

"You can't do too much crap to your neighbors out here because you need 'em," Murphy said. "There's not enough people around. You can't get these big cliques and shove one over there and that one over there and then call them dirty names. Because you need that guy as much as he needs you. And, that's what you call democracy."

Murphy doesn't think you can find that in a town or a city. "Out here you don't segregate and fight people because of what they look like or who they are. It's the way they treat you that makes a difference. You don't even talk to your next-door neighbor at all [in the city]. They just go on and ignore ya. They's so busy scrambling around and scrounging and trying to hoard stuff and then make some more . . . I don't know. It's a funny business."

I asked Murphy if the frontier makes a person any different.

"You got to depend more on yourself than you do on somebody else. I can't expect that guy over there to fix my car tires or haul in my drinkin' water. The frontier makes people tougher, and more tolerant."

Jack Shaffer

Jack Shaffer has been traipsing to Gold Hill on summers for over twenty years to prospect and tend his few claims. Retired from Hill Air Force Base, he has cut a deal with his wife Isabel. She hates it in the forlorn West Desert mining outpost but knows how much it means to Jack. The tradeoff: Isabel goes to Florida in the winter while Jack stays in Salt Lake City and tends the house.

The frontier levels people, too.

"They can see how tough it is and they know the next guy's got it just as tough as they have," Murphy continued. "For little crappy things, well you ain't a'bitchin' about stuff like that. It's got to be something pretty serious before you start causing somebody else any trouble."

Shaffer and Murphy differ when it comes to community improvement. A tidy man, Shaffer wishes Gold Hill would clean itself up. "See that old car laying on its side down here?" Shaffer said. "That's been there I betcha over thirty years. It was there the first day I ever come to Gold Hill. And, there's a '41 Buick sittin' up there. That was old Art's. He got drunk and left it up there. Tire's rotted off of it, and it's still sittin' up there. He was like an Indian. When they quit he got up and walked off."

Shaffer tried to convince the others to call a scrap dealer from Salt Lake to come out and get the stuff. It would be worth something to the community. But he couldn't get anyone interested.

"I always got, 'Oh, no, no, no!' from everybody. 'That's what makes Gold Hill,'" Shaffer reported.

Miners leaving their refuse on the ground isn't new to the West Desert. They considered themselves itinerants in a vast country. Besides, what's wrong with metal left above ground when you're digging for the same thing down below?

Murphy likes his junk around him. He keeps five cars on his yard so that it looks like a lot of people are at home, trying to discourge what he calls "junkers," people who see a ghost town and decide anything can be carted off. He had to pull a gun on two who wanted to haul away his ore car, and they had the gall to get mad at him.

Both Shaffer and Murphy see themselves as conservationists, but not environmentalists, who Murphy defines as "radicals."

"Conservationists want to preserve what there is, within reason," Murphy said. Murphy believes that feeding people should come before wilderness, although he also believes that feeding people and having wilderness would be the best of all possible worlds.

"Don't you wish someone like an environmentalist had gotten on the state sooner to test the water here?" I asked.

"No, why?"

"Well, then you wouldn't have lost your teeth," I replied.

"So what? Then they'd just charge me a thousand a month to come out here and put in a treatment plant. I'd sooner haul a barrel of water once in a while than get mixed up with that government crap. There's no end to it," Murphy said.

"Do you consider yourself a conservationist?" I asked Shaffer.

"I would go so far as to say I am, but I'm not one of these people who say, 'Oh, we've got to save this and we've got to save that.' Hell, this table come from a tree, and I need the table. I believe in this. And, I believe in the mines. That's where you get your silicon for your chips and your transistors, see. All these people who don't want this and don't want that, yet they all have a computer. Well, where the hell do those chips come from. Everything we've got comes from the earth.

"But I believe there's a way for both sides to win. You take one tree out and you plant two more," and Shaffer's voice rose to a crescendo. "But I don't see cutting 'em down and selling 'em to Japan either."

"What about minerals, though. That's more difficult," I said. "You can't put minerals back in and you can't grow them."

"Yeah, but I don't think we've really touched the surface with minerals," Shaffer replied. "I think we've just skimmed the top. For billions of years this has been taking place. It's still going on as we sit here. This mineralization. Hell, like all these mountains [around Gold Hill]. At one time, they all were big. Now, they're all eroded off. All the mineralization we've been looking for and can't find is probably out in that desert."

"So, you also think it's possible to mine the earth and also treat the earth with respect afterward?" I asked.

"Oh, sure," Shaffer said adamantly. "When you dig a hole and take the stuff out, you take the waste material and put it back in the hole. If that isn't clean, I don't know what is."

Always the prospector, Shaffer is an eternal optimist. "And, the leaching process will start again back through that stuff someday. Sure it will. It will start again."

Shaffer picking at overburden

Every day, Shaffer doggedly picks at the overburden from western mining history, looking for rocks that might hide gold, silver, lead, zinc, tourmaline, mica, calcapyrite, or tungsten. In all the years that Shaffer has been splitting leftover rocks, he has never found one with any gold flaking in it. In spite of that, he feels more comfortable carrying a sidearm when he works alone.

3

New Communities
The Second Wave of Pioneers

The first law of inertia guarantees that people leave familiar ground only for good cause. Nor do people eye the horizon for a single reason. That kind of dead reckoning is rare. The motives for leaving home are as tangled as a scrub oak thicket.

When dreams are the reason for moving on, those dreams in practice can become mottled and torn. Stubborn visionaries will clean and stitch them together, but the patchwork often doesn't resemble the original.

People of the West Desert are descendants of this knotted matrix of migration. Materialism was harnessed to spirit. Individuals became wedded to collectives. Those braids became their community.

Perhaps because it was the last frontier in the lower 48, the West Desert remains a seedbed for new community formation. That verity, the land, still beckons. But now its siren strikes a different chord. Typically, it's not material wealth these new pioneers seek. It's spiritual regeneration and the last chance to mold the good society from the good earth. Sometimes, the old myths of the West serve the new communities. Other times, the settlements transplant their own rituals and beliefs into the alkaline soils. Like others before them, the new communities hope for a good harvest.

Each of the new communities documented here have been carved by choice, often after years of study or unsatisfactory experiences elsewhere. Sometimes, mysticism or "being guided by the spirit" lies behind the decision why some people in the last half of the 20th century decided to sink roots and grow in the arid land of the West Desert. When asked, these new citizens often describe their communities as sanctuary, refuge, or cul-de-sac. They see their new homes as a place they ran to, often to escape "what's over there," pointing to the sprawling cities and suburbs of the Wasatch Front, Las Vegas, and Reno-Carson City. These communities define themselves as West Desert communities, and each will extend itself to others in the vicinity. But ties to the urban West are left tenuous. A prime difference between Wasatch Front cities and new West Desert communities is that the former spread laterally, only lightly attached to the earth, while the latter sink their roots deep into the common ground.

In the three stories that unfold here—the Aaronic Order at Eskdale, the Fraternity of Preparation at Vance Spring, and the School of the Natural Order at Home Farm—the people planned their communities. Some are more reasoned and finished than others. One is threatened on several flanks. All reflect the world views of their makers in their efforts to create order from raw land. The key is that each attempt to create community was purposeful and that creation by choice makes these communities attached to their land. With that attachment comes an acknowledged set of responsibilities. Sometimes, those responsibilities are unwaveringly committed to an ethereal principle lying

Singing in the pews
Believing themselves to be descendants of the Levites, the musicians of the Bible, Aaronic Order worshippers sing their hymns with thunderous, animated enthusiasm. On the day this photograph was taken, the pews were half full because most of the teenagers were in Salt Lake City attending a college fair sponsored by the University of Utah.

beyond the land, although nurtured by it. Other times, a community sees its responsibilities on the ground and in its governance.

Each of these new West Desert communities has to wrestle with the puzzle that earlier communities faced—how to strike a balance between the individual and the collective. Western myth glorifies the rugged individualist and his claim to free agency, and urban politicians kowtow to that Bunyanesque icon. The pioneer's will supposedly tamed the West, and indeed, the West has prospered from the energy of the individual rancher, miner, and farmer. But in reality, rugged individualists make lousy community builders. Rugged individualism is the antithesis of practical democracy, a process that clarifies a community of interests and forges it into a common unity—a community.

The united order communities of Eskdale and the Fraternity of Preparation have a much different solution to the tension between the individual and the group than does the new-age School of the Natural Order. The former place the power in the collective while the latter is a looser assembly of individuals on personal journeys. But none of the plans are absolute or perfect. Each of these new communities of the West Desert must still grapple with the legacy of atomism in the West.

United Orders

United order communities are ones where members own no property of their own. All labor for the common good and contribute their earnings to the common treasury. When a decision is made to purchase or build something—whether it's a new automobile, a computer, or a house for a new family—it's a community decision. Correspondingly, united orders are pure, rather than representative, democracies. Everyone has a voice and is expected to offer it.

United orders also tend to be patriarchal. Women in Eskdale are expected to take part in all community governance and can be members of civil leadership councils, but the spiritual echelon is reserved for men. While all men are encouraged to become leaders in the Fraternity of Preparation, and the younger men are purposely elected to the governing council to give them that experience, all final community decisions are made by men and the focus is fraternal, if for no other reason than most members of the fraternity are single.

Obviously, a united order community requires a significant commitment from its members, as it denies the individual the right to own property, a granitic foundation for the rest of the West. United order communities understand the depth of commitment that must precede membership, so they usually have three-year probationary plans. An interested person is invited to look at the community and live in it for two years. After that, a person is a probationary member for another year. He or she can still leave during that time and take all belongings. After three years a person commits to the order and transfers property. Even then, united order communities like the Aaronic Order at Eskdale and the Fraternity of Preparation are like loving parents.

While they have the legal right to property of former members, if a member later chooses to leave, perhaps due to personal revelation, the community sometimes will provision the prodigal son with a small grubstake.

While the economic structure of a united order community is socialist, its members can be devout and successful capitalists. Some members have to generate income through profits because united order communities like Eskdale can rarely borrow money. Banks feel uneasy loaning to collectives where some members don't produce cash flow. Then, united orders feel a responsibility to their older, retired members. They don't want to pledge the common assets of the order to gain a loan because if the loan went into default, the senior citizens couldn't weather the loss, as many of them don't qualify for social security benefits. So united orders usually must raise their own hard cash through their collective labor.

For this same reason united orders try to be self-sufficient. Self-sufficiency cuts down the need for currency. Providing for itself also aids the cohesiveness and strength of the group. Still, most united orders are never totally self-sufficient. Eskdale tries but now doubts that it will reach that goal. The Fraternity of Preparation fiercely maintains that it will, but to do so, it must be more ascetic and isolated.

If a community is not self-sufficient, it must necessarily interact with its neighbors. Inevitably, that brings a challenge, as the group must consider the other as it adapts to a larger, protean culture. Those contacts often are personal, so individualism again begins to rear its head. If the group defines itself in opposition to the other, the seeds for conflict are sown.

Instrumental during sabbath services

Residents of Eskdale play at least one musical instrument and usually several, combining their skills and versatility to perform as trios or soloists during the sabbath services, led by the first high priest John Conrad. When asked whether the community's shared musical talent is inherited or environmental, Doug Childs, the community orchestra conductor, said, "Both."

Child running on grounds

Eskdale envisions itself as a refuge in the 21st century for people who want to momentarily escape the frenetic pace of urban life through peace and meditation. The community is improving its infrastructure by installing concrete pathways and amphitheatres, and upgrading its water system. Guests will not have to be members of the Aaronic Order, nor will they be proselytized.

The Aaronic Order at Eskdale

Like Brigham Young, another visionary and colonizer approximately 100 years before him, Dr. Maurice Glendenning decided that the West Desert would be the place where he and his Aaronic Order followers would create their heavenly kingdom on earth. Previously, he had looked at land in Mexico and around Dugway, Utah, but two vivid dreams warned him of flooding or governmental entanglement. When "the spirit" led him to Snake Valley, Utah, in the 1940s and he saw the tall sagebrush, signifying fertile soil, he knew that this would be the place. In 1954 the Aaronic Order launched their new community at Eskdale, and current leaders still call it "an experiment."

Their first attempts in 1949 to build a united order community under the old Homesteading Act were a failure. That law, giving 160 acres to individual families for farms or ranches, tended to make those clusters of civilization atomistic. It was difficult for members of the Aaronic Order to share common equipment when homes had to be so far apart. It wasn't until they began buying federal land under the Desert Entry provision that they were able to assemble land in a way that facilitated a united order, placing the people in proximal space and surrounding the group with communal land that could be worked more efficiently with shared equipment.

Doug Childs, the second high priest at Eskdale, was one of the first people to settle Eskdale. I asked him what it was like to build a new community on the last frontier.

"In 1947 when I was 16 I'd never heard of the western part of Utah. My dad brought me out one day. We left in an old International truck, driving all night, loaded with old farm equipment that we had at our farm in Springville.

"When we woke up the next day and drove into that valley," Childs continued, "I literally thought we'd driven off the face of the earth. It was totally barren. There was just sagebrush. It was hot. It was in July. I was tired.

"Dad had a little tent set up. There wasn't even a cabin or anything. I went to sleep and woke up in just this sweat. My brother and I went outside. It made him so upset that he just went out and literally threw up.

"It was so barren and remote from anything that he had encountered. There were no roads to speak of, only dusty trails. A little hand well where you'd go over to get a drink of water, surface water, at that. Salty. No vegetation. It was a frustrating experience."

Today, there are homes for 20 families at Eskdale, approximately 100 people, with some homes larger than others. People are assigned a house according to their family need, not according to social station. The houses are set in two semicircles around a common ground. Each family takes care of its own yard. Bicycles and lawn toys clutter the walkways, but unlike the suburbs, there are no fences between neighbors.

In the early 1990s the community began to redesign its physical layout. All utilities were upgraded and utility lines were buried. Eskdale has its own telephone system with backup batteries for a power failure and can direct dial anywhere in Utah without initiating the call with a "1." Six hundred tons of concrete were laid for walkways, an amphitheatre, . . . and basketball courts. A nursery will provide trees and shrubs to soften a currently austere landscape that belies the warm heart of the community.

Eskdale undertook the considerable expense because it wants to become a refuge for people in the 21st century. It envisions itself as a sanctuary where people can come to recharge their batteries and place some distance between themselves and the madding crowd. While they suspect that ministers from other churches will be the likely visitors, the community is opening

Childs giving piano lessons

Doug Childs is responsible for nurturing the root that nourishes Eskdale—the piano. With a degree in music education from BYU, Childs uses a visual-aural approach to teach piano. Like other members of the community, he wears several hats, teaching English in the junior high school and providing driver training to all youth in southern Snake Valley.

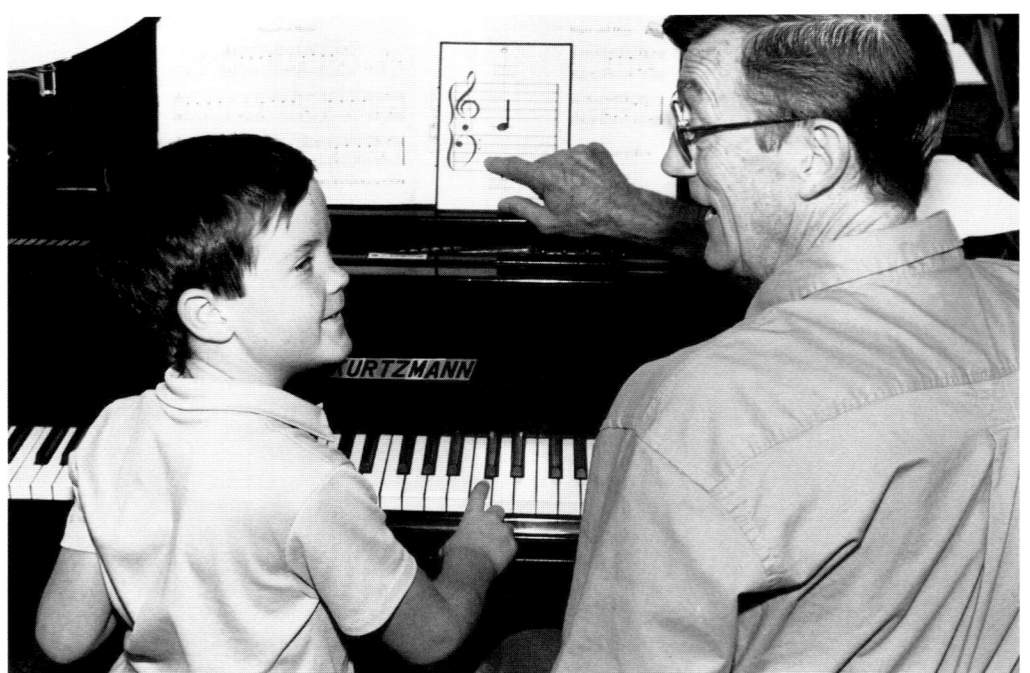

Pianist at prayer

Sabbath services are divided into three parts. In the first segment three candles are lit on the Menorah, symbolizing the trinity, and congregants pause for a moment of silent prayer. The tri-partite cross is fashioned after the Scottish coat of arms of the founder of the Aaronic Order, Dr. Maurice Glendenning.

itself to anyone from any faith who seeks peace and meditation in a family environment.

There are 32 pianos in the compound for the 20 families. If you walk around the semicircle of homes at almost any time of day, especially in the morning after breakfast, you'll hear a cascading medley of piano music. As the tinkling from one house begins to fade, you can hear the rising sounds from another piano in your future. It's almost like a relay, the sound and spirit of piano playing passing from one set of hands to another.

Music is manna for the community of Eskdale, as members of the Aaronic Order consider themselves descendants of the Levites, the musicians of the Bible. Music training is one of the threads that entwines residents of Eskdale to each other and their past. Children are required to take two years of piano in the community's private school, starting in the third grade. Typically, they'll also choose another instrument after that. The other music education requirement is choir in high school.

Instrumental and choral work are one of the three legs of the Aaronic Order church service, too. But while music might be grist for the soul, it doesn't put food on the table. Eskdale tries to be self-sufficient. In addition to cultivating large gardens and an orchard, the community plants 800 acres of alfalfa and barley. Since it tries to be an integrated operation, it will turn much of the alfalfa into silage for the dairy. Presently, Eskdale runs a class B dairy producing bulk milk. Ironically, the community has to buy its butter and will do so until it becomes a class A dairy, when it will begin selling finished products, probably with an Eskdale logo.

Considering it costs Eskdale $40,000 a year just to pump water from its 18 wells, generating cash flow is critical, and members do what they can to bring liquid assets into the community. John Conrad, the first high priest, is a veterinarian and serves a geographic area the size of Connecticut. Joe Beeson worked as a nuclear scientist at Idaho's National Engineering Laboratory. Doug Childs gives private piano and driver's education lessons to other Snake Valley children.

Dean Hayward, the general manager of Eskdale, is an accountant who serves his national accounts by modem from Eskdale. He feels it is his duty to the community to generate as much cash flow as possible. He assumes the responsibility of providing for other members, like teachers in the private school, who are integral to the community's functioning and heritage but who cannot generate income through their teaching labors.

Eskdale women signed a contract with the Border Inn to clean motel rooms. Some women elect not to participate to avoid the drinking, gambling, and carousing that is part of the Border Inn community center. Others like Anita Hansen, Eskdale's bookkeeper, enjoy the opportunity to mix with outside neighbors and tourists taking refuge from U.S. Highway 6/50, "the loneliest highway in America." Like many of the younger women, Hansen is more involved outside the community. Still, she finds her center in Eskdale.

"When I lived in Salt Lake, working as a secretary," Hansen began, "so much went on out at Eskdale that I hated the weekend to come. This definitely was home. On the weekend, where there's really nothing to do in town, except spend money, there was always so much going on [at Eskdale]. We always have a lot of visitors. Someone's always coming to talk. I would get so homesick, to be a part of the activity and excitement. I enjoyed living in Salt Lake. But I had to say they were two different worlds.

"Here, you get to know other people in a way you never would otherwise. And that can be good and bad. You get to see their good points and you also get to see their flaws. And learning to live with the flaws and still love people in spite of that is the way, I think, that the Lord wants you to live, to become more like him.

"Because you get to know people in such a deep way, you really make bonds," Hansen continued. "People who have even left, years and years and years down the road, their only friends and the people they've really bonded to are here, are us. Even though a lot of people have left the quote 'church,' their bonds with anybody are still here. We tap down deep. If you're here over a long period of time, you tap down deep."

Pursuing the grand experiment, members of Eskdale want to see if a community can function as one being. Besides living the economy of a united order, the residents are tied together in a unique social compact. They work together, eat together, pray together, and administer to each other in times of sickness and death. Inevitably, there is a tension between the individual and the group. I asked Doug Childs to describe that tension.

"It's not easy One of the hardest things a person has to do in community life when you come here is give up self. That's tough. 'I want to do this when I want to do it.' You can't always do that in community. You have to think of the guy next door, or the person who has a need greater than yours sometime."

As an example Childs uses the notion of community vehicles. When families first colonized Eskdale, a few people like the Childs brought the cars they previously had purchased with their own funds. They had to share those vehicles with others. When Doug's car began to be lent out, he was personally challenged. A boy carried a screwdriver in his pocket and ripped the seat. Another blew a tire. Another time the fender was mashed.

"I took it personally," Childs said. "It became a real cross. So, as I've seen those things drop by the wayside—I call them 'shackles'— we've been able to slowly throw all that away and we've become more as a complete unit. We're still struggling We will for ever and ever, of course. Because it's human to have our own identity. And we must. If we become like a robot system, then . . ."

That spirit of community giving extends to work organization. Groups divide the responsibilities inherent in supporting a community of 100. One person runs the farm, another the dairy. Still another runs the print shop and machine shop. Usually, members self-select themselves for particular duties, given their skills and backgrounds.

While some residents are permanently assigned to the community kitchen, all members take their turns cooking and washing dishes. Even primary grade children are expected to help the group sustain itself. During breaks in classes, they rush to the community dining hall to lay out the plates and silverware making it a game to see who can finish first. Realizing the risk, the community purchases unbreakable plastic dinnerware.

Homes are built without full kitchens, because members of Eskdale eat all meals together. Every meal begins with a prayer, followed by rousing songs and announcements, the food cooling in inverse relation to the ardor of the speaker. The evening meal is silent, although it's impossible to muzzle the sound of young wiggle worms. Yet while people eat in silence, they telepathically rise in unison at the end of a meal and take their dishes to the washroom window. It seems the rhythms of Eskdale become internalized for all.

Families eat together at long tables. That means the entire nuclear family. Grandparents lift and coo to grandchildren, giving parents some time for themselves. It becomes hard to identify nuclear families. Due to intermarriage within the Aaronic Order, families blend together and children slip effortlessly from one table to the next, visiting cousins.

If dining gathers the community together for physical substance, the chapel brings them together for spiritual leaven. Members of Eskdale try to live their religion seven days a week. Moreover, their religious beliefs shape their economic order and drive their social compact.

The Aaronic Order has 2,000 members, most residing in the western United States. Eskdale is the only unit of the church that is based on a united order plan. A fundamentalist religion in the contemporary sense, it is closer to pentecostals than charismatics. While it is not allied with the Mormon Church, many of its first members were Mormons before meeting Dr. Glendenning, and there are several points of convergence in their two theologies, including the belief in a restored priesthood, available only to men, and a church organization that relies on councils of 12 and 70. They welcome people from all corners, including atheists, and they have opposed polygamy from the beginning. They also lack the Mormons' messianic zeal, despite the fact that the Aaronic Order sometimes calls itself the True Church of God.

"I have nothing bad to say about any group," Doug Childs said. "Every group has their legitimate purpose, and the Mormons definitely do a marvelous job. The only basic thing that I would not want to pattern after is too much emphasis on

Kids on fence

Ironically, the more efficient the community becomes in its business operations, the fewer the number of jobs available for its young people. College poses a different problem. With the upward spiral in tuition, Eskdale no longer can afford to pay tuitions from the common treasury. Kids must find scholarships. Otherwise, families must raise funds from outside sources, like relatives, or leave the united order to earn income they can be entitled to keep.

Stacking hay

Eskdale recognizes it never will be self-sufficient. It must rely on financial support from the larger Aaronic Order. Constantly desiring to increase its cash flow, Eskdale is considering upgrading its dairy from class B to A. Currently, Eskdale can only sell bulk milk, and it would like to develop a horizontal, branded product line.

The business office

Even though it's located in one of the least densely popuated areas of the lower 48 states, Eskdale is wired to the rest of the world through its own digital telephone system, fax machines, and a local area computer network. The community also is looking into the possibility of purchasing an airplane, since they already have an airstrip.

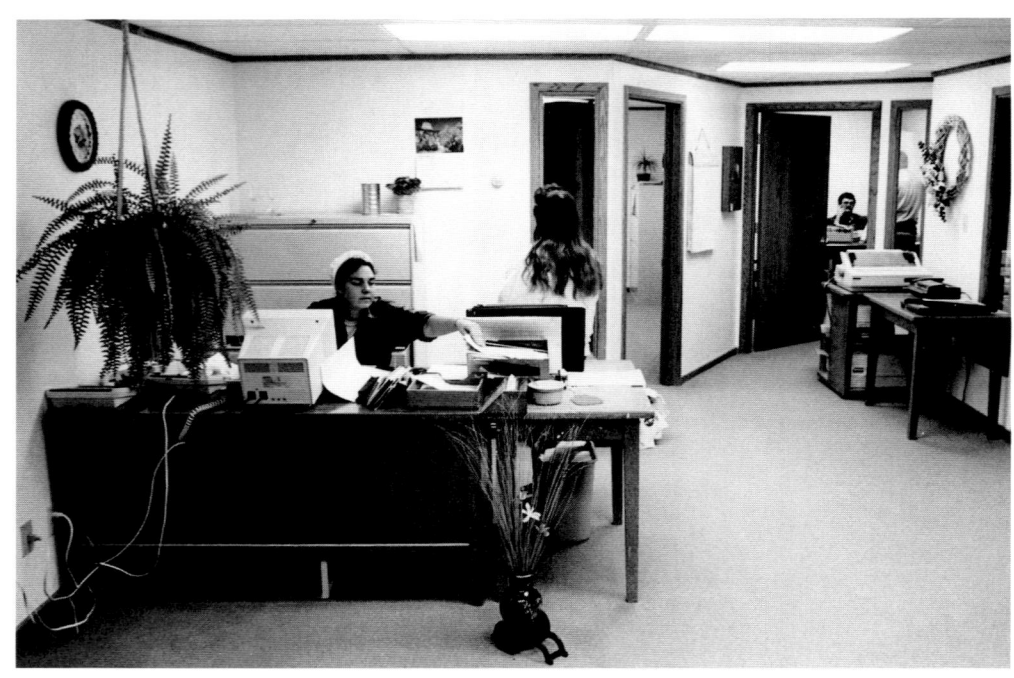

Kathleen Hayward preparing food

Kathleen Hayward is a teacher in Eskdale's school, but that does not excuse her from her turn preparing a dinner meal for all residents. Her son John Paul is exempt from duties until he reaches school age. Eskdale's senior citizens have the right to limit their responsibilities, a privilege granted for a lifetime of giving to the group.

numbers. There are so many who become disgruntled through the conversion process."

There are community uniforms for men and women, both built around blue and white. The men have "Aaron" stitched on their blue shirts. The women often wear what's called the cap of honor, although its use is fading among younger women. The name "Levi" is stitched on the brim, commemorating their belief that they are descendants of the house of Levi, one of the lost tribes of Israel. The cap of honor symbolizes that the woman is joined with Christ and is a witness. To achieve more equality between the sexes, the dress code has been tightened for men at the same time it has been loosened for women.

The Aaronic Order worships on Saturday, the traditional sabbath. The 24-hour service is broken into three segments—the sacrament, a lesson for the adults and sabbath school for the kids, and music and a sermon from the first or second high priest. Both crucifix and menorah grace the Aaronic Order altar. While members do not believe the Old Testment is literal, they do maintain it provides vital lessons, and they acknowledge that Christ was a Jew.

When I returned to Eskdale to show them the products of my first shoot, Doug Childs wondered if my pictures of the sabbath services erroneously made them look too pentecostal. John Conrad, the first high priest, said no, that the images were realistic and truthful, although he smiled and said that perhaps the photographs made them look uncommonly focused.

"We're human beings," Conrad said. "Sometimes we come all fired up. Sometimes we're all drug out. We also try to get away from the division of clergy and the laity, where one performs and one acts like a bump on a log."

Eskdale is not isolated from cultural change. Since 1975, the community has tried to open itself up, to show its good works to the world and to lessen the isolation that bothers some children. Like normal kids, Eskdale children complain, albeit with respect and temperance. Some don't want to wear the uniform. While they understand why watching television isn't allowed at Eskdale, they don't want to feel like oddballs when they get the chance to cruise with their surburban peers at Wasatch Front malls. The community has gotten used to children leaving Eskdale after high school, but in years past a good many of those teenagers came back as young adults to raise their families and join the communal spirit after going to college or sowing their oats. Now, there is a troublesome trend. Young people are returning less frequently.

To help stem that tide, the leaders of Eskdale decided to engage in what a few feel is a dance with the devil. They allowed the school to field an interscholastic basketball team. Basketball is the buzz at Eskdale among the boys, and music is losing some of its preeminence. Doug Childs says that students are increasingly electing not to continue in music after the required courses. Older brothers, who are good musicians, have given up practicing music for practicing basketball. Childs hears reports of younger brothers asking their parents why they have to take piano when their older brothers don't practice, and Childs worries about the future of the Eskdale orchestra, one of the ties that has bound the community together.

But Eskdale has fewer options. While 20 years ago the community might have reacted by cloistering itself, cultural invasion is more powerful and omnipresent now. Like all teenagers Eskdale kids are searching for personal identity. Their parents trust they'll continue to find vitality and meaning inside themselves and their community, even if they march to the beat of a dribble instead of a metronome.

Epilogue

"Part of the beautiful thing we've found in the community is that we've been able to establish our own, quote, 'utopia,' unquote, in the sense that we're not under the thumb of the government in our school system," Doug Childs said. "As far as taxes and regulations and building codes and the whole shmear, yes, we're under them. We recognize that and we try to toe the mark as well as anyone else so that we're not sitting out here in left field being an oddball bunch."

Sometimes, that requires the patience of Job. In 1996, Eskdale began remodeling old dorms for a library and elementary school rooms. One of the reasons for the remodeling was to meet EPA codes on asbestos. It costs Eskdale $15,000–20,000 to eliminate it in one building.

Eskdale has dug a new well to water the freshly landscaped grounds, but it's having problems bringing the well on line. The water, according to the state, is as pure as is possible, the same water quality that came out of the old well. But since Eskdale now has over 25 people, it has to meet the water standards of a class A town. It has to build a $100,000 pumphouse with a filtration and chlorination system to bring the water infrastructure up to code.

In spite of these other-worldly challenges, Eskdale continues to involve itself more with the southern Snake Valley community. For the past five years, it has hosted a fireworks show for Independence Day. Admission is charged, but response has been so great that the community has had to move it away from the common grounds to a larger place near the airstrip. Eskdale also has been hosting an annual Christmas dinner, a fund-raiser for the high school. Doug Childs calls it a "four-star dinner, complete with crystal," which they hold in the dining room. Eskdale keeps the prices down to match the income of the local community: $15 per plate. Still, it has been so popular that the community now has to hold it over two nights to accommodate everyone.

Vance Spring

Vance Spring is the water supply for the Fraternity of Preparation. Flowing at 50 gallons per minute, it could support a community of 300 to 400 gathered at the fount for the Second Coming. Members have developed the spring into a pond and one day hope to plant trout in its clear water for a renewable source of protein.

The Fraternity of Preparation at Vance Spring

They had looked for a place where they could be as far as possible from the seductive lures of government, and they found it at a wellspring inside a dense piñon-juniper forest about 16 miles from the Utah-Nevada border. There are no phones, no power lines, no public services of any kind. Beside the untainted water of Vance Spring, the Fraternity of Preparation is hoping to prepare a refuge for the faithful on the eve of the Second Coming, but another day of reckoning looms 70 miles away in a Beaver County, Utah, courtroom.

Talmage Weis, one of the co-founders of the fraternity, waited patiently in Judge J. Philip Eves's court in May 1993, occasionally cupping his hands to his ears to hear a judgment from the bench. Myron Hamilton, another co-founder, dragged himself around on two wooden canes, due to his arthritis and rheumatism. Dale Lambert of Christiansen and Maack, Beaver County's outside attorney—also supporting himself on a metal crutch and leg brace—was on the other side of the aisle preparing his remarks for a seemingly clear-cut but frustrating case.

Weis and Hamilton were in state district court that day to protect the fraternity's compound at Vance Spring against a forced sale for delinquent property taxes going back seven years. The fraternity owed $8,000, including $3,000 in penalties. In spite of filing affidavits that it was a bonafide religion, the Beaver County Board of Equalization argued that the land at Vance Spring was not being used for religious purposes, and besides, the fraternity could not grant itself its own tax exemption, that it was not a sovereign state.

Weis and Hamilton were having problems being recognized by the court. Judge Eves had said they could represent themselves but not the fraternity, since they are not attorneys licensed by the state.

During a court recess Lambert approached the men and offered them a way to get around the representation problem. He suggested they pay the taxes under protest and then file an appeal. That way they would be able to represent themselves. When, Weis and Hamilton argued that they should not have to buy their way into being heard by the court, Lambert said loudly, "Look, let's not argue semantics. I've thrown you guys a lot of lifelines, but you continue to refuse to use them. You can argue your tax protest case, but . . ." There was obvious frustration in his voice as it trailed off. He seemed to want to be rid of the matter.

"We'll take it to the Supreme Court if we have to," Weis replied.

A few moments later, Lambert leaned over to me and asked if I knew Weis and Hamilton well enough to intercede. I said, "No, I have only recently met them." When Lambert rolled his eyes, indicating his discomfort with the case, I responded by saying, "They are people of principle, and sometimes they can be hard to deal with." He nodded and said he, too, felt they were people of principle, but in a beseeching tone he ended with, "But, ultimately, they are going to lose their land."

The fraternity is not easily pegged. It's a survivalist movement, yet it's not clothed in camouflage. It seeks to sever itself from the outside, but it's not unfriendly. It looks to the Bible and Book of Mormon for guidance, but it claims no special communication with God.

Like many survivalist movements, the Fraternity of Preparation believes the end is near. While the world might not collapse at the millenium, the fraternity thinks the holocaust will come sooner than later, probably in the next 100 years. Talmage Weis explained:

Talmage Weis

Talmage Weis is one of three co-founders of the Fraternity of Preparation, an apostolic religious order whose members have transferred their land and wealth to an Immanuel foundation. Courts have ruled that the foundation cannot hold land in trust for God. Weis is grateful, though, that since the fraternity's inception at Vance Spring, no one has gone hungry.

Brigham Young and sewing machine

While most members of the fraternity were once Mormons, they since have left that church or were excommunicated. Still, the fraternity considers the Book of Mormon as scripture, along with the Bible. Members also try to emulate the self-reliance that is the foundation of the united order plan that Brigham Young and the first Mormon emigrants brought to the inland West.

"John the Revelator talked about the 'six periods of time.' The six seals, you know, or the six centuries of this earth before the seventh. Just what date it will be or when or how or what, you don't know, but we think that things are pretty close and it's about time that people started to do something for themselves."

So growing and storing food is paramount for the fraternity. They want to have a 10-years' supply of corn, beans, and potatoes as an emergency measure. They have no bank accounts. Whenever they accumulate any cash, Myron Hamilton, the steward, immediately turns it into "substance"—things like needles and thread and bolts of cloth for making clothes. Until they accumulate enough substance, they live on the castoffs of society, purchasing their clothes at secondhand stores in Salt Lake City.

I asked Weis if that was his penultimate American Dream.

"I've quit thinking about the American Dream," he replied. "I've given up on it—the one of owning a home and having security, financial security.

"I believe that every human being living on this land has a right and liberty to choose which spiritual life-style and order he attaches himself to," Weis continued. "He has a right [to] which social order he wants to enjoin himself with, and which political order, and which economic order. And that used to be a reality in America. But I don't think that American Dream's going to be available for people much longer. I really don't."

I asked him to explain.

"The American Dream is liberty," Weis replied. "This is the land of the free and the home of the brave. I was talking to one government official once, and he asked me what I thought 'liberty' was. I said, 'Liberty is freedom from government restraint.' And that's what the American Dream was based upon, freedom from government restraint. Not to be regulated, controlled, and domineered by government. Our fathers left Europe to get away from that. They established this republic so that they could not be regulated, controlled, and domineered by government.

"Now, when you see someone trying to stand up and show people how they can capture this American Dream again, they want to tar and feather him. They want to run him out on a rail. They call him crazy. Because he's not in harmony with the mob, the 'sheeple,' I like to call them."

"So, in a sense what you are trying to do," I suggested, "is recapture the American Dream."

"Absolutely. Recapture the American Dream," Weis said.

Part of that dream is to become completely self-sufficient. Slowly, the fraternity is weaning itself from the hard cash requirements and geopolitics surrounding Middle Eastern oil. Residents at Vance Spring generate most of their power from active and passive solar energy, using 500-pound storage batteries they purchase used for $25 from television and telephone companies replacing them at transmitter and microwave relay stations. They have a diesel generator but only use it as a backup.

They build their homes from indigenous materials. While they do have some traditional, four-sided, wood homes and a community center, they are implementing a new kind of architecture. For $200 in supplies, mostly cement and glass, they can build hogans largely below the earth that are more energy-efficient. Eventually, they want to make their own glass too.

Life at the Fraternity of Preparation is spartan. It is close to the life that the first pioneers of the West Desert led. It is what a new community looks like when it must first scratch its existence from the earth.

While the fraternity has one sprinkling system that men can move from the corn to the wheat field, the rest of the irrigating is done by gravity flow with members using shovels to slice into ditches. The men put in a garden without the use of a tractor. One of Larry Briscoe's naturally evolved responsibilities is to milk the cow the old-fashioned way, as he and the cow seem to have developed a liking to each other, perhaps because a childhood bout with rheumatic fever left Briscoe a bit slow and emotional.

The fraternity's membership fluctuates. At times there have been up to 250 people at Vance Spring, although not all were members. Rather, they were there to either celebrate Thanksgiving or the burning of the mortgage

Windmill

The fraternity uses solar panels and a windmill to generate its power. Residents at the compound store the energy in used batteries purchased from television and telephone companies when they replace them at their transmitter and microwave relay stations. Weaning themselves from oil is a philosophical as well as economic imperative for the fraternity.

Hogan

Fraternity members decided to make eight-sided hogans their primary dwellings. They can build them from indigenous materials and about $200 in glass and concrete. A hogan is less expensive to heat, since most of the living area is below ground level. With a skylight at the top, the interiors have a warm, protective feeling, like a kiva.

upon payoff or simply to check out the life-style. Now, the group is down to eight core people, and as Talmage Weis said, "I'm grateful for the unity of about half a dozen men finally gelling and becoming unified, to where they can sit down and talk things over, and we can agree. It wasn't that way in the beginning."

Many of the members spend most of their time in Salt Lake City either working for the common treasury or writing legal briefs, like Weis. Several of the men are married and women have lived at Vance Spring in the past. Weis acknowledged that the spartan life-style is especially hard on the women, and they hope one day to generate enough power to put in automatic washing machines, dryers, and similar labor-saving conveniences. But they can't do anything to control the periodic visits from the Beaver County Sheriff's Office and the Department of Treasury's Alcohol, Tobacco, and Firearms Division that are so intimidating.

"There's a lot of propaganda that's spread about people that's gathered themselves off in a religious community," Weis said. "There's so many of these wackos. But where they get the idea that they have to gather up guns and defend themselves against government with guns I don't know. In the Bible in the New Testament in Revelations there's a very clear statement in there that says, 'If you live by the sword, you're going to die by the sword. And let me fight your battles, saith the Lord.'

"So we don't have weapons to defend ourselves against government," Weis continued. "We have the court. If the court will not heed us, then we will just put it in the hands of God and have him do what he will when he will."

The surveillance mushroomed from rumors that the fraternity is a militant group of tax protestors. Even though Weis deplores the "wackos-from-Waco" types, the fraternity appears suspicious to others. The women, especially, have found the visits by law enforcement emotionally draining. On top of the primitive life-style, not knowing if they would be physically removed has been too debilitating for them. "The constant coercion and threats prevent us from living unitedly under a common purpose," Weis said.

Some citizens of Beaver County haven't treated them kindly either. The fraternity has had to install a 12-foot-high barbed wire fence around their compound to keep people out. It wasn't that way in the beginning. But the protection became necessary when people, usually hunters feeding on that diet of rumors that the fraternity is part of the Aryan Nations and training for war, let their dogs out to urinate in the fraternity's water supply and shot up the irrigation pipe with their rifles.

The core of men of the fraternity is a vanguard group. Weis said that several other groups like them are watching the fraternity to see if they can make things work. Periodically, those groups will send visitors to Vance Spring to study new community building. A favorable verdict on the fraternity's lawsuit would unleash a new wave of community building in the West Desert, according to Weis.

While most of the fraternity are excommunicated Mormons, it embraces Mormon scripture, past revelation, and accepts the Mormon Word of Wisdom that forbids the consumption of alcohol, tobacco, coffee, and tea. Otherwise, the group has severed itself from that church. For one thing Weis said the fraternity is uncomfortable branding those who want a cup of coffee in the morning as sinners. Tolerance of diversity and personal history are important for the community. Moreover, unlike the Mormon Church the fraternity does not believe in current revelation nor does it believe anyone is a prophet. Talmage Weis said that he only knows two things: "That God exists and that I am not him."

Relations between the fraternity and other fundamentalist groups are also strained, because many of those sects are vertically organized under a prophet. In addition, many of those groups espouse polygamy, and the fraternity does not promote the practice. Rather, its moral creed is founded on the Golden Rule and the Ten Commandments, and the latter forbids adultery. So Weis, who used to preach a lot on the fundamentalist circuit, now finds those opportunities dwindling.

At 5'8" and 280 pounds, Talmage Weis is an imposing man. He has the habit of constantly kneading his thinning hair with his hands, like he's trying to wash off sin. His discourse is a mixture of biblical and constitutional reference that comes at you rapid fire, a machine gun of argument. It is his primary responsibility to write the legal motions for the fraternity.

The fraternity bases its *raison d'etre* on a strict construction of the U.S. Constitution and common law. It also supports the more rigid separation of church and state clause in the Utah State Constitution. Ultimately, the fraternity maintains that all powers not granted to government are retained by the people. That means that a group of like-minded people have the right to form their own sovereign community.

The fraternity believes that there are only two dominions on earth—God's and the temporal. They recognize only God's dominion over them, and they refuse to become part of the temporal or civil dominion represented by the state because the devil works through the temporal. Moreover, God's order is more than simply ecclesiastical. In the fraternity's view it extends to the political, economic, and social spheres. In fact, there are only two ways that a person or group can fall under the jurisdiction of the temporal state. First, if an individual violates a state law protecting persons or property, like assault or burglary, then he must surrender to the state and accept its governance. Otherwise, a person can become a subject of the state only through personal choice, like asking for a social security number or by entering into a real or implied contract with government, for instance, by incorporating as a company trust, or foundation. Then, that contract implies the recognition and dominion of government. For example, although Weis was born in 1926 and could receive social security, and while the common treasury certainly could use it, he steadfastly refuses to accept it.

The fraternity is a firm believer in democracy, with an elected committee of six governing the community. For a measure to pass, the vote must be unanimous. The larger fraternity can overturn a vote of the committee with a 75 percent majority. Rather than drafting a constitution that envisions all possibilities, however, the fraternity chooses to deal with situations as they arise.

"We conduct all our business by the voice of the people," Weis said. "If we start laying out rules and regulations about how things are going to be done ten years from now, we're bypassing those people ten years from now. I'm a great believer in one day at a time.

"The law of custom will change as the needs of the people change," Weis added. "People have the right to alter their form of government as the welfare of the people dictates."

The fraternity calls itself an apostolic organization of men and women who have associated themselves to live the law of God. "Apostolic" doesn't mean a direct laying on of hands from Jesus. To the fraternity it means "a body of people living by the teachings of the apostles." "Apostolic" under tax law means that a group has a common treasury.

The fraternity pays property taxes on a hay yard it owns in Salt Lake Valley that generates income. It also pays highway use taxes through the gas tax. The fraternity maintains, however, that its land at Vance Spring is exempt from property taxes because individual members have conveyed their personal property to the unincorporated Immanuel Foundation, which holds it in alodial trust for God. The fraternity is the steward of the land.

Weis believes there is a parallel between this notion of land ownership and the Native American claim that humans can't really own the land. As scriptural support Weis refers to the doctrine among the Lamanites as identified in the book of Fourth Nephi in the Book of Mormon: "All the land belongs to the Great Spirit," Weis said, "and they [people] only have the use of it."

This notion of environmental largesse extends to animals. After reflecting one early fall morning on the fraternity's corn crop being wiped out by a herd of elk from nearby Indian Peak, Weis said to me: "We won't complain to the Division of Wildlife Resources and ask them to come out and shoot the marauding elk. After all, animals have to eat too. But it would have been nice to have had fresh corn on the cob."

The fraternity believes the Internal Revenue Code provides them an exemption from federal taxes under the provisions for an apostolic organization. Therefore, it also is exempt from state and local property taxes. The Catch-22 is that the fraternity refuses to apply for that exemption because to do so, in its belief, would mean that it would be acceding to the authority of the temporal dominion of the state over it, and members proclaim allegiance only to God. Beaver County says that it's a chicken and egg problem; that the fraternity can't grant itself its own exemption. It has to follow established procedures and can't simply file affidavits with the county clerk.

The county's legal juggernaut is moving inexorably to sell the fraternity's land at Vance Spring through a tax sale. The fraternity must try to defend itself in court because it can't hire an attorney, a recognized officer of the court and therefore a representative of the state and the temporal dominion. But neither the Utah state court nor the federal district court have allowed members of the fraternity to represent their Immanuel Foundation, saying they only can represent themselves.

On appeal to the 10th Circuit Court from one of their many suits, Weis and the fraternity did win a momentary victory. The federal appeals court remanded the case back to district court, saying that the fraternity had a constitutional issue that should be heard. Supposedly, that would provide the fraternity the right of discovery, where Weis vows that the fraternity will expose government's corruption of the Constitution.

Weis conceded that they probably should have filed their federal lawsuits earlier, in 1986. That would have given them more opportunities for legal maneuvering, especially being granted the right of discovery in court. Now he fears it might be too late.

Still, there is a calm, fatalistic quality about Weis and the fraternity. Weis recognizes that he and the fraternity are imperfect because they are human. They earnestly believe that redemption comes from admitting one's mistakes and repenting of them. With redemption comes change, and Weis preaches that change is necessary for the health of any body, whether person or community.

So the fraternity's hold on Vance Spring is tenuous. When I asked Weis what would happen if they eventually lose their suits and all possible appeals to the governor and finally the president, he spoke with resignation and a disconcerting peacefulness.

"If that time comes, we'll pick ourselves up, dust off our feet, and move on. Then we will have done all that God asks of us. We will have born witness against them."

Epilogue

On June 24, 1996, six adults of the Fraternity of Preparation and an infant were escorted off their compound at Vance Spring by the Beaver County sheriff. Their land had been purchased for $15,000 by a Nevada corporation at a past-due tax sale, and while they sued Beaver County officials for violation of their right to worship under the Religious Freedom Restoration Act of 1993, since ruled invalid by the Supreme Court, their legal options were running out. The fraternity had lost the first five of its federal lawsuits against the Beaver County attorney, assessor, commissioners, auditor, clerk, sheriff, deputies, and owners of the Nevada corporation.

When Utah Governor Mike Leavitt declined to intervene on behalf of the fraternity in February 1997, and after the fraternity learned that its last suit against the judges was dismissed because they had not stated an "arguable basis" for relief, members gave up their fight to hold onto Vance Spring.

Before they severed the last emotional ties with the Beaver County compound, members of the fraternity, following an 1880 revelation of Mormon president Wilford Woodruff, went back to the land in July 1997. To complete their mission of bearing witness against "the wicked," they took off their shoes and bathed their feet in the waters of Vance Spring "to cleanse them in pure water," according to Weis.

Now the fraternity is making plans to move to a new homeland in Montana. Members have an option on 70 acres in the Flathead River Valley, approximately 3 miles from the town of Paradise. Since it lies at 1800' elevation, they will have a long growing season. Weis maintains the commissioners of Sanders County will welcome them, although the fraternity still will not file for a property tax exemption for the religious community.

"What's to prevent the same thing from happening again?" I asked.

**Briscoe
cutting furrows**
Larry Briscoe puts in the Fraternity's garden largely by hand. At 6,500 feet elevation, the growing season at Vance Spring is short, so the Fraternity tries to put in vegetables that mature quickly and can be stored more easily—beans and squash— besides growing corn and potatoes in an adjacent field.

Weis at stove
A former baker, Talmage Weis does the cooking for the younger men at Vance Spring, whenever he can take time away from his legal work and word processor in Salt Lake City, which won't work on battery power at the compound. The younger men need hearty meals for the hard labor they perform, and none of them can cook worth beans, according to Weis. Even he finds it difficult to bake bread in the old wood oven.

Briscoe irrigating
The fraternity has a moveable irrigation system for the corn field. Otherwise, residents use ditches and gravity flow to water the garden. The sprinkling pipes need repair, however, after hunters shot them full of holes. Weis says rumors are rampant about them, and he suspects the vandals had been fed a diet of lies that the fraternity was arming itself, was a hotbed of polygamy, or harbored fugitives from the IRS.

Praying
At grace on this day, Talmage Weis asked God to intervene in their plight. "Please help the judge to see the righteousness of our case," he prayed. Larry Briscoe decided to fast and pray until the judge's decision. He would go hungry for four days before the men were told that the judge ruled against their request to grant them standing in court.

"Nothing," Weis said. "But time is in our favor now," believing the conflagration associated with the Second Coming is approaching sooner than he once thought, certainly before the next round of legal wrangling works its way through the courts.

The Nevada corporation bought the 640 acres at the tax sale for the thing of greatest commercial value—Vance Spring. Instead of building on a dream, however, the corporation is trying to resell the land. Weis said the buildings on their former religious enclave, constructed from indigenous materials, are fast falling into disrepair. The land is reclaiming its own.

Cabin and pond

Home Farm, the temporal stop for students of the School of the Natural Order, nestles into 325 acres next to Great Basin National Park. Like other new West Desert communities founded by visionaries, the land at Home Farm is a seedbed, well watered with nine springs collecting into a pond. When students turn the soil or irrigate the gardens and orchard, they simultaneously practice metaphysics and pragmatics.

The School of the Natural Order at Home Farm

When members of the School of the Natural Order transplanted it in 1957 from California to a place in Nevada they dubbed Home Farm, the ranchers of Baker, three miles away, worried that the newcomers were strange, perhaps even sinister. By the 1960s Bakerites had become somewhat used to the group, and contemporary culture gave them a label for the harmless oddballs—"hippies." Being a general semanticist, Dr. Ralph deBit, founder of the school, wasn't too concerned with the labels. He'd periodically quaff a bottle or two at the Outlaw Bar with the locals and poke them in the ribs with his own jibes.

Vitvan, deBit's Sanskrit name, meaning "one who knows," wasn't reclusive, nor did he preach spiritual withdrawal to his students. His philosophy was practical and earthy. Although he was a vegetarian, when it came time for Vitvan to leave Home Farm to meet with bankers and the like, he would purposely eat pork chops and eggs in the morning. He felt that a person should get grounded with his audience by first eating what they ate, emulating their "grosser qualities."

Vitvan died in 1964, but the school he founded in the West Desert lives on, largely because it never was conceived as a cult of personality. Rather, it is described as being a "center of light," a beacon or resting place for people stopping by on their individual paths of personal discovery. As Val Taylor, business manager for the school and a resident for 25 years, remembers, "Vitvan said, 'I have made a spiritual journey and here is the road map that I took. I have plotted the road map. You may use my road map, but you have to take your own journey.'"

Vitvan and his school believe in the gnosis, which loosely translated means that there is nothing new under the sun. Each person has internal knowledge to answer all questions. Moreover, knowledge is the key to the mysteries of life, not blind faith. John Woodyard, a longtime student of the Natural Order and Home Farm's resident poet, described gnostic exploration this way: "The meanings of our experiences are inside of us. We just have to figure out how to get in there and look at them. I think [Vitvan's] teachings provide a method and technique for doing that and understanding. For me, that's what all of it is about, and it's not always easy. It's a way of life, an ever going-process. It can be very frustrating sometimes if you don't put it into perspective. It doesn't stop at Home Farm, either. It just opens things up."

Vitvan maintained that his teachings were not original. Instead, he drew from a variety of different philosophies and practices and assembled them into what is called the "wisdom teachings." A student will be exposed to general semantics, a neo-Aristotellian, linguistic approach to life that eschews labels because they erect barriers to understanding. For instance, Val Taylor is uneasy labeling Eskdale, 10 miles away, a "fundamentalist" community, even though it fits her definition, because it might not be wholly accurate.

"It's a foundation stone of our philosophy," Taylor said, "that you can't really label people because it's unfair and inaccurate and sets up all sorts of blockages in our own selves and our own energy patterns. And, in fact, this world is an energy system and everything changes all the time."

In addition to general semantics, students are exposed to the philosophies and practices of Hinduism, the healing arts, and Einstein's field theory. The school believes that there are energy forces in and outside the body that can be read and harnessed. "That's about as mystical as we get," Taylor said.

The school has two missions. One is to distribute Vitvan's assembled wisdom teachings through tapes and books. The school sells over 200 hours of audio lessons from *The Natural*

Order Process. Books are sold in alternative bookstores and through a mailing list of approximately 1,000. Occasionally, a person is drawn to the school after running across a musty copy of one of Vitvan's books in a used bookstore somewhere on a quiet, maple-lined street 2,000 miles away from the sagebrush steppes of Home Farm.

The other mission is to provide a place where people can get in touch with themselves as they try to explore personal knowledge. Val Taylor said, "That's an aspect of the farm that is very valuable to me and that I am very committed to, that most of us in our life's journey need to know that there is a safe place where we can go and experience the changes and perhaps for the first time get in touch with who we really are instead of who our parents and school and church tell us we ought to be."

So people come to Home Farm to be closer to the source and to rub elbows with other people following similar paths. For students who can't live at Home Farm, the school offers seminars twice a year for its peripatetic pupils, who stay on campus for the weeks surrounding Thanksgiving and Independence Day and crowd together into the Centrum, a meeting hall that feels more like a large living room. The seekers of knowledge who live at Home Farm might stay for two weeks, two months, . . . or the rest of their lives.

Sometimes an emotional crisis, like losing or divorcing a spouse, is the spark that begins the journey. Another time it might be a wholesale collapse of faith in urban life. One person described her attraction to the place as a recognition that her quiet spot in yoga was a stream running close to Home Farm. More than one resident wound up at Home Farm because he or she works at Great Basin National Park, two miles away. They became intrigued by the wisdom teachings after interacting with neighbors, or they fell in love with a student of the school.

But "mystical" is the most common reason given when people are asked how they arrived at Home Farm. John Woodyard's story follows that path. In 1982 he and his family were returning from Seattle to their home in Colorado. They stopped at Lehman Caves

National Monument, precursor to Great Basin National Park. The next morning the car wouldn't start. He coasted it to Baker, where Pat Murray from the farm fixed it. Afterward, Woodyard went to the farm and met Jim Dalton, then the school's leader.

"I had been searching, I guess for a long time," Woodyard said, "for what the meaning of life is—all sorts of endeavors in wisdom teaching stuff. Everything clicked. It made sense to me. It was a total accident that we ended up here. It was not meant to be. But when we were leaving, I looked back and I just knew I was going to be moving out here sometime."

After Woodyard's divorce he met Melissa Renfro, a lands analyst with the U.S. National Park Service. When they married and she moved to Home Farm, she began another kind of path, one equally common among students of the School of the Natural Order.

"Home Farm to me embodies more the place, the setting, the animals, and the plants," Renfro said. "Things like that more than the teachings. I'm more of an on-the-ground person. The teachings are a little bit too abstract for me. But I'm trying."

Lynn Bowman, a biologist and one whom several residents call a genius, discovered that the school addressed a dichotomy in her life. "I was attracted to Vitvan because he was the first teacher I had encountered who correlated what we would have called religion and what we would have called science," Bowman said. "I wasn't finding that. This happens because . . . . And you can look at a real reason. Could I do it from a distance? Yes, probably. But I really like being involved with sharing that learning with other people who want to hear about it. This place, whatever this place is, helps us meet more of those people."

Bowman comes and goes, always seeking. When residing at the school, she home teaches her two children, under the official monitoring of Susan Wetmore, the Baker School head teacher who also is a resident of Home Farm. Wetmore praised Bowman's teaching success, noting that her children are ahead of their classes. Bowman thinks traditional school can stifle spontaneity in children. Moreover, she

Trailers

All buildings on campus have meeting rooms and bedrooms for single students. People who need more space, such as families, usually purchase mobile homes and wheel them onto the sagebrush, prefering residences that can follow them on their psychic journeys. Yet, the land and the school are like an adhesive. Often, clapboard and cement foundations grow out of aluminum, anchoring the caravans longer than the residents originally expected.

Taylor cooking

The kitchen in the community dining hall has been described as the "nerve center" of the school. Every resident, no matter how tenuously attached or new, is required to prepare a meal for the group on a regular schedule. When Val Taylor first saw this image of herself, she exclaimed with mock disgust, "You mean I cooked both biscuits and cookies that day!" Taylor says she takes it upon herself to cook "meat and potatoes" dinners because no one else knows how.

Yoga

Students of the school have wide-ranging individual interests. John Woodyard has been studying yoga for over 20 years and is a teacher for Joyce Krebs and Kathleen O'Rourke. The chart on the wall in the Centrum diagrams some of Vitvan's wisdom teachings, and the perforated shield with pieces of metal tails identifies the levels of human abstraction.

Bowman-Hoffmans at lunch

Because Home Farm is a moveable feast, cupboards have to be labeled so that newcomers know where to find particular pots, pans, and utensils. At breakfast and lunch, residents fend for themselves. This loose arrangement is ideal for Lynn Bowman and her daughter, since Bowman is home teaching Alicia and her brother Stefan.

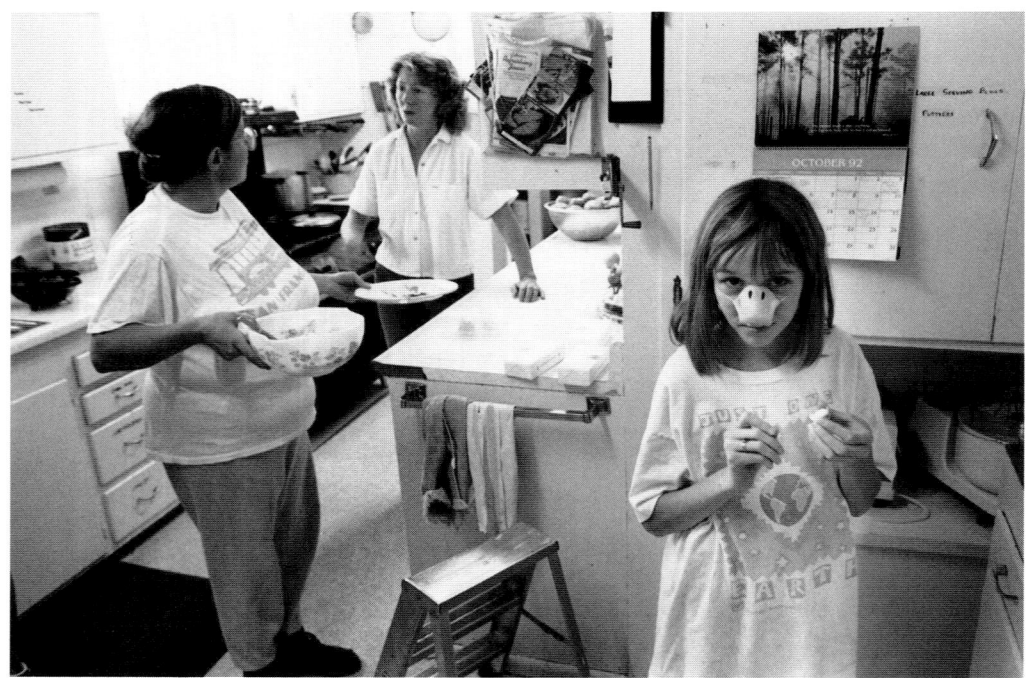

argues that children at Home Farm are in the enviable position of being surrounded by adults who are teachers as well as students themselves.

When I asked Bowman's son Stefan Hoffman what the difference was between regular school and being taught at home by your mother, he replied, "In regular school they always tell you what page you are on."

The teaching of the School of the Natural Order, then, is like water on a West Desert playa. It's fluid and capable of wandering on its own. It's elusive, too, until its earthly momentum stops and it quietly slips into the cracks of a thirsty soul.

Because of the fluidity, the Home Farm compound sometimes looks like an aluminum-sided caravan as it grows outward from the original small cluster of buildings circling the orchard. Although it's not a united order, all residents must agree that if they build a permanent structure on Home Farm's 325 acres, it belongs to the school. To avoid that, some of the residents bring trailers to squat on the land. While the residents worry that it projects an impermanent, sometimes ticky-tack look, everyone laughs and calls the subdivision "Home Farm Heights."

People sacrifice to live at Home Farm, as they must pay room and board to the school. They have to find employment in the area, and high-paying jobs are hard to find. Most wind up working for the national park or in some facet of the nascent tourism industry. For instance, Jane Murray, who has a Ph.D. in psychology, works in the national park visitors' center cafe.

There are few requirements of any resident of Home Farm. People do things out of choice, not out of duty. Sharing of responsibilities, understandings, and knowledge is the watchword. There are only two hard requirements of all residents. You must attend the weekly work meeting, and you must take your turn cooking a communal meal.

There are several long-term work projects for which some residents select themselves—the dairy, cattle, and wood projects—in exchange for room and board. The rest of the duties are the mundane, grubby things that are necessary for a community to function, and they are divvied up. At one work meeting, the residents talked about the loss of electricity to the barn and the failure to put away tools. One person asked what they should do with the geese. The droppings were becoming a real mess on the campus. Someone suggested they drive to Ely one midnight and leave them in the pond at the public park. A lot of laughs all the way around, but there were no volunteers for that one.

Then, someone said it was time to slaughter more chickens. The loaded question became "Who?" The meat eaters in the group leered and suggested the vegetarians do it. In unison the vegetarians replied that they would be out of town that day. Eventually, the meat eaters decided that was their province, and they settled on the day after election day for the blood-letting.

Things work like that at Home Farm. Everyone has the right to choose. If there is one thing that can rail residents, it's restrictions. The people of Home Farm, then, are no different than their older West Desert neighbors. They value their independence and freedom to act, and that can create challenges to the maintenance of community at Home Farm.

Val Taylor talked about the difficulties inherent in bringing new members into a family like Home Farm. In a nuclear family you have to learn to get along. If a sibling has a habit that annoys you, you learn to rationalize. You unconditionally accept, while trying to protect yourself. But at Home Farm the adaptation is more like when a child brings home a spouse.

"The difference is that we're in a physically confined space here, and we're non-blood related," Taylor said. "So, it's intensified. When somebody new shows up, and you've already made these other adjustments and life is flowing pretty smoothly, there's a new mirror held up in front of me. This person represents a whole new set of psychological factors that I've never had to deal with before. In that person or in me. That's where the lesson is and where one of the great values is in living here. This is a laboratory workshop. Everything that I believe philosophically and read and listen to in the books and tapes, suddenly I've got an opportunity in front of me to deal with this, and how I deal with it tells me what type of student I am, what I've really learned, and how much I still have to work on."

Joyce Krebs, a retired special education administrator from Florida and a student of the school, relishes her semiannual sojourns at Home Farm. "When I come to Home Farm I adopt the mental stance that I am going to be with people I likely will not agree with. 'It's going to be uncomfortable,' I say to myself, 'and I'm going to accept it.' I anticipate having to confront people, and I find that stimulating."

Taylor pointed out that Home Farm can be a painful experience, that not everyone is suited for the constructive abrasion. "Home Farm has not been a wonderful place for some people, because we do depend on self-reliance. And there are certain times and certain people who go through certain periods in their life when they need a lot more than we can give. We are not a care center. We are not a therapeutic center. The support is on a less personal, more subtle level. It's like, 'We'll give you the space, the time, and the opportunity to work through whatever it is that you need to work through, but we can't hold your hand 24 hours a day.'"

Taylor also routinely admonishes newcomers not to take themselves or the journey too seriously. One emotionally frail woman saw Home Farm as a retreat. It turned out to be a box canyon. "She's the twenty-seven-year-old who's buried up in the cemetery," Taylor said softly. She added that it was a wonderful lesson for her because she never wants "to kid myself that I'm that special. If I have to go out tomorrow to live in Chicago or Salt Lake, so be it. That's my destiny."

Most recreational activities at Home Farm are solitary. It might be biking, running, walking through Great Basin National Park, meditation, or chanting. Even when students get together to practice yoga, ironically, the focus is on finding the inner self. The only activity that is a constant for every member of Home Farm is reading. All students are insatiable readers, and they breathlessly share what they've learned, like kids reporting on their first field trip. The school's library has healthy offerings in philosophy and metaphysics, natural science and ecology, physical science, social science, and religion.

Home Farm residents inflate the educational level of the Baker area to where at first glance it appears to be a typographical error on demographic maps. Most have college degrees and many have graduate degrees. Because of this background and their willingness to take on individual responsibility, residents of the school tend to be the leaders in the Baker community, serving on the town council, heading the PTA, or working with the national park developing a sewer and water system for the area.

"Part of the reason residents become community leaders is we represent a broader spectrum of education and experience," Val Taylor said. "Those of us who live here have come from all over. So we simply have the background and education, often times. There's no driving philosophy or force here that says, 'We want to come in and move into the community.' There's none of that. It's a very individual kind of thing. People who come here partly get involved because they want to get jobs."

Ironically, leadership is the greatest challenge facing Home Farm right now. Vitvan is dead. His spiritual heir Anita is dead. Jim Dalton, the president of the board, lives in Oregon. There is no one in the community who wants to assume the mantle of Home Farm leader, nor is there anyone who every student would be willing to support. Now things must get done by committee.

"So," Taylor said, "we are trying to learn to function as a group and not operate with one head. We try to come to consensus and discuss things. And we are small enough—we have 20 people who live on the place—that it's still manageable. Things still get done or decided, but not everyone agrees with or understands or knows about what's going on. It's working pretty well, partly because there are a handful of us who have been here long enough that the machinery has been set in motion and it just works."

The conflict, when it is present, is usually between the new, younger people and the ones who have been there the longest. Conflict must be resolved by direct confrontation, but some people, like Taylor, have a difficult time being that aggressive. Taylor thinks some of this is healthy. It's a lot like the current corporate management philosophy of moving responsibility down the line by setting up quality control groups.

Krebs running

Activities of residents tend to be solitary. Joyce Krebs runs and practices yoga. In her sixties she likes to jog for 4 ½ miles in the foothills of the Snake Range. Krebs is more of an on-the-ground person, finding the readings of Vitvan a bit too dense. She is more drawn to the land and the diverse group of people that Home Farm attracts. Eclecticism is manna for Krebs and many other students.

Bowman in library

Reading is the one rabid interest that all residents of Home Farm have in common. Lynn Bowman's self-appointed task is organizing the school's significant holdings of books in philosophy, religion, biological sciences, and ecology. She uses the Library of Congress system of classification, and like all librarians she must be well read.

"It's a harder way to do things," Taylor said, "than when one person was in charge of something and made the arbitrary decisions. But it seems to be the way corporate America is going. Other institutions are moving away from the arbitrary, single head. I think we're in step with that. It's going to be hard and we're going to make mistakes."

Taylor then laughed and quoted from a woman who used to live at Home Farm. "The problem with Home Farm is that everyone here is a fixer, but no one wants to be fixed."

Kids chasing bubbles

Children's lives at Home Farm are unfettered and open. They are encouraged to explore themselves, just as the adults are. On Stefan Hoffman's birthday, he and Alicia play with his new bubble gun with Dusty Murray. Their play is a metaphor describing the journey of students of the School of the Natural Order—life like a bubble, moving in response to the windy course of life, slowly, but constantly rising.

III

Community Institutions

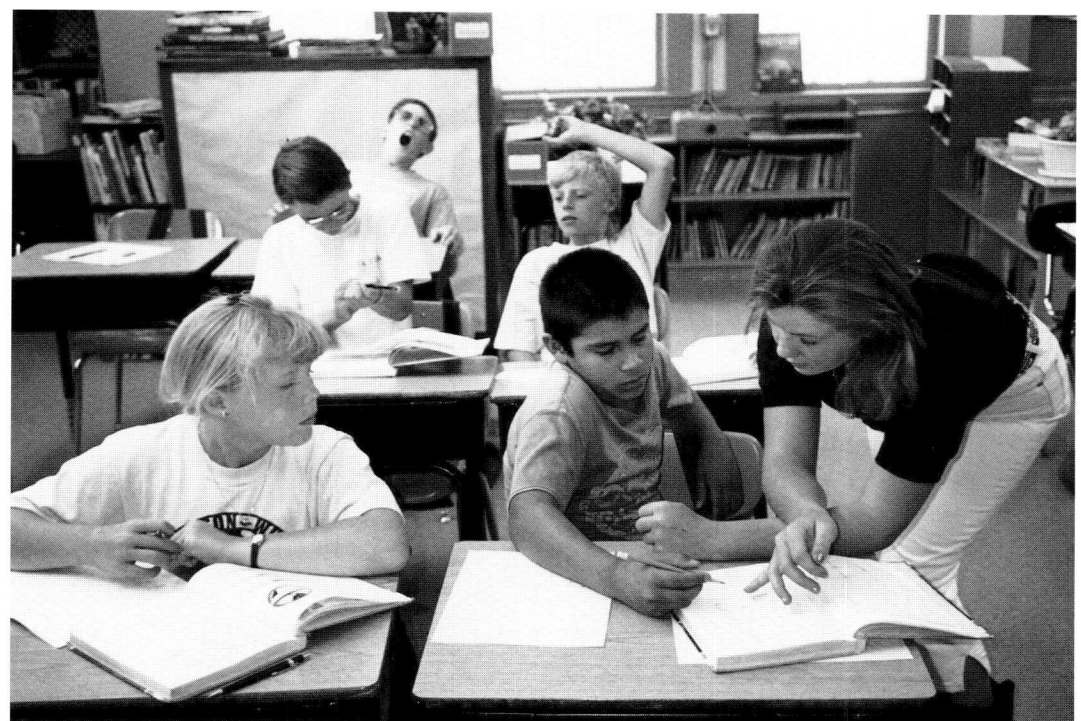

Peer tutoring

Class time at the Baker School is designed to foster peer tutoring, and students naturally fulfill their roles as older mentor and younger tutee. Katie, an eighth grader, willingly helps Emidio, a sixth grader, with his arithmetic work sheet. Older students are especially drawn to Emidio. In spite of being behind grade level, due to attending school sporadically as the son of a migrant ranch hand, he has a positive attitude toward education.

Rebecca Mills

Rebecca Mills, superintendent of Great Basin National Park, brings to her first park command a public graciousness and keen willingness to work with stakeholders. Unlike a vanishing, older guard of park superintendents who thought they could weave political cocoons around their lands, Mills seeks to build coalitions.

Banta at weir

Jay Banta measures a broken depth gauge at one of the weirs on Fish Springs National Wildlife Refuge. Surrounded by mountains whose ascetic strength comes from adapting to little water, Fish Springs is the Shangri La of the West Desert. Not only is water plentiful, it's mysterious bubbling up at 70 degrees. No one is sure from where it comes.

Land Management
Flash Point of the West Desert

In years past when power in the West was rural, the land manager was just one of the boys. He lived and worked in the community and was accepted into that culture because he supported its shared values. His mission was to articulate the local interests first and then serve as the medium for an Interior Department bureaucracy already controlled by extractive commodity interests.

Now that the West looks more urban, another litany of values spoken over the land is creating tension between the resource extractor and his former ally. The land manager wrestles with this devil: a new vision for the land chris-tened in the sprawling cities confronts a formida-ble image print of the past—the sacrosanct cow-boy—while rural stakeholders feel as if they are being thrown to the lions. In this crusade both legions are people of the West Desert, but some cadres on each side see the other as alien, and unclean.

The good-old-boy network isn't even staffed with boys anymore. Nor is internationally acclaimed land management always the moral province of environmentalists. The issues are complex and the sacramental offering of land management is volatile.

Rebecca Mills
Shepherding the National Park Service in the Great Basin

In 1995, Rebecca Mills, "Becky" as the locals call her, assumed her first park superintendency, Great Basin National Park. It was her one and only choice.

"I can't explain it all," Mills began. "One part is the way people do live close to the land here. Another part is the actual physical space, the lack of traffic, the lack of human-made struc-tures. The natural environment. The silence.

"Why I'm so drawn to it probably has to do with the way I grew up as a child, going to parks," Mills continued, "and it may have to do with Girl Scout activity, the spiritual aspect of the Girl Scouts. They wouldn't call it that, but you had these ecumenical services in the Girl Scouts where you really kind of worshipped nature.

"I also really admire this community. I admire the ranchers who make their living off the land and I admire the people who came here for the School of the Natural Order and the people of Eskdale.

"I can only say there are lots of wonderful people in large urban communities but you don't get to know them the way you get a chance here. You don't get a chance to fully because there's so many people in between. And so many mechanical noises in between."

Unlike some in the agency, working for the U.S. National Park Service wasn't a life-long goal for Mills. While she always had been a child of nature, her father showing her how to fly-fish in Yosemite at age six soon after he returned from the war, her degree from Swarthmore College was in history. Then she received a masters in social welfare from Berkeley and became caught up on the civil rights movement of the 1960s. While doing community organization work, she became interested in international park development, especially the preservation of native cultures. At the same time she began asking herself a question she had been asking of other women who had been tracked into certain careers.

"It wasn't until my mid thirties that I decided I had never really asked the question, 'What would you *enjoy* doing?' I'd always asked and answered the question, 'What's meaningful? What do you think is a good thing to do?' But not also, 'Where would you really enjoy working?'"

When an opportunity arose to head a youth program doing conservation work for the National Park Service, Mills joined the agency. Shortly thereafter, Mills became interested in the effects of grazing.

"I had studied grazing management," Mills said, "largely because I got to know the ranchers' point of view because of my partner, who grew up on a cattle ranch in Ruby Valley. I was coming from a 'preserve the natural resources' viewpoint in the San Francisco area where the general climate reeks of 'grazing is ruining the landscape.' And so as I began to talk to this rancher I began to realize how complicated it was. I made a study of it and wrote an article."

Mills doubts that was the reason she was selected to succeed Al Hendricks, who oversaw the transition from Lehman Caves National Monument to Great Basin National Park. But

grazing rights were protected in the park enabling law, and they are one of her personal challenges, because 10 years after the establishment of the park, those grazing rights are in the process of being withdrawn.

The ranchers who own the rights—Dean Baker, Dave Eldridge, and Owen Gonder—have tired with what they see as a constant hassle with changing park grazing policies, even though the NPS follows U.S. Forest Service grazing dictates. Baker area ranchers fought hard to have their grazing rights protected during park negotiations. Deep inside they understood the inexorable forces that would oppose them. Some had wanted the area to be declared a wilderness instead of a national park because they knew that increased visitation of the area by urbanites would mean that waffle-stomped boot soles would wind up stepping in cow pies, and that's a slippery slope to conflict.

While Dean Baker wanted the deputy director of the National Park Service, John Reynolds, to know how difficult it was for he and his family to offer to sell their grazing rights, how dramatically it altered the family's vision of their future, he was a willing seller. With Eldridge and Gonder he believed it ultimately was the best thing for everyone concerned.

Because a grazing permit technically isn't a property right, the federal government can't buy it out. The money has to be raised elsewhere. Enter the Nature Conservancy. The organization conducted appraisals of the permits and put together a package. The three grazing permits would be transferred to the Nature Conservancy, if and when the money could be raised.

In spite of the fact that withdrawing the permits would alleviate one of her problems, Mills would rather see cattle grazing remain in Great Basin National Park. "I think the public needs to understand where their food comes from," Mills said with a wry chuckle. "And what better place to interpret it than a place where you can actually see the ranching. You can literally sit here at the visitors' center and look at the Baker Ranch and see it's a big job. It's a very important job, and I think it would have been a challenge to go along with monitoring, because there's that, the challenge . . . the stewardship, that joint mutual stewardship—management and grazing or any of the uses of the land. It's really the big issue now. It's not the adversarial stuff. The adversarial stuff is already out there. So now, what's really happening that's exciting, I think, is how people are coming together."

While forming coalitions wasn't her official mandate when she was appointed park superintendent, it will be critical for Mills's tenure at Great Basin National Park. If for no other reason, federal budget cutbacks mean that national parks must begin to raise money outside the system. Mills hopes to institutionalize fundraising at her park, and she eagerly wants to help the Nature Conservancy raise money, to be an equal partner with the environmental organization and the ranching community.

The park already had its general management plan when Mills arrived. Her job is simply to implement it. Moreover, due to expected shortages of funding for park infrastructure, the capital improvements plans are modest—cleaning Lehman Caves of dust and lint, some road repair, possibly an interagency orientation center in Baker, and, hopefully, some housing. Many goals, though, require a partnership with the community.

"You shouldn't veer from it [the general management plan] very much," Mills said. "If you do, you invite the problem that you've already consulted the public, and they can rightfully be angry about taking a new direction. So I see the mandate as working towards implementation of what's in the plan but during a time when the fiscal resources aren't there, which I think is actually an adventure. I don't feel depressed by it at all. It's quite an interesting challenge, and that means coordination and cooperation with your local communities above all. You can't move away from main Park Service mission by any means, but the mission is very broad. It's basically, 'Preserve these natural cultural resources for generations to come and leave them unimpaired and provide for the enjoyment of visitors.'"

While park visitation continues to grow, Great Basin National Park hasn't been besieged by people, like parks in the Grand Circle tour. Its most immediate problem is trying to ease the congregation of people, and waiting lines, at the more famous Lehman Caves by encouraging visitors to see the park's alpine country. The only other immediate threat was the one raised by Utah's Representative Jim Hansen when he reportedly said that Great Basin National Park was one of those that could be expendable if the National Park Service had to close some parks due to budget cutbacks.

"How do you feel about Jim Hansen's remark?" I asked.

"I believe what his staff director told me. That he never said it," Mills replied, "that he was quoting a constituent. And I also believe our deputy director when he says Hansen is actually trying to help the parks. I think what happened is he took the ball for what became known as the Park Closure Bill. It really was a systematic way for the congressional end of things to look at proposals for parks to be commissioned and he was going to include the possibility that you would decommission some parks.

"It started when the new Congress was talking with our director, and our director had to keep answering why these various parks were being established. Senator Bruce Vento asked, 'Isn't it true, Director Kennedy, that the Park Service does not decide which parks to establish, that in fact the Congress makes that decision as far as acquisition of land, that Congress makes those decisions?' And the director, with relief, said, 'Yes.'

"So it started in a good way, that this was going to be a bill that would bring some sense to this process, of the establishment of parks, and yes, would consider disestablishment of parks. But it became known as the Park Closure Bill, and given all the threats that were there, the Department of Interior's position was that, 'We're not going to close anything. But if we get cut the way it's looking like, we are going to have to look at that.' And we got a list together of parks that might have to close.

"I don't know," Mills ended. "I have never talked to Hansen himself. That's what Steve Peterson told me. And it's certainly friendly. I'd much rather believe that anyway."

"From my talking to others, it seems you have been well-received in the Baker community.

Do park superintendents have a kind of honeymoon period with the locals?" I asked.

"I think so," Mills said with a laugh, and gave an example. "I was very lucky because we had an issue here: there was a possibility of closing a road," and Mills's eyes lit up in mock horror, "which given the context of land management is a major issue, and given the background of people living here for a long period of time, it was theirs, in some respects. So when there'd been a washout on the Strawberry Creek Road, the staff had tentatively made a decision to just close it there because the general management plan looked like that's where they would close it anyway to establish the new trailheads. I came in with the tentative decision being made and was able then to consult a lot of people in the community and ask them what they thought. Very, very strong opinions against closing it," Mills said with an uneasy laugh. "But it turned out they were just against closing it there. If you closed it here, it was OK. So it really was a good example of, you have to find out what the opposition is actually about. Once you find out, the decision may be very easy."

Mills doesn't feel the antipathy toward either her or the park that some federal land managers feel in the West, especially those in places like Carson City, where a federal office was bombed, or in Nye County, Nevada, where a county commissioner baldly challenged federal authority by cutting a road.

"I don't sense any of it," Mills said. "If people in the community don't like what we do, they tell us why. They tell us what it is that they think we ought to be doing and it's not about, 'You're this awful government agency and you always do the wrong thing.' It's not that way. It's specific to whatever it is we're doing."

Then Mills talked about how the community recently came together in an EMT course. A variety of people from the park, Baker, Eskdale, and the Border Inn responded to the community's need to diffuse emergency medical training.

"I took the class," Mills began. "Talk about a honeymoon! It was this marvelous microcosm of the various segments of the community. And we had to meet three times a week. And we had to take tests together and we had to carry litters together," Mills said rather breathlessly. "And, it wasn't, 'I'm going to get EMT so I can have my career, so I can compete with so-and-so,' which happens in the Park Service. It was, 'I'm going to get my EMT because this little kid has seizures in this community, we have accidents out here, and we're at least an hour and fifteen minutes from the closest hospital.

"Eve, one of the instructors asked, 'Why did you all do it?' And Daisy Gonder said, 'I am here because I've gotten so much help from other people in my family. So I'm here because I want to pay it back.'

"Do you think democracy works any better out here?" I asked.

Mills paused a long time before she replied. "People speak their mind. And decisions get made. It's easier to watch because there are only a few organizations meeting to make decisions. I don't know enough, I think, yet. But if you're going to try to be a participant in community decision-making in an urban area, it's fraught with parties, political lines, late meetings at city councils. I think it's a lot harder to do."

"Do you think it's possible to take some of the problem-solving skills and sense of community that allows people in small towns to make decisions, to listen to one another, and get things done, and transport that back to the urban communities?" I asked.

"I truly believe people are not meant to live as close together as they do in most of the urban areas and that some of our problems actually are that," Mills said. "At some point maybe it becomes too complex for a lot of minds. Mine included. The interdependence means that you're not self-sufficient in any respect whatsoever. It just puts you in a position where you don't even see a bird. There were probably years in my life when I didn't realize that you could look up in the city and there was an actual world there. Besides the pigeons. It really is there. And I noticed in the last several years I was there [San Francisco], walking to work, very few people looked up to the skies.

"It's just such an artificial environment," Mills continued. "Or . . . It's not artificial, but it's not natural. It's a special environment created by human beings for human beings, and they distance themselves, then, from the basic needs of their own bodies and probably their own emotions as well. And, by this complexity, that's so many stages removed from the basics."

"Do you see any evidences of frontier mentality or frontier culture around here?" I asked.

"The Old West? It looks like the Old West in places," Mills replied. "I mean people ride horses and they rope cows. That's pretty neat. I have a romantic connection to it. Where I got it? I suppose from western movies and from western songs. I think it's pretty exciting to watch that kind of skill being exercised. So, it looks like it exists, but it doesn't."

"Is a frontier mentality helpful in building community?" I asked.

"The concept of a frontier as a physical entity is dangerous," Mills replied. "Regardless of how much space there is out here, the world can't afford a concept of frontier. We have to learn to live in balance with the environment, we have to live in balance with each other.

"We're already in a pretty severe state. So that old sense of the frontier, that you can do just about anything, you can throw your beer bottles out, you can mine whatever you want, you can take whatever water you want, you can graze, et

cetera. No, this isn't the last frontier. But if you think of the frontier conceptually, then that's that issue about how can people learn to live in balance, and this is a good place to learn to practice it. I think being in a land management agency and living so closely with people that have lived here and have built an economic base for themselves gives me a chance to interrelate and learn how it can be done and try to help it get done. Not adversarily, but in a truly understanding way.

"This place exists for the people of the United States and for their future generations," Mills continued. "But that doesn't mean that some concept I have coming from my buddies in the Park Service is therefore right. So the frontier that I think of is the frontier of how are we going to manage to live in the world as human beings. And continue to allow the other species to exist. And continue to keep air and water and soil that will sustain us.

"So many decisions are made in urban areas that affect the environment that individuals can't possibly know [about the effects]. In this area, you can. You can understand it. You can work on what you're going to do to develop it, and make it better. You can try to educate the urban people that are coming into the park. That's the frontier that I am excited about."

Jay Banta
Raising Ducks in the Desert

Fish Springs National Wildlife Refuge is the most isolated federal land management outpost in the West Desert. "Great Utah outback," as refuge manager Jay Banta likes to say to his wildlife management colleagues. Allowances for isolation and the lack of police and fire protection bring down the Bantas' monthly rent in federal housing on the refuge to $230. But Banta laments that the family can't save any money on his GS 12 salary. The rental savings are plowed into gasoline and vehicle repair. West Desert road dust slowly grinds engine metal to powder.

Previous denizens of the marsh used the isolation to their economic advantage. When John Thomas, the first permanent resident, would spy dust trails from distant vehicles on the old Lincoln Highway, he'd divert one of the springs and turn the road into a viscous trap. Stuck Model Ts would pay him grudgingly to pull them out with his team of oxen.

Nowadays, Banta goes out of his way to attract and please visitors. "If someone is willing to make the effort and drive out here, and for most people it's a herculean drive," Banta said,

Checking hunting licenses

Banta isn't required to wear a sidearm. Regulations only say he has to have access to it and have yearly training. Banta chooses to wear a pistol when he must deal with larger crowds on the refuge. He says it is "prudent and provides an authority presence." He suspects it has helped at least once when an angry hunter wanted to beat him up but stalled when he noticed the peacemaker at Banta's side.

Banta counting birds

Fish Springs is an important site for birds migrating the Pacific flyway. While too far south to be productive habitat for raising ducks and geese, its rich feeding grounds are essential for birds replenishing calories, as there are few other places for them to go. Consequently, the marsh is a vital counting station, and Banta's figures go into the North American waterfowl census to determine hunting limits for upcoming years.

"when they get out here, I have a standard policy that any organized group that calls me that wants a tour, if I'm here, they'll get a tour. It doesn't matter if it's on Saturday, Sunday, or a holiday. I'll make the time. Because I've always been under the belief that there are two kinds of people, those who are for you and those who aren't. And those who don't know, aren't."

Still, Banta wouldn't define Fish Springs as the frontier. While refuge guests might feel it's the edge of the earth, due to "a degree of inconvenience" with no 7-Elevens around, Jay and his wife Frances feel privileged. For them the frontier would be where, if the weather gets bad, it might be a month before you get mail, a month before the plane can get in with services. "Here, when we get a bad storm," Banta said, "it might be talking three or four days before you can get in."

Nor would Banta like to see any development around Fish Springs. Certainly no paved roads. Part of his privilege is living in a place where time is measured in annual rhythms of wingbeats, while the earth only feels faint whispers of passing.

This passion for isolation doesn't square with Banta's gregariousness. Nor does his dark countenance match his exuberant personality. Only his flashing, light blue eyes with eyelashes so long you'd swear he put them on in the morning hint at the fire inside. If it weren't for his scraggly beard, he'd remind you more of a soap opera swoon than a refuge manager.

In spite of Banta's openness to visitors, Fish Springs National Wildlife Refuge doesn't attract many folks. Most come from Salt Lake City, about three hours away on the road that follows the old Pony Express trail. About 3,200 visitors logged in in 1997, maybe 25 hunters on an average weekend day during hunting season, but mostly birders, with a 2:1 ratio of nonhunters to hunters.

When Banta and his family arrived in Fish Springs in 1990, they weren't overcome by the desolate terrain. They had been there once before and had loved it. Jay Banta never expected to be named manager of Fish Springs, just applying for the open position on a whim. But it's always been hard to find people to manage Fish Springs, and at age 36 Banta became one of the youngest refuge managers in the United States Fish and Wildlife Service. Jay and Frances knew they'd come home, too, when they found one of their son Jed's old toys from their first stay stuck away in a garage.

"Career-wise, I have the greatest job in the world," Banta said. "I have future aspirations, but if I never left here, that would be fine. For me, the American Dream is being able to have the opportunity to be a good steward of the land and to be able to apply those things that I've learned academically and professionally."

Banta knew he wanted to be a refuge manager at age 14 and pursued that goal with a degree in wildlife management from California State University, Humboldt. Early on, Banta sought some place where he could have total control over the resource, to avoid as much as possible the politics of catering to the uses and values of surrounding lands. He desired to be free from pollution external to the marsh. He especially wanted to have total control over the water resources. At Fish Springs Banta has what he wants.

Banta only laments that he has to spend approximately 30 hours a week at his desk, responding to management surveys and information requests, budgeting and fulfilling environmental and wildlife management studies. He'd sometimes rather have the assistant manager's job, since that assignment calls for more hours in the field.

Most of Banta's outside time is spent managing water flows from five springs that feed 22 cfs of the 30 cfs entering the marsh. Starting in September, Banta begins moving water to the various units. Each unit is a pond with vegetation surrounded by a dike to retain the water. He moves the slightly salty spring water by gravity flow to the farthest units to maintain the vegetation and provide more landing habitat for migrating waterfowl. Since water in the outlying units is even more saline, picking up salts from the ground, the vegetation at the extremities of the marsh isn't as hardy as the vegetation nearer the spring sources. Though the water is 70 degrees Fahrenheit when it leaves the spring, by the time it reaches the outlying ponds it has lost much of its heat and those units will freeze in the winter.

In May, Banta begins shutting off water to the outlying units to conserve it because in spring the marsh begins to lose water through evapotranspiration. Banta needs to keep water levels high enough to protect vegetation and cover for the nesting ducks and lessen the threat of toxins or disease in low water.

Banta spends his other precious marsh time counting birds to be fed into North American waterfowl censuses to determine hunting allotments for future years; doing predator studies on waterfowl losses, with most losses coming from ravens and coyotes at Fish Springs; burning units to release nutrients to the marsh for new growth; and enforcing regulations during hunting season.

In years past Banta had to deal with cows trespassing onto the marsh from an adjacent grazing allotment, threatening his plans to nurture nongame marsh birds. That problem has been largely taken care of with the construction of an electric fence. A portion of that fence, however, is in the Fish Springs Wilderness Study Area. The U.S. Fish and Wildlife Service spent $50,000 on fencing and doesn't have the money to reroute it. If it must come down when the wilderness boundaries are established, then the marsh could have problems with trespass grazing again.

Aside from that, Banta has few problems with surrounding stakeholders. He feels that the refuge's relationship with the people of northern Snake Valley is positive, partly because the refuge doesn't appear as a threat to them, nor do they think they could do anything better with the land.

"Most of them are glad that the refuge's here and that it does good things for wildlife. I always joke," Banta continued wryly, "that they like us because they tried to run cows in and that didn't work. So nobody wants to run cows on it. And they tried to grow cereal grains here on the early years of the refuge and it was an abysmal failure. The water has a pH of about 8.2 and the soil is high in salts." Then he added, "Besides that, they have the BLM to hate."

Given federal budget cutbacks, Banta's future plans are modest. He's had one position cut from his staff of four, yet refuge responsibilities multiply. There isn't much opportunity for raising geese and ducks, as Fish Springs is about as far south as one can go and find productive nesting habitat. In the best years Fish Springs can only raise 1600 ducks and 25 geese. That pales in comparison to the 100,000–150,000 duck births to adulthood on more northern refuges. In fact, the generation at Fish Springs is within the margin of counting error at more northern refuges.

Banta believes, however, that Fish Springs could support the propagation of nongame waterfowl and shorebirds like American plovers, egrets, ibis, and avocets. Those future plans run up against politics. Refuges typically have been built or expanded with duck stamp money, paid for by hunters. So refuges are managed for waterfowl production. Wildlife is looked at as a "resource" or "cash crop," and Banta would likely have to search for nongame funding outside the agency.

"The old ways die hard," Banta said.

Similarly, Banta needs to court private funds or seek matching grants from benefactors to carry out future plans like building handicap-accessible blinds or moving geese nesting platforms. Volunteerism, too, is critically important for any refuge improvements. In 1997 volunteers spent 1,000 hours on Fish Springs projects, many of them driving six hours round trip for the opportunity to lend a hand. If federal budget cutters decided to take even more money from wildlife management, the one area Banta would zealously protect from budget reductions would be environmental education and interpretive programs for schools.

Banta believes marshes and wilderness areas provide sites for people to rediscover their understanding of soul and place. Wilderness offers a quick course in natural intuition. There one learns how land marks. Both Banta and his wife would support wilderness status for parts of the adjacent Fish Springs Range, and especially the Deep Creek Mountains, the towering range 30 miles west.

"But it's hard on me," Banta said. "You don't want to breathe that word very loud on the West Desert. They have a hard time realizing that it really doesn't eliminate a lot of the traditional uses. It eliminates methods of access.

At the boneyard

Like all denizens of the West Desert, Banta keeps a spare parts area affectionately called "the boneyard." Fish Springs personnel must look to themselves first for any repairs on the refuge. When the boneyard begins to overflow, Banta holds a liquidation sale, and surplus nuts, bolts, siding, and the like get recycled to area ranches at bargain basement rates.

There's lots of wilderness areas where they run cows. There's lots of areas where they have non-impactive commercial operations, guides that take people in on pack trips. It's a sensitive issue, but I suppose if the time comes, we can uncreate wilderness, but we can't ever create any. We've got all we're going to have, and it slips away every day, much as wetlands do."

"What are your feelings regarding the federal government?" I asked. "After all, it is your employer."

"It's probably a lot bigger than it needs to be," Banta replied. "But then, as soon as you start cutting, it doesn't matter where you

cut, you've got a constituency that's screaming long and loud," and he pointed to the effects of Proposition 13 in California as a perfect example. After taxes were cut, services were cut and people complained.

Still, Banta feels good working for the federal government. Although he said he can't speak for all the federal agencies, "I think the mission of my agency is a critical mission. I think we are the people that keep the pulse on those things that really tell us about the quality of life on the earth. As they go, we go.

"I'm always amazed that people refuse to accept that" Banta continued. "If it's not a good place for wildlife, it can't be a good place for people, because our requirements are exactly the same. Our basic requirements to stay alive are identical. If we in our efforts have made the quality of life for animals as well as people better for a longer period, that's certainly a worthy thing to me to be involved in."

Banta believes that stewardship of clean air and water must be a federal responsibility. Migratory resources, especially, would be threatened if they fell into state control under the guise of new federalism. "States tend to look out for themselves. That's not state nature. That's individual human nature," Banta said. "I don't think you'd see the cooperation internationally that we see on a lot of things if it occured at the state level. Regulation certainly is an unpopular

thing," Banta added, "but I really believe it's a function of having too damn many people."

Slowly, an anxious tone began to shape Banta's words, as his affability slipped into angst. The man whose work is devoted to nurturing life fears a toxin is invading the nest. "It's probably only going to get worse," Banta said, "as we try to come to grips with dealing with exceeding our carrying capacity as a species. And we in fact have [exceeded that capacity.] There's no doubt about it. And the average person doesn't want to admit to having to come to grips with it. But regulation is just going to get worse. I question whether any administration has the capability to deal with a lot of the problems we face. I guess it remains to be seen."

Paul Rokich
Restoring the Landscape

"**W**hen I was a boy, about six or seven years old, I remember standing with my father right here by that [Kennecott] smelter sign," Paul Rokich began. "I looked at that mountain and I knew then that I'd go there and replant that mountain. It's what I had to do. It's hard to tell people, but it's like being commanded. And I never changed. I've never left it."

When Paul Rokich began his life's work in the early '50s, revegetating the Oquirrh Mountains, the easternmost mountain range in the West Desert, they couldn't have been in worse condition. Eightieth West in Salt Lake County was the gray line; west of that point sulphur dioxide would kill mules, let alone vegetation. Black flue dust coated everything, including Rokich's father's lungs. Rather than becoming embittered, however, when his father died early in his life, Rokich became more committed to his vision. When other boys built sand castles, Rokich planted sandbox forests in the foothills behind his Smelter Camp home.

As a teen Rokich became serious, sowing seeds in the northern Oquirrhs behind the

smelter. He'd buy them with his own money at 25 cents a pound and carry them in a five-pound sack high on the mountain.

"Did you plant them or tamp it in?" I asked.

"Oh, no," Rokich replied. "I'd get a good windy day. One of my favorite pasttimes is throwing that out and watch that seed how it acts in the wind. It'll take it right down, like an artillery shell. It will plant itself."

For years Kennecott Copper Corporation, inheritor of the old American Smelting and Refining Company (ASARCO) smelter and its environmental damage, tried to prevent Rokich from reseeding company land. Paranoid about bad publicity and union sabotage, Kennecott guards would try to chase Rokich off corporate property. A "walking fool," Rokich would devise elaborate cat-and-mouse games to avoid the guards, hiking in the dark hours of the morning when no one could see him or slipping up a side canyon he knew was invisible to the guardposts. By the time they could spot him with their binoculars, he would be climbing in terrain they couldn't reach with their four-wheelers.

Concurrent with the first Earth Day, Kennecott corporate environmental culture began to change. At the time Rokich was working on a master's degree in botany with Walter Cottam at the University of Utah. When Cottam and Rokich decided he should do his thesis on the Oquirrhs, Cottam suggested Rokich write Kennecott for its permission. Kennecott sent their top attorney and biologist to see what Rokich already had done. Impressed, someone in the corporate halls with an enlightened mind then reasoned it was crazy to thwart Rokich's work. They gave him permission in 1971 and eventually hired him in 1973 as environmental engineer. He turned out to be a gold mine.

"I was hired at this job and stayed at this job. They weren't going to promote me out of my job," Rokich said. "Every time they call me in for my job evaluation I say, 'I don't care what you think of me. I'm going to do it whether I'm working for you or not,'" Rokich chuckled.

A company man all the way, and 1 of only 150 employees Kennecott retained during the corporate shutdown in the early '80s, Rokich underscored that RTZ Ltd., the London-based mining giant and parent of Kennecott, is committed to restoring the mining landscapes they work, unlike Kennecott's previous owner, British Petroleum, which faced a money crunch. Rokich's budget isn't unlimited, but it is much bigger than it used to be. In fact, he never uses all his allotted money.

"They want to make sure that everything is done proper. 'Don't be cutting corners on a project. The money's there. Use it,'" Rokich related. "But I never like to spend a lot of money on reclamation. You can get into these reclamation programs where they are spending $20 an acre. That's a bunch of baloney. I'd rather see that money saved and put into a scholarship program to teach students [ecology]."

With the support of Kennecott and RTZ, Rokich is able to get more work done, and the effects of his reclamation are accelerating. Also, work for Rokich is seven days a week. It's a lot like having a milk cow, Rokich said. It has to be tended daily.

In fact, it was a Sunday when we jumped into his pickup for a tour of his restoration efforts in the northern Oquirrhs. We took a truck only so we could cover more ground. That was some relief to me. Otherwise, Rokich would have walked, and though born in 1933, he still exhausts younger men. As a teen he'd walk his pigs to livestock shows in North Salt Lake from Magna, approximately 50 miles round trip.

As we slowly drove through Rokich's verdant June undergrowth, he had to tell me how it used to be because the evidence was disappearing. Never quite finishing sentences, his mind propelling to another topic before the last words could leave his lips, Rokich began his environmental history of the Oquirrhs.

"The moon was in better shape than this," he said.

The original environmental damage began with heavy logging of the native douglas and white fir and aspens. Lumbermen would cut the timber, slide it down the mountain, and stack it on a barge for shipment across Great Salt Lake to Corinne, where it would be loaded onto trains for homes, buildings, and barns. Aspen was used to make fences.

"They were rather wasteful," Rokich said. "They used to cut that timber when snow was on them. About four feet of snow. They cut 'em high, about snow level."

Later, in the 1930s the stumps and any remaining trees were clear-cut for firewood. In the meantime there were the sheep. "In the old days this used to be the main migratory route for all sheep herds," Rokich continued. "You know, we used to have upwards of six million sheep in Utah. They'd stop here and graze all this country. They used to have a big loading dock and pens here for the railroad. They'd bring their stock in and hold 'em. They let 'em graze up on the hill before they loaded them.

"And then the steam engines and the fires. Every year, burn the place. Most of those native species can't tolerate fire.

"Nobody really had control of this and everybody used it," Rokich continued. "Then the smelter came in and the public assumed that the smelter did all this damage. It just finished it off."

So when Rokich began his work, there wasn't time for slow, deliberate testing. Annual spring floods would tear down raw Smelter Canyon, once covering two-thirds of the smelter with mud and boulders. Water from denuded Little Valley would bury Magna in debris. Rokich had a good idea what would take hold from his earlier work on ASARCO property and experiments in his greenhouse. It was essential that he quickly stabilize the soil, hence his five-pound sack of seed.

"If you're well trained," Rokich said, "you can see what I was doing. I'm not so much a botanist as an ecologist, an ecologist in the style of Doc Cottam. If you're an ecologist you should be able to interpret. Like, my mind reads it right now on the land. When I walk through the Oquirrhs, I feel it with my feet if I want to plant a tree."

Rokich never used any topsoil or liming, nor does he to this day. He reasons that once something starts growing, the plant draws up minerals and other nutrients from below ground level. When the leaves drop or the grasses wither, that becomes the duff that creates topsoil. Then natural succession takes over with native plants blowing in. On more devasted sites Rokich will be more active with his planting, but he still believes that plant seres will take over.

For grasses he's planted yellow sweet clover, cheatgrass, alfalfa, penstemon, Mormon tea, and late yields like vetches and sego lilies. Wheatgrass, intermediate wheatgrass, sage, and four-wing saltbush came next. Then he added some orchard grass and rabbit brush.

In lower elevations he'll plant what people like, a honey locust to memorialize a loved one, a giant sequoia someone brought from California. At higher elevations he sticks with native plants—chokecherries and elderberries, snowberries, serviceberries, and mountain lilac. Still higher are the aspens, maples, oaks, and, eventually, conifers. Rokich knows in his soul that a greater force will eventually sort things out, and that what takes hold has its season. That philosophy has drawn complaints from the Sierra Club.

"The Sierra Club has a hard time looking at the big picture. If I took them on a trip like this, all they'd be doing is bitching about some plant that shouldn't be here. They'd never see the life that was occurring.

"What I do is just a sere in time. And it doesn't do you any good to point fingers and spend your life arguing over really *nothing*. Like Louis Pasteur said, 'The microbes will have the last word.' The land has a way to heal itself too. Read Carl Sandburg. On grass and things.

"I know that these things I've done are going to change. They're going to be overshadowed by the native species again someday. You're a steward of the land from the time you're here. But that's all you are, a steward. You're not the boss.

"So, ya gotta look at things the way they are today," Rokich continued. "If you sit there and stomp up and down, you freeze yourself worrying about that, and the race is going on. If you stop, you get run over. Like I say, if I stand still on the Oquirrhs, I get buried by plants."

As we drove through the range, he'd reminisce as he periodically pointed things out to me, identifying things growing unaided. "This is squawbush," he said. "The chukars really like this. This was really an achievement in the old days to get this to grow, because of the SO_2. That's my [wild] rose garden over there."

All Rokich's planting decisions are based on biodiversity and wildlife management. He is looking for a healthy, complete ecosystem. A vibrant undergrowth will bring herbivores and with them carnivores. With any new planting project, Rokich asks, will it provide more feed? Will it provide cover for security and birthing? Will it provide feed during droughts and snows?

"There's nothing I like better," Rokich said, "than coming up here on a winter day and seeing a big bull elk standing up on that ridge. And he looks down on me like he knows me."

That reverie was momentarily interrupted as Rokich noticed a plane flying low overhead. "Look at that airplane. What the hell's he doing there?" Rokich asked. "He's harrassing an elk, the damn yahoo! God, I get so mad at people! They get up there and do that and they kick down the elk and they come down and get in the tailings pond and I have to go get them out. They run out there and get stuck."

The feed is now so thick in the northern Oquirrhs that elk tend to congregate. Rokich has a hard time moving them to the middle and southern Oquirrhs, and some of his conifers are growing in a most undignified, flat trajectory because they are being munched at the top.

"Is there more wildlife now in the Oquirrhs?" I asked.

"Oh yeah. There's more wildlife here now than you'll see in the entire West," Rokich replied. "I'd match this against Yellowstone."

"What have you seen?" I asked.

"Deer. Elk. Cougar—I saw one the other day on a field trip, in the early morning out on the ridge. The cougars work this [area] quite a bit. There's one that works high and one that works low. That one up there, he follows me all the time when I go up there to work. I don't see him. But every time I come back on my trail, I see his tracks behind mine."

He's sighted a black bear, too, suspecting that it crossed the Jordan River around Point of the Mountain.

"What do you think of the Wasatch Range?" I asked.

"I see the Wasatch as a dead mountain. It doesn't interest me. It's deteriorating. The Oquirrhs are just the opposite. It's growing. It's alive. It's changing."

We then began a discussion of Allan Savory and his theories of holistic range management. Savory maintains that cattle grazing is good for the land, as long as it's done properly. Cowpokes need to actively manage the herd, keeping the cows bunched together so that their droppings become concentrated and their hooves work the manure into the soil. Rokich believes the essential flaw in Savory's argument is that about 60 percent of a plant's remains have to go back onto the earth.

"When you're using forbs, grasses, and shrubs, especially shrubs, they have taproots that reach down and pull up the mineral reserves that lie deep within the soil structure. They bring them up into the leaves. When they die and fall they bring those vital micronutrients to the surface and they revitalize the soil. They build that A horizon.

"With Savory," Rokich continued, "he's talking about cows. He's talking about increasing cow production. Okay, so that cow takes all that mineral and you take him and kill him. You take him off the land. So, you're talking it off the land. You're not going to move ahead with building an A horizon. His whole philosophy is an economic one, not a biological one."

Suddenly, there was an explosion of wings 50 yards away that diverted our attention. We both spotted it at the same time. "Hey, there's a duck!" Paul said. "A mallard, too. Of course, their young uns have gone off now."

Although he's the only person directly attending to the land and the person who makes all the planting decisions, Rokich does have the help of outside contractors now to move large amounts of earth. He also is overcome with the offers for volunteer labor.

"I have no shortage of finding tree planters. Oh, in the early days *I* used to get kids. Now I have a standing order with scouts and school groups."

Rokich likes to work with the American Forestry Association, Tree Utah, Kids Organized to Protect the Environment, and the Learning Tree. Then, there are the Arbor Day groups and the Wildlife Rehabilitation Center. He also works closely with county extension agents, Utah State Fish and Game, and the state Board of Forestry with its prison program planting trees and collecting seeds. On the federal level he has close working relationships with the Forest Service, EPA, and the Soil and Conservation Service.

"What's the American Dream for you?" I asked.

"The American Dream is . . . First of all, be honest and appreciate what you have."

Rokich's voice began to rise and his delivery quickened. "Respect for the land, and make it better. And not worrying so much about yourself and how many days off you got, or what I see in America today, everybody worrying about their damn weekends.

"By God, make a contribution," Rokich continued, with an edge in his voice. "If you believe in something, then you go put yourself on the line. You make a commitment. If you care about health care, you go into a hospital and work for free cleaning bedpans. If that's your contribution and all you can do, that's what you do, and don't ask to be patted on the back for it. I don't believe in rewards. You're supposed to do these things. It's supposed to come from you."

On the horizon was the tailings pond, probably Rokich's most challenging reclamation

Rokich walking through undergrowth

Rokich measures the success of his reclamation work by biodiversity. As we walked through this thick undergrowth, four bucks lazily got up from their resting spot and slowly began ambling up the mountain. A flock of ducks exploded off a wetlands nearby that Rokich had created. All the while a herd of elk looked down on us from a ridge. Kennecott zealously prevents hunting and human trespassing on its land.

project. Before Kennecott installed its new sprinkling and wet tailings diffusion system, and especially during the company shutdown in the 1980s, northern winds would lift the dry, talcum-like tailings and rain them from a great cloud over Magna. Rokich showed me his "farm," the first reclaimed area in the tailings.

"Isn't that something to see," Rokich said. "The only thing that's different from this to that over there," pointing to fresh tailings, "is this road. We just keep picking up this road and setting it in. As soon as that's done, I'll step in and seed it to grain and alfalfa. In seven days it's up about an inch. Last Sunday I was here watching a doe having her fawns right here."

The newly planted area was only a year old, yet at four feet high the plants could hide a deer and her fawns. Ducks also nest on wetlands created on the tailings. The water is agricultural quality and potable.

Rokich is moving away from planting Russian olives, reed grass, and tamarisk around the tailings berms now. He's using willows, poplars, and wheatgrass instead. The former ones are "weedy" and tend to invade the duck marshes.

"But twenty years ago, we needed something fast, if you knew it would even grow at all," Rokich said. "I have no qualms about planting anything out here now. Tomatoes, potatoes, corn,

Colorado blue spruce, grapes, fruit trees." He said he wouldn't have to fertilize fruit trees any more often than he would do at home. "You aren't limited to growing particular species on tailings. It's just a question of what you want to plant."

The last stop on our journey through the northern Oquirrhs was a wetlands in the undulating foothills above Magna, along the old Lake Bonneville shoreline, that Rokich had begun reclaiming nine years before. When he started his reclamation work, it was a dustbowl. The willows the pioneers had planted in the area had shriveled up and were just stumps. Rokich had turned it into a wetlands by bringing water in the table up to the surface.

Three ducks took off when we approached, although it was impossible to see them beforehand because of the dense vegetation. The willow trees had come back and shielded the pond with a generous canopy. Cattails and wild rose bushes were thick. Even Rokich couldn't believe how much it had filled in the four years since he had last been at the site. Life in the northern Oquirrhs is like that for Rokich. He wanders around planting a string of jewels. He comes back to them periodically and it never ceases to awe him. He has a childlike ability to be continually fascinated. Everything is always new. But he also doesn't get too attached to his creations. It is a process, not a monument he is creating.

For a brief moment Rokich stopped talking and pointed, as if into the future. "Look at those two out there!" he said.

"Egrets," I cried.

Rokich surveying new willow tree canopy.

Paul Rokich's reclamation work in the northern Oquirrhs is widely recognized. He's received the national Arbor Day and Freedom Foundation awards. His most recent accolade was the first international The Man Who Planted Trees Award, named for the character of Jean Giono, who planted acorns and beans in Provence, France, the fictional clone of Rokich. Rokich was nominated for the award by the American Forestry Society. Rokich's success wouldn't have been possible without Kennecott installing its gigantic smokestack with its scrubbers. Because of it, the PH value of the soil has dropped from 14 to 8.

Education
The Soul of the West Desert

Education in the West Desert is a wellspring of pride and profound pain. It binds communities together more than the extractive economy. It is the link between old and new communities.

It also is a reason why some West Desert communities are at risk. While the education delivered is personal and individually tailored, the educational opportunities are limited. Northern Snake Valley has a high school in Partoun, and Eskdale has its own, private prep school. But southern Snake Valley, centered around Baker, Nevada, and Garrison, Utah, has none. Families reach the Rubicon when the oldest child reaches the eighth grade. Ninth-graders either must attend high school in Ely, Nevada, or Delta, Utah.

Rather than board out their children to distant schools or have them commute on a bus three hours a day, young families sometimes teach their primary grade children at home. Other families leave the West Desert at the onset of the eldest child's maturity. They always pledge to return, but inside they doubt they can. That constant fear of parting is a ghost that lurks beside the children in the lower grades.

Baker School
The Two-Room Schoolhouse

Baker School is the repository of history and dreams for the community. Reverberating inside its 1910-era walls are echoes of the town's births and farewells. It also represents how communities on the distant, tenuous borders of government apply invention in democracy and overcome provincialism.

Baker School is part of an interlocal agreement with the Garrison School, five miles distant but over the Utah-Nevada state line. With the blessing of White Pine County School District in Nevada and Millard County School District in Utah, the two communities divide up their children. The single-room school in Garrison takes southern Snake Valley's kindergarten through second-graders, and the Baker School houses third through eighth grades in two rooms. The communities' cooperation is necessary, since neither Baker nor Garrison have the critical mass to make separate schools work.

Wetmore and Chris

Seventh-grader Chris thrives in the Baker School. Small class sizes enable Susan Wetmore to give him individualized attention. When it had more money, White Pine School District stretched the rules a bit and provided Chris a special education teacher, who doubled as a teacher's aide for the lower grades, even though the number of students wasn't large enough to qualify for the aide. Chris went to space camp with funds raised in the community.

The school bus

Two buses ferry students to the Baker School. One picks up kids spread out to the north and east into Utah, while the other meanders between the distant ranch outposts on the other side of the Snake Range in Nevada. The Nevada trip must be done with two buses and in two segments. One bus can't cover enough distance to pick up all students and deliver them to the school on time.

That cooperation is somewhat remarkable when one considers the nature of the two communities. Some family ties stretch between the two towns, yet Garrison is older, a predominantly Mormon ranching community, while people in Baker tend to be more transient and religiously diverse or nondenominational, due to the influence of Great Basin National Park and the School of the Natural Order.

Class sizes are small in the multiple-grade classrooms, but oddly enough, in proportion to the size of the school district. White Pine County, approximately the size of Massachusetts, has a school-age population of 1500. In 1992, the Baker School had 24 kids in the two classes, 10 students in the sixth- through eighth-grade class and 14 kids in the third- through fifth-grade class.

Susan Wetmore is the head teacher. Schooled at Mt. Holyoke College and the University of North Carolina, with a bachelor's degree in comparative literature and a master's in education, she came to Baker in 1976, attracted to the region because of the School of the Natural Order, where she lives. She'll teach her daughter, Cassie, beginning in 1993, and will be forced into that wrenching decision of high school placement in three more years.

Heather Harvey's first year teaching was 1992. She's perceived as a "local girl" by the older folks in Baker, although she doesn't share that description of ethnocentricity, having moved between divorced parents. Harvey never wanted to be a teacher. Since both her parents are teachers, she couldn't imagine a worse job. During her occasional forays into Baker, however, she was a teacher's aide for Wetmore. Then, she said, "I fell in love with teaching."

Both teachers group their students by literature textbook level, an important difference in the multiple-grade classroom. Harvey, for instance, will teach two grades of kids from the same social studies textbook, regardless of the grade level for which it was intended. The next year, she will teach the same two grades from the same science textbook. That differs from the usual curriculum of teaching social studies to one grade and science to the next higher grade. If a teacher in a multiple-grade classroom couldn't have the flexibility to make this change, "We'd

all grow crazy," Harvey said, because they can't teach at one and the same time to multiple grades from multiple textbooks. Rather, because they have the same children for three years, they can work over a longer time line.

While the kids are grouped by literature, they tend to sit by grades. That is not inviolable. When there are only one or two kids in a grade, that creates a problem of critical mass. If a child is new to the community, constitutes a single grade, or has a personality problem that means she or he needs more integration, the teachers will break up the sitting-by-grade and try other arrangements.

Sometimes, the kids work on the same subject at the same time. When I arrived for the first week of school, the older class practiced writing similes together. They all recited the same Carl Sandburg and Emily Dickinson poems in front of the class. For an exercise commemorating Labor Day, they broke into groups to come up with A–Z listings of occupations.

Other times, the activities were broken into grades. During science, students worked with worksheets that were particularized for their grades. But it had to be silent table study. It wasn't directed to the class by the teacher because of the problem of "having to speak with too many tongues." Instead, Wetmore was available at her desk for the students to consult individually.

The ability to incorporate peer tutoring more effectively is one of the greatest advantages of the multiple-grade classroom. For instance, during an independent work period, students would be working on different worksheets. When they had a problem, the kids had two options. They could raise their hands and ask for the teacher's aid, or they could enlist the help of an older student who had that same material the previous year.

"How do your kids respond to peer tutoring?" I asked.

"They love it," Harvey replied. "It's just sometimes easier for a student to ask an older classmate for some help than ask the teacher. They don't feel dumb that way."

Wetmore talked about the advantages to the older child. "It's like that old maxim goes:

'The best way to learn a subject is to teach it yourself.'"

Peer tutoring frees up time for the teacher to work with individual kids. For instance, when the class worked on a math exercise in the morning, the peer tutoring and quiet study time gave Wetmore a chance to correct that math exercise and then show the student where and how mistakes were made. The student got immediate, individualized feedback. Wetmore gained from having one-on-one interactions with students, building rapport and learning more about how her kids process, a distinct advantage when you are working with a child for three years.

The rigidity of grade divisions in the traditional classroom forces certain curricular and teaching approaches. Not so in the multiple-grade classroom. The "slopover" effect facilitates a skills mastery approach. If a student shows exceptional talent in a particular subject area, science for instance, it is easier for the teacher to "promote" that student into the subject material for the next higher grade level. Students can work at their own speed. The "promotion" is an "effective promotion" for a single subject, not a formal one, like having a kid "skip a grade."

"That could be damaging in a small class of multiple grades," Wetmore said. "It would call too much attention to the student, and when the consequence of a formal promotion would mean working with the same kids in class, rather than getting a new sea to swim in, that can create interpersonal problems."

The Baker School has no principal. Wetmore is paid an extra $50 a month to be the head teacher, essentially being responsible for the paperwork. Harvey laughed and said, "I am the assistant principal." There used to be a kind of roving supervisor from the White Pine District office in Ely, but that position was cut several years ago. Now, Wetmore's direct supervisor is the district superintendent, and she has little interaction with him.

"You know," Wetmore said, "in the entire time I've been a teacher here, no one has ever come by to check out my teaching. I'm not sure that they even want to know."

This "have-I-died-and-gone-to-heaven-dream" provides Wetmore and Harvey more decision-making power. They needn't automatically run things by a superior when they want to implement a new idea. As long as it doesn't violate a district or state policy, they feel they can be more innovative. More importantly, they find themselves thinking along those lines, of innovation and change, simply because they know they won't have to go through multiple levels of clearance.

This idyllic period could fade. One reason there is relatively little contact between the Baker School and the White Pine School District is Kennecott Copper Corporation's withdrawing from the Ruth/McGill mining district outside Ely. Wetmore said that when Kennecott was in the Ely area it was the prime organizing force in the community. When something had to get done, Kennecott brought the necessary forces together to get it done. When Kennecott withdrew, White Pine County found itself on its own. Suddenly, all public institutions had to learn how to get things done on their own, and some things still fall between the cracks.

Budgets, however, were not an immediate casualty. Nevada's gaming industry provides steady income to the state's schools, and once their yearly budget is provided by the superintendent, Wetmore and Harvey have ultimate responsibility for it. The $2,000 per teacher is twice as much as Millard County's Cecelia Phillips receives in the Garrison School. While the Utah teacher always feels she never has enough money, both Wetmore and Harvey laughed over the fact that in her first year Harvey didn't know how to spend it all. "I got it up to $400," Harvey said, "and then I got stumped." Wetmore helped her see where other monies could be spent usefully. Nevada teachers on average are also paid $10,000 more than Utah teachers.

Wetmore reported that the Baker community is generally financially supportive of the school. Several years ago when White Pine School District patrons were offered a "pay as you go" approach to capital improvements, a conservative funding approach that doesn't require tax levies or bonds, Baker residents voted for approval. Wetmore felt they probably voted for it because they knew that if it passed, Baker would get a new school building. They

Two rooms

During silent study and reading periods, the door between the two classrooms is opened for community ventilation. It really isn't much of a sound break, as the paper-thin walls allow experience to ebb and flow between the two grades. A new school will have sound insulation between the walls and no intervening door, and while the two teachers are thrilled over the possibilities, something will be missing.

Ringing the school bell

Several Bakerites tried desperately to preserve the old Baker School, even while supporting construction of a new school. They tried to designate it a national historic site, but the Catch-22 was that the old school would need to be moved to make room for the new school, and historic buildings that have been moved no longer can qualify as historic sites with strict preservation status. The new building will have its own outside bell tower, however, so the tradition of every Baker kid getting a chance to ring in the school day would continue.

knew there would be immediate return for the community.

But, Wetmore also said, "This is a conservative community and those who have money want to hang onto it." So when there was a bond election to raise money to pay for a new high school in Ely, which is almost as old as the Baker School, the issue did not pass and Wetmore said most Baker residents opposed the bond issue. Even though a lot of their kids go to the Ely high school, it just seemed far away—another community's problem.

Wetmore added that the Baker School has a very strong PTA. They are supportive and not adversarial. She does get a bit disappointed when the PTA will organize a meeting on a school problem and only 30–40 percent of the parents of school kids attend. Then, Wetmore also asked, "I wonder if the percentage is higher or lower in an urban school? I suspect it probably is lower."

Both Wetmore and Harvey waxed ecstatic over the new school building. Even though it, too, would be a two-room schoolhouse and might lack some of the character of the old school, the benefits of starting from scratch would be obvious. Lavatories wouldn't be cramped appendages added after outhouses became passé. The teacherage would be housed in the same building.

"Imagine," Wetmore said. "We'll actually have a hall in the new school. We'll have to have a hall pass and a bathroom pass. We'll have to do that because we won't be able to see the kids congregate. Why, they could sneak to the bathrooms and have a grand old time. Now, it'll have to be like a regular school."

"What are the disadvantages of a two-room school?" I asked.

Wetmore and Harvey turned toward each other and drew blank stares. At first, they couldn't think of any disadvantages. When I suggested that students get new teachers, and a fresh start, every autumn in single-grade classrooms, both Wetmore and Harvey conceded that they have to be careful to provide multiple perspectives and outside counsel whenever possible.

For one thing, they try to organize a lot of field trips. Denys Baker, owner of the Border Inn and a college political science teacher, was going to take the school to Topaz, the Japanese-American internment camp outside Delta, the following week. Periodic fund-raising provides scholarships for things like summer space camp in Alabama. The teachers rely on the pulling power of Home Farm to bring in speakers. Then, "anyone who looks interesting" who comes through Baker is corralled, hog-tied, and brought to the Baker School.

Wetmore also said it is especially important not to let any problems develop or fester with kids or their parents. Since teachers have them for three years and interrelate in the community on a variety of levels, it is imperative that lines of communication remain open. It's important, too, not to have a teacher's pet or whipping boy. Both could be more destructive to the child and the class than in a traditional school.

Wetmore said, "Every day has to be a new day. You can't let things carry over from day to day or year to year. If something goes wrong, you are forced into a lot of introspection. Maybe the kid was arrogant or disrespectful, but ultimately it falls on you. You have to ask yourself, 'How did I handle it? How can I make sure it doesn't happen again?'"

Disruptive children have to be handled differently. "Let's say you have a kid with a personality problem who is disruptive," Wetmore said. "In a large class it might not be so apparent. But when you have ten kids in a class, like me, that problem then gets magnified. It's like it's ten percent, when it might be less than a one percent problem in a large classroom." That problem kid might have more of a distracting effect on the other students and it might be harder to isolate him or her effectively to help mitigate the problem.

Norms can vary widely in the small class of multiple grades, unlike the traditional class where abilities likely reflect the standardized, national norm in all subject areas. In the small, multiple-grade classroom, you could have five very talented kids in one subject, and Wetmore takes that into account. In those situations she tends to disregard national or state norms and pitches the material to the norm reflected in her class. More importantly, she doesn't design the instruction for the two slowest students, which often happens in a larger classroom when the slowest learners constitute such relatively high numbers that a teacher tends to speak to them in order not to lose them, frustrating the normal and faster learners. Wetmore can meet the needs of the slow learners through individualized instruction.

"What about the problem of younger kids having to compete with older kids?" I asked.

Wetmore replied that really isn't a problem. She said that students tend to see things over the long haul. They know how the multiple-grade classroom works because it is their only experience. They know they'll get their turns to be "class stars," due to developmental differences, in the future.

"Besides," Wetmore added, "it doesn't always follow that the oldest students will necessarily do the best work on a group assignment. It's that numbers game again." Sometimes, the best work is done by a younger student who has a particular talent in a subject area. That student shines, and peers, regardless of grade level, can see, acknowledge, and freely accept that person's talent.

Like most teachers Wetmore and Harvey take their work home with them. Unlike teachers in large urban areas, however, home for Wetmore and Harvey still is the small Baker community. They really can't become lost or separated from their jobs. Does that make their work even more enervating?

"Not so," Harvey replied. She said the kids actually show them great deference, and she especially enjoys that part of teaching in a small, multiple-grade classroom. "The kids automatically give you more respect because they see you all the time. You aren't just their teacher. You might also be a friend of their parents. They see you in their home. And, like in my case, they know I grew up here, at least during summer vacations."

Baker School is the open heart of the community. Townsfolk live large lives in its small spaces, so that life seems to spill out the cracks where the foundation has settled. Even when they graduate, Bakerites never spiritually leave the two-room school because school was the center of the community and, hence, their formative lives.

All school functions are supported by the community. It isn't just parents of school kids who turn out. Senior citizens come to the school plays or fund-raising bazaars. Folks from Eskdale come, even though their own kids attend their private, Shiloah Valley Christian School. Eskdale's four- to five-man basketball team, depending upon the size of that year's high school class, plays its games in the adjacent, aging Baker gym. Families come to marry their children and eulogize their parents on the polished, hardwood floors.

"It has become the focal point of the community," Wetmore said. "We have no movie theater, no [professional] sports teams. The school is it."

Epilogue

Later in that academic year, Wetmore and Harvey moved their classes into the new, two-room schoolhouse, hallway and all.

In 1996, when Cassie reached ninth grade, Susan Wetmore and her daughter moved to Ely for the high school, and Wetmore took a position in town teaching fourth grade. They return to Home Farm on the weekends and summers.

Heather Harvey became the sole teacher at the Baker School. The White Pine School District decided that falling enrollments didn't warrant replacing Wetmore with a credentialed teacher. Instead, Harvey got a paraprofessional, a kind of student teacher who might become the second Baker School teacher when he finishes his degree. In the meantime Cecelia Phillips would teach grades K–3 in Garrison and Harvey would handle the 16 students in grades 4–8 herself in the Baker School.

Part of Wetmore's senior teacher salary was converted into funds to pay for students living in Pleasant Valley, Nevada, to attend West Desert School in Partoun, Utah. The greater student numbers in the largely polygamous community at Pleasant Valley warranted the decision.

The loss of a credentialed teacher for the community, albeit perhaps temporarily, rankles Bakerites for two reasons. First, they feel their

Rosary

Each day begins with mother and children reciting the rosary. A devout Catholic, Frances Banta is determined that her kids will be raised that way. It means traveling 120 miles every Sunday to attend church in Dugway, Utah, despite the priest telling her distance would excuse her from a few masses. On the other hand, Banta says that if there were no church anywhere, she could accept that. The virtues of living at a place like Fish Springs are sufficient for her.

taxes are going to support what they call a *de facto* parochial school. Second, they also maintain the Pleasant Valley community doesn't contribute as much to the tax base, and their larger families create the school population imbalance to begin with.

Home Teaching at Fish Springs National Wildlife Refuge

The kitchen doubles as classroom, while the living room is the library. The master bedroom also is the computer workroom. "These units were not built for families," Frances Banta said.

Nevertheless, the two-bedroom, red brick house provided for the refuge manager at Fish Springs National Wildlife Refuge must serve two ends—home and school. Since they arrived in 1990, Frances Banta has been home teaching her two children Jed and Marsha. Their assignments clutter most walls in the home, except the one near the potbellied stove, the sole source of heat in the house. One can't avoid brushing into their papers while walking through the house, generating a kind of electricity that reflects intellectual inquiry and growth that is as much a part of the Banta decor as family portraits and western landscapes.

Home teaching is a privilege as much as a necessity for the Bantas. There is a school 50 miles away, the West Desert School at Partoun, Utah, and if Frances or her husband, Jay, ferried their kids to the bus stop 26 miles away, Jed and Marsha could make school on time. But the dirt roads are treacherous in winter, and time on the bus is time taken from education—and family.

The Banta school day begins in the kitchen after breakfast with catechism and prayer over rosary beads. Next, Frances, Jed, and Marsha stand and pledge allegiance to a small, thin flag that clings to a far corner in the kitchen. The first lesson is a writing session, and all three are required to write in their journals for 15 minutes. On the day I visited in 1992, Jed quickly became absorbed in the process, but Frances had to admonish Marsha to stay on task, as the third-grader's mind tended to wander past the muse.

Whenever possible, Frances Banta tries to coordinate her lesson plans so that Jed and Marsha's activities dovetail. For instance, on that day I observed, both Jed and Marsha were involved with a project on India. Utah state curriculum states that students in sixth grade will be exposed to world cultures. So Jed was responsible for researching the soup that Marsha would make for her homemaking unit. He found a book entitled *Food in India* at the library and picked out a representative soup. He also made a map of India using their home computer and map-making software. As a test, Frances asked him to fill in the names of the countries surrounding India.

Sometimes, studies would diverge. While Frances quizzed Marsha on spelling in the kitchen, energetically kneading bread dough while her daughter recited, Jed worked on a geography project in the living room. He was charged with plotting a route to Lake Havasu the family would take the following day to attend a wedding. He totaled the expected mileage, which they would check against the odometer.

Frances supplements her home teaching with weekly visits to the Army's Dugway Proving Ground 60 miles away. The trek is important for several reasons, besides picking up the weekly mail for the refuge. The kids get a chance to socialize with other children. Jed and Marsha also enroll in after-hours classes there, Jed taking a class in cultural anthropology and Marsha in money. Frances would teach a class later that year in wildlife. In addition, the kids get to use the two libraries, the post library and the school library, for research and pleasure-reading books. Frances said that Jed checks out approximately 10 books a week from the library and finishes them before the end of the week. "He doesn't get more than that," Frances said, "because his book bag always rips."

Dugway is important, too, for the religious education of the kids. While her husband only belongs to "the great church of the outdoors," Frances Banta is a devout Catholic and wants her kids raised that way. To do so, they

Pledging allegiance to the flag

Pledging allegiance to the flag generates complex feelings for the Banta family, as it does for many employees of the federal government. In an era when some Americans label government bureaucrats as alien, especially those like Frances's husband Jay who are charged with managing federal lands, the national rampart is symbol of embattlement and neo-frontier isolation as much as a sign of community.

Marsha looking at "words" chart

Besides the whole-language approach to teaching, there are other topics and pedagogies that link large sub-urban, rural two-room, and home schools in the West Desert. Learning about the environment and endangered species is a required unit, a thread that weaves through regional elementary grade curricula. Conservation, then, is likely to become a value that graduates of New West schools will consider as adults.

must drive to Dugway a second time each week on Sundays.

"How much would Fish Springs feel like home if you didn't have access to a full-time priest?" I asked.

"If I didn't have that, I would go in once a month to Tooele and attend there [96 miles away]. I would feel good about that. That would be fine. Our being here is a real blessing and almost a guidance. So it feels very right."

Before their current stint at Fish Springs, the Bantas worked on the U.S. Fish and Wildlife Service's unit at Lake Havasu in Arizona. They had access to schools there, and Jed did quite well. But Marsha, who is learning disabled, was one to two grades behind her peers. Moreover, the Bantas noticed mounting stress in the system, as the conservative community voted against a school bond five times.

Then the Fish Springs position opened up, and the Bantas eagerly jumped on the opportunity to relocate to one of the most isolated refuge outposts in the lower 48 states. But the Bantas don't see the place as isolated. They prefer to call it "insulated," the ideal place to raise and teach children.

"Was Fish Springs a place you purposely came to, or was it a place you ran away to?" I asked.

"I really felt it was more of a going to," Frances said. "Of course, the boon in that is that you do get away from. But that was secondary for me. If we never moved again, it wouldn't bother me in the least."

The only deal Frances and Jay made with their children to soften the idea of moving to a place where Jed would have no one his own age and Marsha only one peer was to buy a satellite dish. Before that, the Bantas had no TV, and even now they place strict limits on television watching.

Jay said Marsha gets frightened by the violence on TV. "Our friends say, 'Oh, that's just because they're not used to it.' But I'm concerned about them 'getting used to it," Jay said. "That's just the problem. They shouldn't become used to it. It should frighten anyone. Certainly a ten-year-old."

Marsha has shown dramatic improvement under her mother's teaching. Now she tests at grade level with her peers, and is slightly ahead in a few subjects. Jed is capable enough that he would likely excell in any teaching environment.

Those improvements are largely due to Frances's efforts, and after two years, she is feeling more confident about her home teaching skills. At first, she was intimidated by the double-loaded responsibility of being both teacher and mother. She had hoped that the state and school district would be able to help out, and by law they are supposed to assist home teachers with periodic visits and computer software.

The parent-teacher dichotomy hasn't been the problem Frances anticipated. I noticed that Frances didn't change personalities when she was speaking to her children as parent and then as teacher. If anything, there was more teacher in her demeanor than parent, if indeed there is any distinction between the two roles.

Both the teacher and mother were patient, and Frances was focused at all times. She was quick to spot and address mistakes, especially with Marsha, who tended to make more mistakes. There didn't seem to be any frustration from Marsha, the kind of frustration a child sometimes shows when an adult is constantly monitoring them and watching for errors. At that moment Marsha recognized her mother as her teacher, and she willingly corrected the mistakes she made, with energy rather than rancor.

Frances did point out, however, that her kids can get cross with her during the course of a school day, which typically begins at 8:30 and ends at 1, 2 or 3 P.M., depending upon the week's activities and the total amount of hours logged for a quarter. Frances thinks the ability to get cross is an advantage with home teaching. In a regular school setting, a child naturally feels more constrained toward the teacher. That tends to keep some emotions bottled up. With home teaching, Frances's kids know they will always have her unconditional love, no matter how they act or what they say. That creates a different, perhaps more vibrant, and volatile, learning environment.

Frances and Jay know that there are natural limits to her teaching role. In three years Jed will be in high school, and Frances might have to withdraw at that time. Her bachelor's degree in

Marsha Banta daydreaming
Partly because she has a learning disability, Marsha Banta has occasional difficulty staying on task. When her mind wanders, Frances is able to spot the departure quickly and with firm but loving admonition get her refocused. Because of this parent-teacher interaction, Marsha Banta is performing better under home teaching than she did in public school.

Bantas interacting
Home teaching provides a family an avenue for extended familial development, as domestic living and learning form a symbiotic relationship. Baking bread becomes a teaching opportunity that provides manna for body and mind. Peer tutoring between older brother and younger sister becomes as natural as sibling rivalry.

horticulture from College of the Redwoods doesn't provide the background necessary to teach all high school subjects.

Jay thinks they might have to move away at that time. At those times when Jay would say, "When we leave," Frances would immediately reply, "Take that phrase out of your vocabulary."

Frances hopes that Jed can go to West Desert High School once a week for things she can't provide and receive home teaching the rest of the time. Jay isn't sure that would work and worries about the quality of education in rural schools with fewer resources.

"In the smaller communities with the education and the money available to the educators, it's just not there," Frances said. "This generation is suffering. But it's a trade-off. If you go into a big city area where they have the technology and the money available and they have this wonderful lab, they have these pretty severe social problems."

Besides, there are intangible benefits to using Fish Springs as a teaching resource that couldn't be duplicated anywhere. Frances related her first experiences at Fish Springs in a short stint before Jay became refuge manager in 1990.

"When Jed was a baby, I was a new mother, and I remember Jay being out hunting and Jed would be just fussing and fussing. And I'd be trying to wean him from this feeding and that feeding. It's hard to do when you're nursing and there's no one you can give the baby to. So I'd put him in a backpack, stick him on my back, and we'd walk. We'd just walk. His second word was 'duck.' His first word was 'poppa.' 'Momma' came after that.

"So the kids spend a lot of time in the outdoors," Frances continued. "And they're comfortable with that. I don't know many nine-year-old little girls who would feel comfortable riding a bike in the dark, hearing coyotes howl and owls hoot, and enjoy it."

Home teaching means more to the Bantas than state-mandated proficiency in certain subject areas. Natural education and family become intertwined. They are not separated by place or spirit. "To really have a family. Not farm off to this scouting group or this group or this lesson or that lesson. We are responsible for our children," Frances said. "Being here, you are truly responsible for your children. You're responsible for everything—their education, their health, their recreation. It's nice because it's coming back to basics, and I'm a very basic person. I don't require a lot of things. There's no shopping. It just really challenges you to be a family, and that's important to me."

For the Bantas, home teaching has become a refuge on the refuge. Fish Springs National Wildlife Refuge is a place where two parents can take small control of the universe, where they can establish boundaries. It's a place where a mother can protect her children, a place where she can forestall for just a moment the forces that inevitably split the child from the mother. Home teaching is a refuge where a mother, teacher, and her kids grow up together.

Epilogue

In 1995, Jed enrolled in West Desert High School full time. Frances commutes 50 miles a day over dirt roads to get him back and forth from the bus stop. With 225,000 hard miles on it, the family Volvo is starting to break down.

Jed is excelling at regular school too, getting better than a 3.5 GPA his first year. He still wants to be an archaeologist. Jay Banta reports that his son enjoys verbally sparring with his classmates at West Desert High School. Jed calls them "conservative, Mormon Republicans," and they dig at him for being a "liberal, Catholic Democrat," the only one in the school. For Halloween in 1996, Jed went dressed as a Catholic priest. Ed Alder, the principal, called him "Father" all day long.

Marsha continues to maintain her grade level under her mother's tutelage.

Shiloah Valley Christian School
Parochial Education

The motto of the Shiloah Valley Christian School, the parochial school for the children of Eskdale, is "Education Unlimited." The people of Eskdale feel strongly enough about the slogan that it's become one of the few bits of ostentation they allow themselves. They inscribe it on the ball-point pens they buy for the community.

Probably more so than publicly funded schools, Shiloah Valley represents a deep commitment on the part of the community. It requires substantial shared resources to make the education "unlimited," because the school's teachers are also members of the united order community. They are not salaried. The united order must generate enough income to completely support them and their families.

The school consists of several schools. Besides elementary, junior, and senior high schools in separate buildings, the community also has a Montessori preschool. In fact, Eskdale's head Montessori teacher, Larue Young, organized the first Montessori school in Utah, and even now Eskdale teachers tutor prospective Montessori educators.

The school is growing. In 1996, the community decided to spend $20,000 to convert some old dorms into a new elementary school with an expanded library. Much of the outlay includes the costs of removing asbestos, a financial commitment that will expand when the community has to tackle its junior and senior high buildings.

Eskdale's levitical tradition permeates the Shiloah Valley curriculum. While other arts are offered, music education is the lyric thread to the community's soul. Each student is required to take two years of piano and sing in the high school choir. While Doug Childs, who teaches the piano, drivers' education, and junior high English, maintains that not every member of the Aaronic Order is biologically ordained to be a musician, most students elect to study a second instrument after piano.

The school is committed to computerized instruction and incorporates units using interactive software at all grade levels. But the school doesn't have the resources to offer more than a chemistry lab and one foreign language, Spanish.

At one point in his career, Doug Childs doubted that Eskdale's good intentions were enough for the children, wondering whether they were deluding themselves about offering a quality education. Part of his angst was due to an impending site visit by the state superintendent of schools.

"I used to worry about the fact that we don't have all the facilities and things modern and up-to-date," Childs said. "Then the state superintendent came out here one time about twelve or fourteen years ago. I was giving a tour, and of course, there were no sidewalks here then. He put his hand on my shoulder and said, 'Doug, you don't need to worry about that. What comes out the front door when you're done is the necessity and what you're pulling out the front door speaks for itself.' So, I've always remembered that, and I don't apologize for anything. We do what we can the best we can. So if kids don't get all the chemistry labs they should have had in high school, they get the chemistry textbook and a great teacher to go with it, and they have to do more later on if they need it."

It would be misleading to suggest that the Shiloah Valley education only meets the minimum. The school offers a 13th year, college preparatory program. Consequently, Shiloah Valley graduates tend to perform better in higher education than their publically educated peers. Childs thinks that's due to Shiloah Valley students being one year older, and their choir and junior orchestra experiences providing them

**Doug Childs
giving spelling test**

Most teachers at the Shiloah Valley Christian School wear several hats. Besides offering piano instruction and driver's training for all Eskdale children, and many other Snake Valley residents, Doug Childs teaches English in the junior high.

**Karma Childs
and elementary school**

Because her elementary grade class has more than ten students, Karma Childs has a teaching aide, an Eskdale teenager who aspires to become a teacher for the community. The younger woman chooses not to wear the cap of honor, but like most older women at Eskdale, Karma Childs feels more comfortable covering her head and identifying herself as a descendent of Levi from the Old Testament.

more opportunities to travel, and therefore, more life experiences.

College educations, however, are becoming a problem for Eskdale. In the past the community often was able to pay the bills for students willing and able to enter college. But tuition inflation has eaten away that promise. Now, would-be college students have to find scholarships or seek family funds outside the united order to support themselves.

In some ways Shiloah Valley Christian School is becoming a victim of its own success. Non-Eskdale parents with problem children have discovered the parochial school with high standards and strict discipline and plead with Shiloah Valley to enroll their sons and daughters. At first, the school tried to oblige beleaguered parents, but now has to use more discretion.

"We'd open the door, have an interview and try to help the child," Childs said. "Some we've helped and some we haven't. But more and more, the phone rings off the hook, even during the school year.

"So we've really had to upgrade our standards," Childs continued. "We're going more and more to academic standards, and also recommendations from people other than parents. Parents will lie to you every time. They're desperate. They won't tell you the whole story. It's sad but true. And we've had so many encounters that way that we've just had to become hard-nosed about it."

Shiloah Valley reserves the right to use corporal punishment but rarely exercises that option. If there is a problem, the school goes to the Eskdale parent, explains the problem or infraction, and turns it over to them to provide punishment or counseling. The parents back the teachers.

In the case of an outside student boarding, the school takes on the responsibility of *en loco parentis* and corporal punishment. One of the priests assumes the task, although, "There is always one or two adults there witnessing,"

Childs said, "so that we'd be able to verify what actually took place. We're very careful with that."

Usually, the corporal punishment alternative works, and Shiloah Valley has had success with borderline students. Doug Childs said, "A borderline child is a lot different than one who has slipped over the edge. That's why we don't know for sure where that edge is. That's why we have to be so careful."

I asked Childs whether or not they would use a school psychologist if they felt one was needed.

"We would not necessarily use the school psychologist in Delta that works for the county. We've used him a time or two. We're human, too. We have our problems. But for a lot of it, we just get together. We have counseling here, too. The principal and the teachers. And what we can't work through we try and get somewhere else—we get down on our knees and work through it."

Epilogue

Increasingly, Shiloah Valley is seeing applications from Baker families, and as the public Baker School loses students, that creates some strain in the southern Snake Valley community. A few disgruntled Baker patrons claim that Shiloah Valley is recruiting Baker children. Doug Childs says that is not the case. Parents are asking Shiloah Valley Christian School to enroll their children.

Nor is Shiloah Valley recruiting for its Utah class 1A high school boys basketball team, although they probably should. In the 1995–96 season the Warriors lost every game. Their hearts were in it, but they could only put four boys on the floor.

Karma Childs retired from teaching in 1996. At Eskdale that means that a person doesn't have to work as hard and can sleep in if she wishes. Karma is looking forward to spending her time painting.

Two boys reading

In most rural communities the book is the medium of choice, partly due to the lack of other media. Video tapes are sparse, few television stations can be received without satellite hookup, and public radio is the only channel that comes in loud and clear. At the Shiloah Valley Christian School, reading is even more fundamental, as watching television, except for programs like Ken Burns's epic *Civil War*, is forbidden at the Eskdale community.

Ed Alder, principal of West Desert School

As part of his job as principal of West Desert School, Ed Alder must be a diplomat. He has to negotiate school finances with two school districts, each in a different state. Then, he has to bring together three groups in northern Snake Valley who sometimes eye each other warily—polygamists, Mormons, and Gentiles. His school is the place where community must be made.

West Desert School
Two Nations, Separate but Equal

A school's population triples in four years. Modular classrooms begin to sprout, seemingly cloned from the sheet-metal-clad mother building, clustering around it like a fort. The picture of a school in one of the New West's burgeoning suburbs? Not even close. It's the West Desert School in Partoun, Utah, a town in northern Snake Valley whose houses spread out according to the Homestead Act, not urban sprawl.

The school scrambles to keep up with the infusion of new students. The number of teachers has doubled in four years: from two to four in the elementary school; from two to four in the junior and high school. The school uses Utah state's EDNET frequently and boasts more technology than most schools in the state. It is linked interactively via video camera and software to the Tintic School District headquarters in Eureka, and classes and one-time video conferences are downloaded and uplinked with regularity.

Unlike growth in suburban schools, however, where the numbers climb steeply but regularly over several years, forecasted by building permits, the influx of new students to the West Desert School was startlingly swift. A new community of equal population, Pleasant Valley, Nevada, wheeled into the area on trailers and effectively grafted itself onto the old ranching society. While the two communities don't physically touch, separated by approximately 10 miles and a state line, Partoun and Pleasant Valley have become uneasy partners in the West Desert School.

An interlocal agreement between Tintic School District in Utah and White Pine School District in Nevada attempts to smooth out the edges. White Pine is furnishing one of the modular units and a school bus and driver to transport the kids from Pleasant Valley. Extra teachers and monies for books and athletic supplies have been promised too, but those promises haven't always been kept because the White Pine

District is cash-strapped. In spite of Nevada's booming economy, the sparsely populated county, too far from urban centers to attract gaming dollars and taxes from tourists, went into financial arrears in 1994 due to soaring costs for the new high school in Ely. The state of Nevada had to kick in emergency funding.

Utah is picking up more of the funding slack for the Nevada kids than it probably should, but Pleasant Valley folk don't really care that their property taxes go to a government entity in Nevada, not Utah, to pay for their children's education. It's all one, big, distant government. While they are pressuring their financially ailing district for their own school, that won't happen soon, due to water, building code, and continuing financial problems. So the communities have no choice. Kids need to be taught and the West Desert School has opened its arms.

This interlocal agreement is more ticklish than usual. It's not as graceful and efficient as the one between Baker and Garrison in southern Snake Valley. The problem? Pleasant Valley is a polygamous community. Those offspring from unions that are constitutionally unrecognized in Utah have more than doubled the size of the West Desert School.

Yet the infusion of kids from a polygamous community into the West Desert School isn't like an invasion by aliens. Northern Snake Valley always has had a large polygamous population. Due to its perceived isolation, the West Desert has been a kind of zion for adults seeking to practice a plural marriage life-style. Now polygamy and its attendant ecclesiastical doctrine is the dominant culture of northern Snake Valley, followed by Mormons, and then two non-Mormon families, locally called Gentiles.

How does Ed Alder, the principal of West Desert School, handle the challenges? Partly, he relies on his laid-back personality and wide Irish grin to try to bring folks together—students and parents. He balances that easiness with organizational skills developed as an officer in the Naval Reserve. He's in a unique position, too, because polygamy has weaved its way through his family's history.

"Has polygamy had any change on the school, the dynamics, how kids interact?" I asked.

There was a long pause while Alder thought through the scope of the question. "No. Because, and I'll say it this way, kids are kids. And I think kids when they're six years old to sixteen years old, the ecclesiastical leanings of parents, as hard as we try to get our children to go one way or the other way—they're much more interested in each other than in what our beliefs are. They're much more interested in who likes who and who doesn't like who. And trying to work the adult system for their own personal gain, than they ever are in 'What does God look like?' and 'What is the 'truth?' With the influx of kids that we've had here, I see a melting."

"Is there or could there be a schism in the school between kids whose polygamous parents followed one prophet and another group whose parents followed another prophet that would affect the dynamics?" I asked.

"Well, basically we have that," Alder replied. "We have a group of kids whose parents follow the fundamentalist belief, and a group of kids who follow the LDS prophet, and then we have a group whose parents don't believe one way or another. At this time, I don't think we have two fundamentalist groups.

"Where the schisms happen is when the parents get involved," Alder continued. "Because parents have very set beliefs and very set ways. Legitimate concerns. We've faced that the last two or three years, trying to keep it out of the school."

"Does it come up over certain episodes?" I asked.

"It comes up over worrying about associations. About who is playing with whom. Not in the school, but in extracurricular things. What's unfortunate about it is the kids are so parallel in beliefs that most of those beliefs are just lockstep. Like the Word of Wisdom [the Mormon dictum that members should eschew alcohol, tobacco, coffee, and tea].

"But out of the school setting, when both of the religious groups are so small, and the kids have intermingled so much during the day during school, that when their various churches want to do something, with just their youth, it's kind of like having a family reunion and only having half your family there. Because their best friend is over here, and their best friend is over there. And yet, the churches are always trying to pull the kids apart that way. The kids wouldn't care. They want to go camping. They want to play volleyball together. They want to play basketball together after school under a 'church setting.' But it's raised some real concerns with some parents and with some higher church [authorities]. And it's usually by people who are not familiar with what's going on. They get very paranoid about that."

There is the perception among some parents in northern Snake Valley that behaviorial problems in the West Desert School have increased with the incidence of polygamy, and that there is more alcohol and drug abuse, in spite of the cultural taboo among both Mormon and polygamous cultures. Those families argue that when a culture is used to breaking one law, through plural marriage, it doesn't have much respect for other laws, either. Periodically, one of those families might send their kids to even more distant schools. But the overwhelming majority of northern Snake Valley residents is happy with its schools.

I asked Alder if he has seen more behavioral problems at the West Desert School, not from polygamy and its cultural conflicts, but from the larger problem of having more dysfunctional families.

"I think there are more [behavioral problems in the West Desert School] than fifteen years ago. We aren't any different. People say it's wonderful that you're out here. But we really aren't any different."

Yet, violence hasn't come to the West Desert School. "I don't go to school worrying that a kid is going to draw a knife on me," Alder continued. "But I have just as many dysfunctional families out here. It comes from fundamentalist sides, to Gentiles, to LDS. Being married and getting along and having a warm relationship with a family isn't a function of religious preference."

"Are there any specific problems that would tend to be localized that would make a family dysfunctional?" I asked.

"Financially, it's a very strapped area," Alder said. "Everyone's in the same boat. Very few people have a new car. Everyone's baling wire and chewing gumming their vehicles together. We are more functional in the sense that when we go home, most of the time both parents are there. We have as much of a divorce rate, but usually divorces have happened before the people came out. I did a count one time and three-fourths of the kids in my classroom were not living with their same biological parents. Lots of mixed families."

Alder then added that single parent households aren't a primary cause of dysfunction in the West Desert. "I think where the dysfunctions come in is a lack of opportunity for individual fullfillment in a family. I see a lot of frustration in that there's really no kind of employment outside [the home]. It doesn't matter what it would be. Even if you took a four-hour shift at a 7-Eleven. It would be a sense of the individual adding to the family. It would be a change. You know, dad's out there busting his butt all day, every day, and getting a sense of accomplishment out of it. A lot of times, the other half, there's nothing." Alder was quick to add, "Although they work just as hard.

"The educational opportunities for the adults are not there, although we're working on that. We're trying to get the EDNET system going. But that's where the dysfunction is."

"What are you most proud of about the school?" I asked.

"Oh, a lot of things," Alder began. "Our reputation with the other schools we compete with. We're known for hustle, heart, and sportsmanship. We win a lot too. But our kids give everything to it. It's not like, 'Well, I'll go out and play a basketball game and *then* I'm going to my job and *then* I'm going to go on a date.' My kids: 'We're going to play basketball!' It's a big thing."

"I'm proud of the kids I've graduated," Alder continued. "They're out there and productive. A large portion go on to college. Some are not as successful as others. That's normal. But for the most part, they're going to go out and they're going to be good at things like hard labor. They're going to do it with the desert hard work ethic. It goes with them.

"When I send out my kids, they may be one of six. But when that six have a problem, when they have to sit down together, that one who came from West Desert has the common sense and courtesies and social aptitude to work things together, to say, 'Here's a problem. Let's solve it together.'"

"How many kids come back to the community?" I asked.

"Very few," Alder replied. "Not by choice," he added. "It's just, economically, that's it. You look at the kids coming up, and I look at my own kids, and I know what's going to happen. Ninety percent of the kids don't want to leave. You'd think maybe from a small area like this they'd wanna say, 'I'm on the first bus out of here. I want to go where the life is going on.' But no. And when they do leave, they do everything they can to get back.

"You know, you've got to set those kids with the tools they've gotta have," Alder continued. "And we don't have the best math program or English program or science program. To tell you the truth, probably the bottom. Hell, a bunch of Coke bottles with chemicals in them. No. But my kids, I think, will have people skills to facilitate them. And, as I see it, [the successful person] is a guy who gets along with people and who can see resources and put this to this and that to that."

"It's like that old ranching and farming know-how," I said, "of taking what you've got, scavenge, and put it together and make something work out of it."

Alder agreed.

3

Community Activism

There are people who are rawboned activists from the get-go. Born as burrs under the saddle of the status quo, those activists are like itinerant hell-raisers, taking their personal shows on the road when one righteous cause wends its way to conclusion—or a dead end. They tend to seek the revealing light of the media wherever they go.

Activism in the West Desert isn't like that. While egos certainly play a role in public life, these cattle prods for community stay in one place. In fact, they are motivated by a sense of place. They are committed to change, public involvement, and improvement because they choose to live in their communities. Like drought resistant plants with deep taproots, they draw their perseverance and commitment from their environment. They might be coaxed initially into activism by the land or the dynamics of their sub-community, but inevitably, they take responsibility because they choose to serve.

Typically, West Desert activists self-select themselves for community work based upon their personal skills or backgrounds. A waitress with a Ph.D. involves herself in the Baker School. A Callao rancher carries his sense of place to the Soviet Union to lobby for peace with other people of the land. An engineer tries to educate his southern Snake Valley community on the need to bring integrated computer telephony into their homes and businesses.

In the stories below one person teamed with others to successfully fight the federal government and continues to lean against intractable institutions whose public consciences are lost or too diffused. Another became involved because he was a wanderer looking for a new home. A third was looking for additional income to support her decision to live in the West Desert, and in so doing, hoisted the weight of grass-roots law and justice onto her shoulders.

JoAnne Garrett
Peacemaker

In the late '70s the United States government, in the name of peace, announced a plan to turn the West Desert into a nuclear sponge. By siting the newest generation of ICBM missiles, the MX, on train tracks carved into eastern Great Basin valleys, the theory was that the Soviet Union could not possibly mount enough firepower to wipe out the constantly circling warheads. There would be effective, final deterrence in the nuclear arms race. Just wasteland would be affected. Now, who could argue against that?

Only people who lived there, and one of the three who led the West Desert opposition to MX was JoAnne Garrett. While it's tempting to label her a matriarch, since she was born in 1925, her physical description doesn't fit. The lines in her face, etched over years of living outdoors, are the only clue to her years. Otherwise, her radiance would be the envy of anyone half her age.

As the door to her locally renowned Rock House, a labor of love constructed from native materials by JoAnne and her late partner Joe Griggs, swung open for me, I could hear a familiar voice in the background. To break the ice I said, "Oh, you're listening to KRCL [the community radio station in Salt Lake City]."

"One of the nicest things about living here [in the foothills near Great Basin National Park] is being able to get public radio from the Wasatch Front from the three university stations and KRCL. The music, the reading tips. I can't imagine living here without that FM connection," Garrett said wryly.

Garrett doesn't have a generational attachment to the West Desert. She didn't arrive in Baker, Nevada, until 1963, and even though having grown up on a ranch outside Billings, Montana, she had spent most of her adult life in California, getting an English degree at UCLA and Berkeley and raising her two children in southern California. Her pedigree, then, wasn't the reason she became the community's anti-MX organizer. The incident that did most to propel her to an environmental consciousness grew out of the social turbulence of the 1960s. Like other parents, she became aware of issues through her children.

"Before then," Garrett said, "my thinking had been somewhat auxiliary to my husband's, and he was a pretty conservative person, a chemical engineer who was very much dedicated to technology, and not concerned in those days with the environment. So the '60s experience catapulted me into beginning to think for myself and to ask questions rather than to be part of the machinery."

Garrett's oldest son had started a recycling program at Berkeley. A TV station in the bay area did a story and came to southern California to interview his family. "That was the time that precipitated my self-consciousness about being something of an environmentalist because in that video my husband and I came off on very different sides of the fence. And it was a major event in our marriage and a contributor to our eventual divorce," because her husband felt threatened by their difference of opinion.

Having nowhere to go, Garrett found herself "magnetically drawn to Baker" after her 20-year marriage failed. Even though she and her ex-husband had purchased a lot near Baker, he never was fond of the area, preferring the beaches instead. She also had a friend at Home Farm, so it seemed natural that she put down roots in Baker and build a home.

"For a long time after I got out here, I thought, 'What on earth am I doing here?' At any rate when I got divorced, why not move up there and keep building, because I've always liked to build, to make houses and mess with them. So it was an opportunity to do that, without too much supervision," she chuckled. "The building inspectors are not very evident out here."

In college the most she had been involved in the environmental movement was at the level of conservation. Garrett believes it is part of human nature to conserve. She wonders if it has something to do with growing up during the Depression, but she really thinks it runs deeper than that.

"I think it actually hurts us when we are wasteful, at some level of consciousness. Having the privilege of living out in the country like this and depending on a well and having to scrounge for soil, having the immediate experience of having to deal with the earth for your livelihood, at least for water, is instructive. I don't know that from my years of living in the city I would have had that experience, when water is delivered through a faucet. There is just so much that stands between a person and the source that I don't know if the people of Las Vegas, for instance, can be inspired by the challenge of doing with less water, although other southwestern cities have done it. I would assume that they'd find some satisfaction in not wasting water, not having it run down the gutter, in realizing that it increases our consciousness of what a privilege it is to be here at all."

Not long after her arrival in Baker, however, Garrett's inclination toward conservation flowered into environmental activism. Parallel to that change of consciousness was an evolving understanding of place. For her the term "activism" is less idealistic than simply "doing the things that need to be done." Activism grows naturally out of being present in a place, seeing and understanding it, rather than traveling through a place. One has to be grounded in a place to be an advocate for it. She appreciates her place, and "that has a heuristic meaning that facilitates learning."

"I also appreciate all that centralized thinking and caring that goes on in Washington," Garrett continued. "But the particulars of a place and the particulars of a conflict are, it seems to me in my very small experience, on the ground. They can paint with large brushstrokes from a distant high place, but perhaps without understanding the very essence of what matters, with all due respect."

Garrett's baptism into activism came through Citizens Alert, a watchdog group focusing on military activities in Nevada. Through that organization she got early wind of the Air Force's MX plans. Deeply concerned, she visited her friend Mia Miller, a '70s Democratic candidate for the U.S. Senate, who gave her some tips.

"I wanted to find out if it was feasible to fight the U.S. Air Force. Because the general tone out here, the consensus, was that you couldn't do that. You had to bow down—that together with a certain amount of good, old-fashioned patriotism."

Garrett next went to a $10-a-plate dinner that the Ely, Nevada, Chamber of Commerce hosted where an air force general would address the locals as to the need and benefits. The Ely Chamber of Commerce had jumped on the bandwagon early. A black activist from Las Vegas who had been visiting Miller when Garrett dropped in gave explicit instructions on how to behave at the banquet. She advised Garrett to "drop your napkin and slide your chair back just as the general's speaking or go to the restroom. She had a

variety of interesting ploys that would infringe on his dignity. They were just slightly irreverent. They were used to interrupt the sacred tone of the occasion, to bring it down a little bit to human level." She also had suggested some picketing by mothers.

"It was all news to me," Garrett said, "that one could begin to think about various ways to be effective rather than simply to wring one's hands. It tipped the balance a little bit, because it was all pomp and circumstance. It was this wonderful thing that was going to happen to us. And property values were going to go up."

Garrett's brother-in-law was working for TRW at Hill Air Force Base at the time, and he was all for MX. "He knew about the Russian threat and was a true believer," Garrett said. "He advised me on how to make out on real estate out here. He knew where it was going to go."

The economic benefits were implicit in the rationale: jobs, schools, swimming pools, golf courses—carrots dangled in front of poor rural communities. But the driving force was the necessity of MX to the national defense.

"It was a nice process around here, in my view," Garrett continued. "People who had not questioned the authority and competence of the military anywhere . . . . I think they've always questioned the competence of the government," she smiled. ". . . If the military said it had to be, well, you'd have to knuckle under and move the cattle and try to make do. But then, the utter unfeasibility of their plan, when it came to rearranging the ground and building the roads—all the engineering things—were hatched without any understanding of the terrain and soil for siting. These ranchers had plenty of experience with construction. That caused them to doubt the competence of the military. And then you think, 'Gee, if they don't know how to plan a project, do they really know how to plan our defense?'

"I don't mean that this was necessarily articulated, but it was disillusioning. You put your faith somewhere. That's an area you don't have to worry about. It's all taken care of. But on close examination, the foundations of your faith begin to crumble," Garrett smiled. "It's a nice, healthy process."

In the initial stages of organizing opposition to MX, Garrett and her partner Joe Griggs, a Baker Ranch foreman who had been a field organizer for the Sierra Club some years before—until he cooled to what he thought was its narrowing vision—received encouragement, tutoring, and a bit of funding from other activist groups like Western Action and Clergy and Laity Concerned, which had successfully foiled the basing of MX in Nebraska, with a coalition of clergy, farmers, and environmentalists. They convinced Joe and JoAnne to lead the efforts in the area. "We were very halting in our efforts," Garrett said, "totally inexperienced."

Garrett first met Cecil Garland, the outspoken Callao, Utah, rancher, who earlier had helped initiate the wilderness movement by lobbying for the Scapegoat Wilderness Area outside his then home in Lincoln, Montana, at a scoping meeting in Delta, Utah. Garland had sworn that he'd never get involved in activism again, but MX was just too much a threat to his family's well-being in northern Snake Valley. "That was the first time I laid eyes on Cecil, and he was a wonderful surprise." With him the trio formed the Great Basin MX Alliance.

"It was carefully forged after a bit of trial and error to be a single issue outfit, and was carefully disbanded afterwards, too, for that reason—that this was an unlikely coalition that couldn't agree on a single other thing," Garrett said.

Joe Griggs knew that involvement of environmental groups meant that the coalition couldn't extend beyond MX, that environmental groups' ways of organizing and proceeding were "offensive to rural people." It was an urban way of proceeding rather than rural.

"Joe insisted that we weed out these 'customs' so as to be more inclusive and to watch our assumptions as to values. To be respectful in that regard and not to assume that everyone in the room shared our values," Garrett said.

I asked if the Mormon Church ever contacted JoAnne and Joe. They did not. The two did get a lot of support, however, from Ed Firmage at the University of Utah law school. When the Mormon Church announced its opposition to MX, Griggs felt Firmage had a lot to do with the creation of the church's public position.

"Joe was innocent enough at the time to say, after the church's announcement, that Ed Firmage had a lot to do with convincing them. Ed took exception to Joe's assessment and chastised Joe. He seemed to be embarrassed by Joe's remark."

"Have any effects of MX lingered in the West Desert?" I asked.

"You betcha," Garrett said with force. "The mistrust of government in Baker no longer is just of the social arm. That mistrust includes the military. Skepticism is the residue of MX.

"What came out of the MX experience was a feeling of power, that is, that it is possible to effect things, and the realization that nobody's in charge. Where corporations and the Department of Energy are concerned, there's not a conscience running things there. There just can't be. No matter how nice and whole the individuals are who represent those large organizations, and how winning they are and how humane, the organization itself doesn't have a conscience. There's no central intelligence that cares. So who's going to do that," Garrett asked rhetorically, "but the people on the ground? Wherever you happen to be and whatever the issue is, it falls on you if you happen to have the energy or the time. So that was a change in my understanding of how the world works, that is a bit of a burden," Garrett said, "but really a privilege to know that it matters. It also increases one's appreciation of where you are."

The MX controversy brought together previously atomistic groups in the West Desert. By forging some alliances it forced people to cross over cultural lines of separation subconsciously drawn. Ironically, the federal government initiated an unintended wave of community building in the West.

Much of the reflexive opposition to MX grew out of western understandings of land. For years people of the West Desert have turned the rock and soil in search of gold and foodstuffs. That experience with an extractive life-style gave them insight and strength in opposition to the government, but that same exploitive history worries Garrett on another level, especially the mining heritage.

"An exploitive attitude maybe sounds powerful, but basically there is something really weak and undermining about the hit-and-run attitude," Garrett began. "And the spoiling attitude that comes out of mining. It's not intentional. Those mining guys love being out on the ground just as I do. I like going out and moving these rocks around. I assume that's why they love what they're doing. I respect that, although they surely have made some big messes.

"But I think that in the process we get wounded when we make those messes, and then we get a kind of scarring that takes place, and we get a little embittered and embattled. We've led this hard life, and it's been hard on us to make those messes. The failure of Nevadans to be more progressive in their politics and environmental attitude, I think, is somehow tied into that wounded psyche. You get hardened, and then you are hurting."

In short, when you spoil the garden, you suffer original sin.

Garrett also thinks men have a tough role given to them in a capitalistic, paternalistic society that wounds them more than women, who haven't been given, or allowed, that role. "It really seems that men are exploited in a paternalistic, or maybe capitalistic system," Garrett said. "Exploitation is the order of the day and someone is assigned that role to carry it out. Once again, those wounds set in and people suffer horribly. While women's liberation is all well and good and absolutely necessary, I think women in some very profound ways are better off than men because they have not been divorced from themselves. Men have been assigned an impossible role of oppressor. They have to implement. They've been assigned the role of exploitation and oppression of the earth and the labor force. All that hurt is visited on men, starting when they are little children. They are kept from their humanity."

I asked Garrett if exploitation and oppression of land and peoples reveal an inherent flaw in the American Dream.

"I always turn off a bit when I hear 'The American Dream,'" Garrett said, "because I associate it with the negative of getting more than they need. What amounts to greed. It isn't intentional, but it's losing track of what on earth you're trying to do. It's shorthand for making it big.

"But for immigrants, it maybe meant having a little piece of ground. And that's no small thing. I feel really grateful to have a little piece of ground. I think it's a privilege."

Garrett believes the weaknesses of the American Dream are entwined with a problem in public values, although she doesn't feel the Republican nostrum of family values hits the mark. Since it's a product of partisan politics, it's a polemic and lacks a foundation of inclusion. Still, there is a paucity of values that she feels is a problem for society. She attributes it to a growing realization that the values of a materialistic society don't hold up over time.

"Capitalism encapsulated is singularly unsatisfying finally, and I think that one of the things that sends people off to addictions is this need for some kind of transcendence and no clue in our culture where to find it if you don't get inspired by a given religion. But even spiritual values aren't very evident in the offerings of organized religion. They aren't inspiring. They are tied into our culture so much that they don't seem transcendent."

When asked, then, if she opposes the standard idea of the American Dream, Garrett felt that would be misleading. "Well, I can't say that, because I live off the proceeds of my divorce and interest on investments and social security, so I'm right in there. I have two and a half cars, so I'm part of it. But my very self is very much in opposition to having more than I need, and I'm actively paring down and trying hard to get rid of those habits of having more than I need."

The demise of MX did not mean the withdrawal of JoAnne Garrett from the arena of environmental activism. She remains an advocate of the earth, but in all instances, her motivation for protection grows out of her sense of place. She trains her sights on the local environment and its impact on community.

Currently, she is involved in several projects. Standing up to another Goliath, she is marshalling grass-roots opposition to what is dubbed the Las Vegas Water Grab, the on-and-off-again attempt by the gambling mecca 200 miles south of Baker to claim all unused water rights in White Pine, Lincoln, and Nye counties and convert that desert lifeblood to swimming pools for

JoAnne Garrett

To be one for the people, a person must first be one with the land, JoAnne Garrett believes. An early anti-MX missile community activist in the West Desert, Garrett's sense of place grows out of her grounding in that place. Appreciating a locale offers a heuristic understanding of it. Knowledge of the land creates strength when it comes time to defend it. For her, advocacy of place is a natural response, a kind of humane outcropping.

its dolphins. The conversion of rights would effectively preclude any future development in the three counties, freezing them in amber.

Garrett also keeps her eye on expansion plans for Great Basin National Park, especially the siting of a new visitors' center. To help steer people away from the overused Lehman Caves, the focal point of the park, the master plan calls for a new visitors' center to be carved out of currently pristine juniper and piñon forest on BLM land, an idea that would also mean approximately five miles of road building to reach the center. Rather than laying more asphalt, Garrett would like to see the new visitors' center located in Baker, where tourist services already are located, instead of nine miles away. Those construction plans are on hold with federal government downsizing.

But growth in Baker is inevitable, especially since the town became the recipient of federal government largesse by being included in a new sewer system for Great Basin National Park. Baker is the only Nevada town bordering a non-gambling state, like Utah, that isn't experiencing dramatic construction growth to meet the gaming needs of tourists. Some in town worry about the spectre of rampant growth.

Garrett said it can be helped with planning, but acknowledged that the townsfolk seem to have a natural and historical aversion to planning.

"We don't have very much response [to planning]. They are so used to being unfettered that they don't naturally like to think about making rules and regulations," Garrett said. "People don't want to change zoning if they happen to have commercial zoning where they are. They're hedging their bets because there's always that sort of speculation. Very few citizens are willing to relinquish the possible killing they might make," Garrett said with a chuckle.

With her membership on the Baker town advisory board, Garrett helps build a commercial base through effective zoning. Sensing the personal irony, she talked about how the "embattled" syndrome sometimes plays out in town business. Garrett said some Baker merchants feel their competitors are in the way, "rather than realizing that, to some extent, the more of them the better." Garrett supports the notion of critical mass in business, that there has to be enough commercial infrastructure to lure more business.

Finally, I asked Garrett if relationships with land and a sense of place have an effect on American democratic values.

"The importance of the individual, if that's what is central in democracy, is tied to our realization of our relationship to the earth. But I don't know where that leaves urban dwellers who have less of that experience. But feeling part of the world, and the sense of belonging, must be important." Primitive peoples have a real sense of place, in spite of being so confined and having so few amenities and advantages, Garrett added. "Their sense of belonging seems palpable, not just a romantic notion of mine. They really know who they are and where they are. A real relationship with the earth, that in a way, makes them seem kingly."

As Garrett's closing words drifted into the granite boulders in the wall behind her, rocks that she had lifted from the earth, I reflected on the community spirit that seems to grow from an individual's interaction with land. If one digs into the soil, is she liable to find the grains of American democracy, as Thomas Jefferson thought? Or does interaction with the land ultimately create an aristocracy, with stewardship of that land more noblesse oblige, a grace reflected in those like JoAnne Garrett, who make peace with the land?

Bill Rountree
Host

There are those who say you'll never be accepted in a small town unless your grandparents are buried in the cemetery. It's wasted effort to try.

Bill Rountree has never listened to them. When the budget for the new Baker School didn't allocate money for a bell tower, someone needed to assume responsibility for raising money and building it. It was no small concern. Pulling the clapper rope was a tradition binding four generations of Bakerites to their school and each other. Because he grew up in overcrowded Los Angeles schools, and because his skills made it an opportunity, Rountree stepped forward.

Being a transplant was immaterial. He knew that the bell tower job should be his.

"I have a love affair with working with metal," Rountree said. "If a welder fastens metal together, it's more than that. It's the working with metal, primarily with steel. Whether I've made any money working at it, through the years, I've always been around it."

His Silver Jack Motel became the fundraising headquarters. Rountree scrawled the usual thermometer onto poster board and began corralling the spare change of townsfolk. When it came time to dedicate the new school, the bell tower was in place, seared with new energy, the continuum ready to be stroked.

"Hands on." That's the kind of community involvement Rountree prefers. "Not having to petition some government entity for permission or funds. Just do it. There are people who have that talent [working in councils]," Rountree continued, "but I don't particularly have the talent for committees and groups. Partly because I have a really short attention span. When it comes to protracted negotiation, I start to nod off."

When Bill Rountree returned from Vietnam in 1970, Baker wasn't in his sights. Instead, he became a motorcycle vagabond, driving around the West with a big chip on his shoulder, looking for a place to land. "I was in a state, to put it mildly, of confusion. I was twenty-one and felt like I was eighty. Confused. Dark, pretty dark."

Rountree landed first at Home Farm. He lived there for about a year. Val Taylor gave him a place to stay and odc jobs to earn his keep. "It was a revelation, when I first came out here in 1971. And I drank that up like a thirsty person," Rountree said. "I did not have it in Los Angeles. Anonymity was the rule. One of the first emotions I experienced when I moved out here was a sense of regret that I didn't have a chance to grow up in an environment like this. Based on that knowledge, I immediately regressed to eight years old, and I've been there ever since," Rountree said with a wink.

"Was it the landscape and environment that attracted you or was it the people you met?" I asked.

"All of it," Rountree replied. "I was particularly struck by the people—by their lack of fear and the way they stood on their feet when they talked to you, their innocence. I sensed that this was the country where your word was still your bond and you would be judged by it.

"I think of Baker as being one of the last cul-de-sacs, one of the last little safe pockets in this dangerous country of ours. It's a safe little place, and yeah, safe in that perhaps we are simple and naive. But it seems to be that a lot of the old-time values are still practiced here.

"One thing I've noticed since I moved out here is the generational interplay. Grandchildren and grandparents, young people and old people, everyone knowing each other all their lives and together going through the years. Babies being born, growing up, being kids; riding a bicycle for the first time, playing softball, going to high school; going off into the military, coming back and getting married, going through the middle years, and dying. In the way that all of that goes together with the families. That was something that really struck me as being perfectly wholesome."

"Did you feel like you were received fairly quickly in Baker when you first moved here, or if not, how long did it take?" I asked.

"I'd say I was fairly quickly received. Some people reserved judgement for awhile, but that's fine. I didn't have a problem with that. Of course, I was really responding to the general openness of people, so it was a general kind of high and happy time for me. I enjoyed myself. I had an irrepressible enthusiasm that was not going to be denied."

"Has that changed or is it the same? Could someone come in now, over twenty-five years later, and still be accepted as quickly as you?" I asked.

"I think so, except for old codgers like myself," Rountree said with his irrepressible tongue in cheek. "I tend to stand back and give them a year or so to prove themselves. But the more enlightened, open types, yeah there is generally fairly quick acceptance."

"Does everybody basically get along pretty well?" I asked, incredulously.

"Yeah, yeah, even if we don't all operate on the same level or necessarily understand one another. Or have the same politics. There's still a common ground and this common love."

"Do the politics tend to break down into traditional liberal/conservative, or are they more localized?" I asked. "More localized like ranching versus tourism versus park interests."

"A little bit of everything," Rountree said, "as far as everything comes into play, everything must be considered. I guess it partly depends on how you derive your living, as to what's more important to you, or less important. In terms of ranching, [Kathy and I] have no economic interests in ranching, but we are sympathetic to their situations and life.

"It's a quilt, or a weave," Rountree continued. "I don't know about clear lines of demarcation about anything."

"It's been said that deliberations about creating a national park helped to coalesce the community, to make it stronger, more organized. Would you say that's true?" I asked.

"Yeah, I would agree to that. The town council essentially came out of that. Things had to be addressed. There's a sense that from the period of time from the formation of the park to the present, and into the foreseeable future, that these are milestone years for Baker. I sure have that feeling. The formation of Great Basin National Park was really one of the milestone events in this valley's history. Good, bad, or otherwise."

"How able is the community to change and how willing is it to change?" I asked. "And maybe that's the same question. Does change come easier here than in other small towns?"

"What brings about change?" Bill asked. "I think a distinction should be drawn between evolutionary change and cataclysmic change, thrust fault change. For instance, this community has been changing evolutionarily ever since the advent of the national park, almost microscopically, almost imperceptibly perhaps, but it has been changing."

"In what ways?" I interjected.

"Oh, I don't know. Look around," Rountree said. "People have gone to work up at the park who haven't worked there before. So their whole lives have changed."

"What about the sewers?"

"That'll be cataclysmic," Rountree said. "But that sort of evolved, the whole process of bringing about this. But this thrust fault, this cataclysmic change for me is the closing of the dump, via a bureaucratic ruling."

Before now, garbage was being taken to a dump two miles outside Baker. But with the landfill full, the town has to come up with a solution. Complicating that decision is an order coming from the EPA saying that, in spite of having available land, Baker can no longer dump into an unlined, open pit. Garbage has to be hauled off. White Pine County has given a hint of things to come by assessing every property owner in Baker $180 a year for a landfill tax.

"Now, that's cataclysmic!" Rountree continued. "Not that it's destructive as such, but it's a radical change. It's 'boom!' going to happen," Rountree said, snapping his fingers. "And what's that going to bring us? Nobody seems to know.

"So, are we adaptable?" Rountree continued. "I think the human species is very adaptable to whatever the condition is that presents itself. There's a lot of cursing and grumbling, but what the hell are you going to do?"

Still, change is likely to come faster to Baker now that the water and sewer system is in place. Once he taps into the sewer and can free himself and his motel from septic tanks—"And I'm going to push old people out of the way so that I can get to the front of the line to sign up"—Rountree will consider adding a few more motel units. Regardless, Rountree guesses Baker will feel the influx of more people, initially on U.S. Highway 6/50, five miles away.

"How much development would you like to see in Baker?" I asked.

Rountree began making a sneering sound, but I added, "You really need a certain amount of steady development don't you [for the tourist business]?"

"How is Baker going to go?" Rountree interjected. "I hope to see Baker to continue to evolve and not to experience an explosive growth. Whether that is in anyone's power to direct remains to be seen. I think a master zoning plan for this town is in order. One fear I have is that it will be developed along the lines of all the city lots, which are fifty feet by a hundred feet. Of it getting carved up into city lots and cement pads being poured and snowbirds coming up for four months in the summertime and taking off. I would hate to see that. I would like to see families, to have the mix that we do now, not to become predominantly geriatric. Not just a bunch of old farts that all they have to do is tell you how great the grandchildren are and be against all improvements, especially those involving taxes. That's a fear I have."

"Is the community doing anything proactively to manage growth?" I asked.

"That's coming up," Rountree replied. "The master zoning plan will be addressed and that will be hammered out, and that is going to be pretty interesting. It probably will be acrimonious."

Bill Rountree

Bill Rountree was looking for refuge after Los Angeles and Vietnam. When he settled in Baker, he found something else—community. Now, from his central vantage point in the only motel in town, he gets to watch a continuing flow of characters and live an American Dream, "Recognizing that part of the human condition is to have frustrations with things not being as perfect as they could be or should be, but also realizing that if we could create at the speed of thought, things would be all built."

Drafting the document will be a cooperative effort between the town council and all citizens, with assistance from the state department of planning. Rountree said he is very concerned with the outcome as an individual. He doesn't fear competition, only that arbitrary, bureaucratic change.

While he had to drag an odd job seining net when he arrived in Baker—welding, operating a backhoe, and eventually buying the motel—things are better for Rountree now. The motel is turning a profit, and the niche business he and his graphic artist wife have developed selling T-shirts and other artifacts capitalizing on changes in popular culture have provided the extra that allows them to travel during the winter when the motel is closed.

Rountree's motel business comes predominantly from California, Nevada, and Utah. When he opened, Wasatch Front tourists provided most of his cash flow. Now, because Great Basin National Park no longer is a notoriety, Utahns are a harder sell.

"It's better for me now in that Californians and Nevadans are an easier sell.

They don't quibble [about prices], and I don't lose near as many towels," he jabbed at me.

Rountree noted that since Great Basin became a national park, he has seen an "incredible" jump in the number of Europeans staying at the motel, upwards of 30 percent. "Four years ago, when we had a mild recession, I would have been in a real bind had it not been for the Europeans. They were here in droves. They made the difference between another good year and a marginal year."

"How would you characterize the relationship between Baker and the Wasatch Front?" I asked.

"There's the peeking over the fence at the cultural phenomenon of Mormons, but they're all around us here, too. The Wasatch Front is the destination of choice for provision runs, entertainment, and so forth. Not only for its geographic location and beauty, but for the fact it's close. It's a clean place and relatively safe. I don't feel uncomfortable there. I'd far rather go that way than to Las Vegas for a weekend of entertainment. Las Vegas seems to be totally foreign to me," Rountree said, adding that most Bakerites feel the same way. "That's the anomaly of this state."

In retrospect, Rountree wouldn't change anything about his life. He'd like to become a mechanical engineer, and still might do so, but he's content to live out his years in Baker, living his American Dream.

"I kind of see Baker as a stage, if you will, with a cast of characters, entering stage left," Rountree said. "Some of us stay around for quite a while and exit. And some come back. It's a continuing flow of characters. I'm the stage manager—and janitor."

When we concluded the session, Rountree confessed that he had agreed to it only reluctantly, having earlier sworn to never be interviewed again. Like other people of the West Desert, he is no stranger to reporters. The opening of Great Basin National Park and periodic stories on U.S. 6/50, "the loneliest highway in America," have brought *National Geographic*, the *Los Angeles Times*, and local media to the area. Rountree then talked about an interview he had had with an underhanded reporter from Boise who was doing a piece for PBS on the national park five years after its opening.

"She beat the hell out of me," Rountree said. "In fact at the end I said she had a real good shot with the *Enquirer* given her talents. She spent a lot of time prepping you, then you went through the interviewing process, and then she'd drop a bomb on you like, 'What about this feud you have with so-and-so?' And there you are on camera, and you get to stutter around, 'What the hell are you talking about?' She was a muckraker. A cheap shot artist."

Val Taylor
Mediator

"I make $200 [a month] for being justice of the peace," Val Taylor said. "We figured at one of the meetings I went to, since we have to be on call for twenty-four hours, that I make fifty-six cents an hour." Since the first appointment, she's run for office two times, unopposed. "Who wants a job for two hundred dollars?" she laughed. "I look upon it as my public service."

The work is uneven and irregular, more work in the summer with the tourist season and traffic cases. There really isn't much crime in the area. A few years ago they had some incidents with vandalism and were pretty sure it was some kids. The people who were vandalized really didn't care if the people were tracked down. Nevertheless, sensing a teaching opportunity, Taylor called the sheriff in Ely and asked him to visit the Baker School and talk to the kids about justice, juvenile hall, and what happens to people who are caught and punished.

Taylor calls her charge largely mediation work. Moreover, the position of rural JP provides her with flexibility. "Rural justice out here is kind of funny because I'll just call the parties in and we talk about it. I fine them or write restraining orders."

She had a rash of domestic violence once, her saddest cases, since not much can be done. In one case the couple moved away and in another they separated. In a delicate matter of logistics, Taylor once had to divide up the local bars. There were four in the Baker area and the couple frequented them all, often using them as venues for violence. Taylor wrote a restraining order parceling out the water holes.

"She had to do her laundry at the Y and she worked for the Outlaw. [Those became hers.] He worked at the [Baker] ranch, so I let him go to the Hitching Post and the Border Inn. That kind of thing is unheard of in a big city, but out here, that's the way life is."

Judges are always supportive of small towns and the fact that, "We can do things differently. We can cut through a lot of the paperwork," Taylor said. "I mean, the ACLU is not sitting

Val Taylor

Few people dispute charges in Val Taylor's justice-of-the-peace court. A fine could be writing on the blackboard, "I Will Not Speed Through Baker."

She's never had to issue an arrest warrant for an unpaid traffic ticket.

"I just write them a nice friendly little note and say, 'My records show that you haven't paid your fine,' and they send it to me. And, there're mostly tourists." When I look amazed that out-of-staters would remit, Taylor said, "Yes, it's really remarkable. People are so good."

on my shoulder. I don't do anything blatantly wrong, but I do a lot of mediation and hopefully avoid some of that."

Taylor is not a lawyer, so she carefully avoids the semblance of practicing law. "I tell them out-front. I can go to the statutes and read the law to them and help explain it, but that's all I can do. I say, 'This is the law. How you choose to use it and apply it, what actions you choose to take, you've got to see an attorney.'"

Because they have non-lawyer judges, Nevada has a model educational program at the University of Nevada at Reno. When she was appointed JP, the first thing Taylor did was attend a two-week crash course at UNR. Then, twice a year the state has educational conferences for the JPs where a JP gets plugged in. She has met the Nevada supreme court justices, and the governor and senators learn the JPs' names. It's a small state.

Labels don't mean a great deal to Taylor, though, as labeling runs counter to her School of the Natural Order philosophy of general semantics. Nor does she consider herself a judge or require that label for self-definition. Yet, Taylor pointed out the power of labels regarding her JP position, and how it's important to other people.

"I've been in places where I've been sitting and visiting and somebody walks in and the waitress or proprietor says, 'Oh, here's the judge,' like that makes me something special. And it isn't that I'm so special, it's that they know the judge. And so they have to slip into the conversation that I am the judge."

Although previous Baker JPs held court in their homes, that isn't an option for Taylor. One of the White Pine County commissioners' stipulations was that, "You cannot hold court up at that place where you live," referring to Home Farm. Commissioners thought they were separating church from state, although Taylor and members of the School of the Natural Order laughed at that assessment. So Taylor holds court in the Baker Hall in a former classroom off the gymnasium.

The elementary-like location belies the seriousness Taylor brings to her charge. As an example, she cited the time when two guys got into a bar fight. One of them pressed assault charges against the other. When the plaintiff came to her court two days later, both he and his corroborating witness were drunk. Taylor was infuriated at their behavior.

"Here I thought I was this classic Chicago, bleeding heart liberal. But I was incensed when they came in drunk and treated my court like that. I threw out the plaintiff's case and then gave them a real tongue-lashing lecture. 'Don't you ever come into my court like that again and treat it with such disrespect,' I said."

Deputy Sheriff Jim White is Taylor's law enforcement cohort. Deputized in White Pine County, Nevada, and Millard, Beaver, and Juab counties in Utah, White has the largest geographic beat of any law officer in the United States. Baker used to have a part-time policeman, but it was an unsatisfactory situation from the beginning.

"He was a little Barney Fife kind of guy," Taylor said. 'Everyone hated him. No one respected him. Everyone complained bitterly about him. Then I would say, 'Do you want the job? I'm sure the sheriff would be happy to get rid of him if he had a replacement.' But no one wanted the job. When he left, we didn't have anybody. When the Millard County deputy was placed in Garrison, Denys Baker instigated the arrangement. She could not live out here and run [the Border Inn] without law enforcement. So he got deputized in Nevada. And I do get questions about that."

Taylor talked about one episode when someone complained about the deputy arrangement. "We had a young man driving a hundred thirty-eight miles an hours down this highway and his father called me from Utah, very officious, and said, 'I think this is an illegal arrest and duh . . . duh . . . duh . . . and it was in Nevada and it was a Utah patrolman, and . . .' And I said, 'Sorry, Sam.' It was really amazing. He was more concerned with his image than he was with the fact that his kid had been driving a hundred thirty-eight miles an hour."

4

Community Centering

Like a dog seeking security, small towns will find their centering spots. Sometimes, churches can play that role. For instance, before the construction of tribal headquarters and gymnasium on the Walker River Paiute Reservation, the Methodist meetinghouse was the community gathering spot. But some Paiutes see churches as vestiges of colonization or assimilation of Indians by whites, so those congregations remain small, reaching a quiet equilibrium with the practice of traditional Native-American religion. Most Paiutes, in fact, claim no religious affiliation. In the West Desert like so many other small communities in Utah, the Mormon ward is a central meeting place for the majority of residents, possibly the most important congregational point in their lives, and there are LDS churches in Ibapah, Trout Creek, and Garrison. But churches have limits as common gathering spots because faith has a way of too crisply circumscribing the boundaries of community. As buildings are symbols of community, churches can signify a safe spot for a soul but not for a whole body of diverse interests.

A community center ultimately will be secular. It might be a cafe, bar, or school gymnasium. Often, the centering spot is tied to commerce, a truly democratic activity that brings all people together. It is no different in southern Snake Valley. Two bar-restaurants are the local oases of civic communion. In northern Snake Valley it is the West Desert School, largely because there are no businesses in that more sparsely populated locale.

Another time community centering might be found in a brief moment snatched from time that the community momentarily drapes with bunting and celebrates as its own. Small towns have their founders days, reunions, and if they've really survived as a community, their centennials. Sometimes the celebrations of life aren't delineated on a continuum. Rather, a community marks a spot on the circle to commemorate its belief that life is a cycle and it is the seasonal harvesting of that life that brings people together. Another time community celebration is the province of a family, inviting their far-flung friends to revel with them in their ongoing attachment to land and their homestead. Music forges a larger community at Christmas when one community performs the *Messiah* for its neighbors. Then, there are the children of the West Desert. At once present and future, the community gives them images of its past and asks them to remember.

Border Inn at night

The Border Inn stays open all night, and although Nevada law allows 24-hour liquor sales, Denys Baker, the owner, closes the bar at 2:00 a.m. Not many people drink much past that hour, and since most of her business in the early morning comes from tired traffic off U.S. Highway 6/50 drawn to the sentient light, she rationalizes that it's not a good idea to serve alcohol at that time.

Miguel Torres outside

The Border makes a little money in the wee hours on gas, motel rooms and slot machines. Subtract free coffee from that bottom line and the equation still works, because Baker really wants a night man for security and cleanup. Graveyard is an especially long stretch on the desolate high desert, but cool breezes provide a wake up for Miguel Torres, watchman on the loneliest highway in America.

"The Border"
Outpost and Inn

The Border Inn rests on 2.3 acres at the bottom of Snake Valley, its parking lot the size of a gravel prairie seamlessly merging with U.S. Highway 6/50. A speeding car coming from either east or west could run out of gas miles from the service station-bar-restaurant-motel complex and still coast to the haven because there are no curves in the highway to slow momentum. Dubbed "the loneliest road in America," that stretch of highway in front of the Border Inn is like the land— unbending and relentless.

Most automobiles leaving the road for the Border Inn haven't run out of gas. Usually, the occupants just need a break from the numbingly insistent up and down, never left nor right, cadence of driving U.S. 6/50. Denys Baker, majority owner of "the Border," as the locals affectionately call it, says that 80 percent of her business comes from travelers on the road. Residents of Snake Valley account for the other 20 percent, but it's an important percentage because it carries her through the slow winter months.

Standing on the line separating Utah and Nevada, the Border also straddles cultures in Snake Valley. On Sunday mornings ranchers, teachers, and itinerant construction workers put two long tables together and sit down for brunch. Later in the afternoon the poets' group meets in the quiet corner away from the slot machines. Peter Ford from Baker started the literary group. Wally and Faye Carlson and Lois Faber from Eskdale always drop by, as does John Woodyard from Home Farm. Cecelia Phillips from Garrison comes when she can find break time from church or from preparing lesson plans for the one-room school in Garrison.

Mostly, kids have their birthday parties at the Border, but one time Tom Brewster's four children, ranging from 14 to 6, asked Baker if they could bring the cakes and have his 60th birthday party there. They wanted to make it special, thanking him for raising two families without the benefit of mothers.

In 1995 out of the blue, a couple who met in the area six years before while working on a seismograph crew called Denys Baker and asked if they could get married at the Border. They moved the pool table, put up a screen, and decorated the back half of the room. Val Taylor, the justice of the peace from Home Farm, performed the ceremony. Susie Douglass, daughter of George and Veronica, married Terry Hale in front of the Christmas tree. Then, Tom Knutson, a *New York Times* reporter who fell in love with the area when he came out to cover the dedication of Great Basin National Park, brought his fiancée to the Border to get married. For her it was site unseen.

People gather at the Border for election night returns, always getting aggravated when the only area TV news they can receive is from Salt Lake City. They have to call the newspaper in Ely to find out who's leading in the local Nevada races. In 1996 the Border was becoming a Friday night hangout for teenagers until Denys Baker put the kibosh on that. Drinking only ice water, occupying all the tables and chairs, and playing the jukebox at heavy metal decibel level was having an effect on Baker's bottom line. She organized a meeting with teachers, parents, and 40 teens to help them organize more productive activities.

The Border Inn works like any real property development. It's location, location, location. "Where I'm located, I know more people in the valley than other people do," Baker said. "It's real easy for the Baker [Nevada] or Garrison or Eskdale [Utah] people to isolate, but I interact with all the different groups."

But Baker (no relationship to the area's founding family) is more than a uniquely situated innkeeper. She's a mixture of small-town banker, community organizer, and pundit.

Graduating from the University of Utah in 1970, doing graduate work in history at Utah and Long Beach State, and teaching basic government at the community college in Ely, Baker has a long view. She's shrewd, compassionate, and seasoned. She's never lost more than $100 a year in bad checks, in spite of the fact that she cashes all types of checks, since there's no bank in the vicinity.

"Paychecks. Big checks. Coming up with cash out here is a problem for people," Baker said. "I've never lost money with a local check. If I lose it's somebody coming through who gives me a sob story about not having enough cash to get to California, so can they please cash a check here. Generally, I don't, but once in a while, if there's ten kids . . ." and Baker's voice trailed off. "That's when you get burnt."

Baker extends credit too, helping everyone from locals to migrant workers. Many of the itinerant sheepherders in the area are Mexicans. Baker lets them run a tab over the season, in spite of the fact she doesn't keep their names straight. When they return in the fall, if they didn't zero their account at the end of the previous spring, the first thing they do when they walk in the door is say, "I owe you $100 for my tab," in broken English. Baker doesn't have to ask. That debunked one stereotype for her.

"You think about that when you listen to some cowboy at the bar bad-mouthing Mexicans," Baker said.

Not that Denys Baker keeps her opinions to herself or shies away from sharing sharp-edged historical facts when the need arises. In fact, that's one of the reasons she decided to stop bartending at the Border, a move that led to an increase in her bar business.

"I now hire people who have personalities to bartend," Baker said. "That was part necessity because I couldn't take it anymore."

"People crying on your shoulder?" I asked.

"No. It's just a tough job. I get too edgy. I want to say what I really think," and Baker punctuated that thought with a deep belly laugh.

"You can't get into politics when you're a bartender," I added, referring to Baker's reputation as a local Democrat activist.

"Oh, that's fine," Baker replied with another laugh. "I can do that anyway."

"What kind of opinions can't you get into when you're a bartender?" I asked.

"The local gossip, and we've had some fairly serious scandals the last few years. Criminal charges," Baker said. "I just refuse to talk about those, and fire the gossip at all. Telling people how to lead their lives. Telling them they don't need another drink. When they start on somebody else and it's none of their business. That kind of thing."

The Border Inn is a significant local employer. Baker will hire any teenager who wants a job. There also is a symbiotic relationship between the Border and Eskdale. Baker has three people from Eskdale working at the restaurant—one cook and two waitresses. Eskdale also has the contract to clean the motel rooms. But the relationship flowers only because Eskdale residents decided to open themselves to the larger Snake Valley community.

"So Eskdale's becoming a more important part of your business then?" I asked.

"Yeah," Baker said.

"If you took them out?" I asked.

"It would be catastrophic," Baker replied.

Baker's biggest staffing problem is getting people to relocate. The problem isn't pay. She basically pays the same wages as in local towns. But housing is tight and Baker usually has to offer board if people aren't residents. Her biggest problem has been finding someone to do the graveyard shift.

"I advertised that position in Ely and Delta and Milford," Baker said. "A job, a forty-hour week with housing provided as part of the pay. Never got one response. Miguel [the current night man] had just come up from Mexico and didn't have good English. But he let me know he would work really hard if I would hire him, so I gave him a chance. And he's working out fine."

Baker only makes a little profit on her early morning sales, but she likes to keep the Border open 24 hours a day for security reasons, especially since an arsonist burned a building in the complex in 1981. Baker also was glad when Jim White, the local deputy sheriff, was assigned to Garrison, because she now has someone to call and he shows diplomatic sense dealing with Border customers. Originally, he was sent out to control the increasing cattle rustling in a three-county region.

"Where do most of his problems originate now?" I asked.

Baker laughed and said, "He'd probably tell you here. I had one day this spring when I called him three times. And they were legitimate police calls. An automobile accident, almost in my yard, first thing in the morning, and then we had a report of a lewd man out on the desert from a tourist and he went out and he got him, and that night I had an employee shoot herself in the leg. Had two ambulance runs and an arrest on one day. That third time I was the one who was a little upset because I don't have a gun in here and she was bringing a gun to work and I didn't know it. She had a little pink semiautomatic she kept in her purse and she was putting the clip in and shot herself in the leg." The woman was a Utah state resident with a concealed gun permit.

It never was Denys Baker's dream to own a roadside stop, although she admits to having hated the years she was a suburban housewife. When she graduated from college, most of her jobs were as a librarian or teacher's aide. She thinks the American Dream is a meaningless term in the West Desert.

"Because everybody out here is sort of escaping what I think of as the American Dream. The suburbs, the two cars, the two kids," said Baker, who has two sons, one who helps manage the Border.

"So what's the American Dream for the people out here?" I asked.

"To be left alone," Baker replied.

"Just to be left alone?" I asked. "But that's not possible is it?"

"Nope," Baker said.

"How do they react when they find it's not possible?" I asked.

"They get really mad," and Baker broke up laughing. "They get really, really mad."

Baker found her way to the West Desert via California. Her first husband wanted to own his own business. But he had no skills for the tasks. "He didn't have a clue how to do it," Baker said. "Neither did I, but I figured it out. So I ended up with the business and he left. I'd never even waited tables before when I was a kid."

Later, she would marry Dean Baker, the largest rancher in the area, but that didn't work out either. Her only regret is that she spent too long in each marriage trying to make it work. For her the Border became a healing place. It facilitated her interaction with the community and from there she began to put together a new family.

Now she'd like to begin a majority ownership transfer to her son Gary. First, however, she wants to purchase the 20 acres on the Utah side that the BLM has proffered to her. She'd like to install an RV park, a convenience store, and more housing for workers, realizing that that employee benefit is going to become increasingly important to managing the business.

Then, she'd pull away from the Border and accelerate her traveling. Since she moved to the West Desert, she's developed an appreciation for space. Typically, Baker takes one exotic trip yearly, usually in the winter, "When you get trapped, when all the people you see are the same locals every day, telling the same stories," Baker said. An innkeeper and protector of the community's center is like others in the West Desert. Living on the border between the automobile and the last frontier, sometimes she needs to be alone.

Halloween Party at the Outlaw Bar
Coming Out

The Halloween party at the Outlaw Bar in Baker, Nevada, is the social event of the year, even more important than the Snake Valley Reunion. Tourist season is over so visitors can't take up valuable space that local folks need to display their costume wizardry. The occasion is so important that in 1992, when Halloween actually fell on a Saturday, the Outlaw decreed that local kids would have to trick-or-treat on Friday night so the adults could have their party on the usual Saturday night. That didn't sit well with some adults, Al Hendricks in particular, the former superintendent of Great Basin National Park, who called himself "a sucker for little kids." He felt that Halloween is for kids and they should get the priority.

So Hendricks didn't attend in protest, but he was about the only local who didn't. It's the one time at the Outlaw where drinking slows down. The costumed folks and the gawkers are so intent on studying subtleties of masquerade and identity that they don't have time to drink.

The ingenuity, planning, and time that went into many of the costumes was remarkable. The winner of the best costume was Bill Rountree. He came as a horse's ass. He built a shell that looked like equine haunches and covered it with a gray tufted material. His legs ended in black hoofs. There was a small hole for the rectum and a black tail that he could swish back and forth from inside. Once inside, he had a bag full of tricks. He'd make a clippety-clop sound periodically from pieces of wood. At appropriate times he would squeeze out a blast from a whoopie cushion. Rountree said he "worked like a one-man band" inside the costume to create all the visual and audio effects.

But the pièces de résistance were the droppings. After the whoopie cushion, Rountree would shoot red potatoes out of the horse's rectum. Eventually, potato turds began to litter the floor in the Outlaw. In between the evacuations, Rountree would stick out a straw and sip a bourbon and water tendered by a kindly groom.

Dean Baker took second place. He came as Church Lady from *Saturday Night Live*. The reason the judges were so impressed with his effort was that he stayed in character all night. With his handbag lifted high to his chest, the successful rancher, businessman, pilot, and former Republican Soil and Conservation Service appointee tiptoed through the tables chatting with all the ladies about teas and doilies, tittering all the time. In past years Baker came as a Mafia don and Jack Nicholson. In both cases he carefully selected the right kind of nuts to stuff in his cheeks to give him the requisite jowels, using walnuts for the Mafia don and pecans for Jack Nicholson. The insides of his cheeks were lacerated in the mornings.

JoAnne Garrett also won a prize. She came in drag, too, as an Old West gambler and snake oil salesman. She tinted her hair a dark brown and folded it under a hat. She added a bushy mustache and long sideburns. A soft deerskin jacket and checked shirt completed the costume. Like Dean Baker, Halloween gave her the opportunity to shed her accustomed public role of social activist and flirt with the devil.

Garrett and Baker in drag
Halloween is as important to adults in Baker, Nevada, as it is to children, because it's time for the social event of the year—the Halloween party at the Outlaw Bar. JoAnne Garrett and Dean Baker, two granitic pillars of the community, come in drag, sharing brief openings to their playful fantasies.

Melodrama
To help celebrate the community's centennial, Eureka kids script their own Old West melodrama, with continual performances every 45 minutes. They localize the play by including icons of shared history, weaving the story around the dominant Sunshine Mine. The good couple in white plays the leads, and the miscreant is sent to jail. The girl on the right holds up cue cards: "Boo," "Laugh," "Applaud!"

Eureka City Centennial
The Sound of Different Rattles

In its official *Centennial Celebration Calendar of Events*, Eureka City, Utah, describes itself as "a city that refuses to become a ghost town." Once the center of one of the largest mining operations in the United States, its mines have produced over $550 million in silver and other precious metals. "It has twice been flooded, been burnt, plagued by epidemics and buried in snow. From its mining-boom peak of 7,000 residents, it has declined with the price of silver to one-tenth its size. Yet it struggles to maintain its dignity as the hub of the Tintic Historical District."

"Struggles to maintain its dignity." There always is a bit of wistfulness wafting through the public braggadocio surrounding centennials. The cobwebs of memory and spectre of an unsure future float in the vast labyrinth of tunnels and stale air under Eureka. The Burgin and Trixie Mines periodically become objects of mining promotion and some production, as the price of silver fluctuates, but old mines in the West Desert come with weighty baggage that cools the ardor of promoters. Pollution left by former operators becomes the reclamation responsibility of new owners, no matter how environmentally friendly their operations are.

But hey, 100 years. That's something to celebrate for a mining town, and on January 1, 1992, Eureka teens kicked off the year-long commemoration with a 1950s dance. March was the Miss Tintic Pageant, although the Miss Tintic Fund Raiser didn't chip in until May. St. Patrick's Catholic Church decided its namesake day was the best time to hold a fund-raiser. In April the Methodist Church followed suit with its sing-along and bake sale. The Elks Club weighed in in May with its Centennial Mother's Day Brunch, while the Ladies Order of Eagles opted for grace with a Mother-Daughter Tea.

The pace began to quicken once summer arrived, the Elks holding a Flag Day ceremony, despite the fact it fell on a Sunday. The Parade Committee feted dads with a Father's Day Brunch. Kids got their Little Buckaroo Rodeo a week later. The community celebrated Independence Day with the Firemen's Circus. Mormons held their Primary Parade and Carnival on July 24th, the day their ancestors arrived in Salt Lake Valley, 80 miles north.

The weekend of August 15th was the penultimate—the Silver Festival—the moment the Eureka Centennial Celebration Committee had sweated for eight months. There was the parade, the sidewalk sales, the nonstop entertainment in the vacant lot between two buildings, the Old West melodrama produced by local kids, and the mountain man rendezvous.

September is harvest time, even in a mining town, so Eureka ladies staged the Old Fashioned Quilting Bee and Luncheon at the LDS church. Poking fun at the traditional disappearance of men in October, the centennial committee hosted the Deer Widow's Chili Cook-Off. St. Patrick's church held another fund-raiser the Saturday following Thanksgiving. Santa made his usual appearance in December, and the elementary school capped its centennial celebration with an operetta. Opera was just too much—for everyone. Then, the celebratory year ended with the Mormon ward hosting the Community Christmas Dinner. It was free for all.

Products of a ghost town
The centennial parade highlights Eureka's Silver Festival. The Fire Department hauls out its vintage trucks, the Tintic High School marching band struts its stuff, and Miss Tintic and her two attendants wave from a late model convertible. Floats are small and personalized, sometimes loaded with a community's hopes and fears.

Teaching use of musket
Mountain men are part of the Eureka centennial parade. Walking down Main Street, they periodically fire their muskets, playing the crowd like any good street entertainer. When they sense a curious parade-watcher, they give a young girl the chance to feel the power and recoil of a weapon's discharge.

Saddam Hussein target
The musket shoot is one of the competitions held at a mountain man rendezvous. Clothing and weaponry are authentic, the participants usually stitching their garb by hand. The only artifact in the ceremony transferred from twentieth century culture is a bull's-eye for the 1990s.

Loading muskets
The mountain man rendezvous is a traveling subculture committed to preserving an era from the Old West. When an occasion like a town's centennial celebration arises, the group of creative anachronists will move its tepees and caravans to available vacant land and stage its reenactments of life in the 1820s. One culture and mythology become grafted onto another, and time is collapsed.

The Memorial Day Barbecue
A Family Celebrates Its Life on the Land

Community reunions like the Snake Valley Reunion in Baker and the Deep Creek Reunion in Ibapah salute a frontier past. Often, organizers hold them on Independence or Pioneer Days to link them with sacramental moments that already have been publically annointed with ritual. Grandparents show grandkids from the suburbs where they sat in a two-room schoolhouse. Former residents return and local patriarchs like Joe Eldridge in Baker, who gets tired of always being proclaimed the oldest person extant, are thrust onto center stage. As heritage is celebrated, reunions reify the community power structure.

Ties to political community can become tenuous, however. As oldtimers die, the second and third generations, none who ever lived in the West Desert, come back to the homestead to honor the tradition, but the homecoming has an oddly distant feeling. Communities become like aspens. The original stand might still be there, but the roots have long since migrated elsewhere, sprouting new clones that are identical in makeup but also wholly different, having adapted to a new environment.

Reunions are more about families, and gatherings that stay centered in one family and commemorate that community more likely resonate with original meaning. Such it is with the Douglass family's Memorial Day Barbecue. On a continuous run since 1966, it evolved out of George Douglass's professional community of students, faculty, and biologists at the University of Utah and Dugway Proving Ground. All talked about getting a toehold on that wild West Desert landscape that they had come to love. Each year they would try out a different spot to celebrate their attachment to the land. When George and Veronica Douglass made their leap of faith and purchased the old Falkenberg Ranch, the Deep Creek Mountains became the site to commemorate their shared but ineffable feeling that the land had become part of them.

The reunion has evolved. Biologists dwindled in ratio as families sprouted offspring. Some older locals stopped coming when kids began their tradition of water fights. Then children began to invite their friends, and as children began to find lives outside the West Desert, newcomers from the cities began attending the Memorial Day lamb roast. Now, it is indeed a moveable feast. George and Veronica never send invitations. Those who have been touched know to come on that same Sunday every year.

When I asked George and Veronica to stock me with crisp anecdotes from past celebrations, we were surprised with the outcome. George could remember when Bob Jacobsen's dog ate all the sheep fat, slept in the family tent, and when they couldn't get the tent open fast enough to let out a pleading dog, they had to burn the tent. Both George and Veronica laughed about how George's brother, an athlete, was going to show five girls how he could beat them in a tug-o-war and promptly got pulled into Indian Farm Creek. But that was all that came to mind. Their reunion had become less a memory and more a feeling.

George Douglass roasting lamb

Every Memorial Day weekend George Douglass roasts a lamb on a spit he made for the 50 to 100 guests who attend the family's annual celebration of community and place. A keg of beer stays cold in Indian Farm Creek, although it usually runs out long before the meat is done, and kids take turns cranking the handle of the ice cream maker. The rest of the the menu is a potluck affair.

Reunion entertainment

Entertainment varies from year to year. George Douglass has led nature walks, and Buck Douglass periodically sets up rappelling routes off Deep Creek Mountain cliffs. There's caving, trap shooting and the usual horseshoe tournament. One year a belly dancer showed up, and someone always brings a guitar and lusty songs.

The Eskdale Orchestra
Musical Ties That Bind

Most families and communities that live off the land plow their capital and profits into the operation, buying tractors, barbed wire, steam compressors, and the like. Eskdale finds itself under this lion's paw of extractive machinery, but the united order also has made a commitment to another set of community-building tools. Believing themselves to be descendants of the Levites, the musicians of the Bible, residents of Eskdale decided early on that they would scrape together extra money to purchase musical instruments and assemble a community orchestra.

Trips to the city on errands always included hunts of five-and-dimes and second-hand stores, asking proprietors if there might not be a dusty, old violin buried in some corner in the back of the store. Slowly they built a basic strings collection. Now they have all the strings in the orchestra.

The size of the orchestra has varied from 20 to 55, depending upon who is residing at Eskdale. Usually, several musicians from surrounding Snake Valley join the ensemble, a blessing for Doug Childs, the musical director, during those down years when he frets that the orchestra has a shallow sound. Given the emphasis on musical instruction at Eskdale, however, Childs never has failed to find enough willing musicians, especially since many Eskdale kids take up a second instrument in fifth grade. Students make their own choices, despite what Childs envisions he might need in the future, because they already have a feel for it.

"They all know the orchestra," Childs said. "They all know the instruments. Their mothers and dads all play in it. A few times we'll be practicing at night and the little ones will be right there by them in a basket or playing out on the floor. A lot of them like to play with their parents."

Music also links Eskdale to other communities. Each Christmas the Eskdale orchestra teams with the Delta City choir 90 miles away to perform Handel's *Messiah.* The show rides the circuit in the West Desert, playing to packed houses of ranchers dressed in suits and ties and Sunday go-to-meeting dresses.

Musician numbers were up in 1996, another "blessing," Childs called it, because the governor asked the Eskdale orchestra to kick off Utah's centennial. Dignitaries in pioneer dress gathered in Fillmore, the territorial capital, while Eskdale's 42-piece orchestra charged the air and the year-long celebration with verve and a reifying nostalgia. Eskdale's musical threads extend a long way, too. Al Hendricks, former superintendent of Great Basin National Park, flew from Crater Lake with his bassoon to join the performance. He continues to take time off from his new superintendency for the yearly *Messiah.*

Walker River Pinenut Festival
The Celebrated Life

It's billed as "a traditional Indian thanksgiving," and the Walker River Paiutes' annual Pinenut Festival does have a few things in common with the 1623 version and its modern changeling.

There is the mixture of races, with Indians now the host. There is a giddy, foolish overabundance of food, although the menu has evolved for a modern palate—moist, long simmered beef, prepared

Childs family and Hendricks

Each year the Eskdale orchestra teams with the Delta City choir to perform the *Messiah* for West Desert communities. The music weaves together families, with Karma and Ryan Childs accompanying each other on cello. The chords reach Oregon, too. Crater Lake National Park superintendent Al Hendricks takes vacation leave each Christmas to join on bassoon.

Handgame

Gambling is an honored pastime when Native Americans gather to celebrate life, not tinged with moral weakness as in the Judeo-Christian ethic. Handgame is often the game of choice, and it's one tradition that isn't in danger of fading away from lack of practice and practitioners. In fact, young adults are as common on handgame teams as Indian elders. It's also a cross-cultural tradition, with Anglos sometimes becoming part of a team when they join the culture through marriage.

for 1400 people by caterers, instead of tough, stringy game birds.

However, there is one significant difference between the Walker River thanksgiving and the Anglo one. The Pilgrims and their cultural offspring use the celebration to mark linear time and progress. For Paiutes the Pinenut Festival is a signpost rather than a milestone. It signifies the circle of life. When I asked the dynamic, down-to-earth, former Walker River tribal chairwoman Anita Collins how long the tribe had been doing this, she surprised me when she said almost dreamily, "Forever."

At first I thought she meant "forever" in a chronological sense. The tribe had gathered pine nuts every fall when the rabbit brush turned yellow as part of their hunting and gathering culture, making sure to leave some cones on the ground for squirrels, rotating gathering places in three-year intervals. That was the cultural history of the ritual. That was real time. Later, I understood the allegorical allusion. As far as Indian conception of cyclical time is concerned, both Anita's people, the "Numa," and pine nuts had been on earth for all time. God created them together and for each other. Anita was acknowledging the mysticism in the practice, an eternal linkage to the past, to the elders, to the earth, and to the next cycle of life. That was the homage we were celebrating for four days the second week in September.

Preparations for the festival began early in the week, with tribal members climbing high onto Black Mountain west of Schurz, Nevada, to harvest a single piñon pine for the round dance later in the week and enough cones to provide a bag of nuts for every festival goer. A backhoe operator dug a large hole in the tribe's festival grounds. The cones were placed in the pit with burning pine embers on top, covered with dirt and cooked over night. Willows were used in the past to cook and open the cones to the seeds because the branches burn quite hot and don't leave ash attached to the nuts. But willows are too rare now, and the tribe has to use piñon pine as fuel, which can leave a pitchy taste in the nuts due to uneven cooking.

Shucking and winnowing the nuts took three days, with a core of about six women doing the lion's share of the work. They wore surgical gloves to protect their cuticles, digging out approximately 20 seeds from each cone with their thumbs. The few men who shucked disdainfully refused the gloves.

Winnowing gets rid of the chaff and sandy soil that sticks to the hard brown outer shells of the pine nuts. In years past Paiutes made winnowing baskets from willow. Long, straight, thin strands would be carefully selected and then laced together so that there would be just enough space between the reeds so that pine needles could fall through but not the nuts. Expert winnowers would throw a basketful of nuts into the wind. The breeze had to be strong enough to separate the nuts but not so strong as to blow them helter skelter. If the winnowing was done correctly, the chaff and nuts with no meat, being lighter, would be blown farthest to the side by the wind. The good nuts, because they were heavier, would be blown only slightly to the side. The wind wouldn't catch the weighty dirt and pebbles, and they would fall straight down. The expert winnower would position the basket to catch the good nuts. The trick was to get the nuts hot enough to cook completely without burning the reed baskets.

With willow rare and winnow basket-making skill even rarer, the old baskets are now too valuable to use. Today, the winnowers employ more practical, stainless steel baskets. Purists say they don't work as well, the winnowers cleaning much of the nuts of debris and dirt by hand.

Conversation among the shuckers had the tenor of a ladies' card game. So-and-so was sick and needed help from tribal social services. They lamented the work they still had to do at home. But, mostly, the conversation danced with sex. There was talk about particular men and their current objects of desire. Any statement became grist for a double entendre. "Riding high in the saddle." "Stroking that motorcycle." "Going full bore with him." I couldn't tell if I was being teased, seduced, or if being Anglo and helping clean pinecones made me a eunuch.

Occasionally, men would come by and the women would playfully chastise them for being tardy or leaving early to sneak a beer. The men talked fatalistically about liquor as if it were a temptress and their fondness for it a tragic flaw.

The women would tease the men about that other "woman," but there was a haunting sadness in the tête-à-tête between men, women, and liquor.

By the end of the third day, everyone became punchy. Anything anyone said was followed by raucous laughter. A phrase would get worked over and over, placed into different contexts, each new context bringing another round of guffaws. Tears began streaming down cheeks. Perhaps it was the pungent smell of pine that, breathed over the course of three days, had the effect of laughing gas. Probably, it was exhaustion from the tedium, mixed with great expectations and togetherness—a contagion and a purgative. Laughter and tradition are like that.

In Native American tradition gambling is a respected, much anticipated segment of any gathering, and expert practitioners are held in awe. At the Pinenut Festival, there were two forms: card games and hand game. Men and women played all day and well into the night, moving for water but seldom for food.

Women, exclusively, played cards. Twenty-one was the game of choice for some, while other tables played show-your-pairs, a fast-paced game where one player can play over another if she isn't fast enough, the object being to get rid of your cards first. Elveda Martinez, tribal public relations person, said she'd be leery of getting into a game with some of the older women.

"They pretend they have no money. But they have money everywhere. Stuffed in pockets, in hems, and pinned to skirts. Also, those old women cheat. You have to watch them too carefully," Martinez said wryly.

Hand game is a traditional Indian game played by men and women and common to all tribes. In years past two clans would play one another. Now teams are formed across tribes, ages, and gender. Even Anglos take part, if they are married to an Indian or were raised in the culture. The purse in 1992 was $1500 and the winners received champions' jackets.

In the version played at the Pinenut Festival, two teams of five people face each other. Each team has five sticks and two pairs of bones, with two of the bones white and two with black stripes around them. Any two members of a team

hide the bones in their hands, first cloaking their hands with handkerchiefs or hiding them under their shirts. Then, the other team's appointed guesser points to the two hands where they think the solid white bones are, by pointing with a burned stick to one of two sides, to indicate inside or outside hand, or pointing the stick straight ahead to indicate the bones are in one hand. The guesser will sometimes feint a gesture, trying to lure a response from the opposing team, but once the stick is pointed the guess is fixed. If a team guesses right, it gets one of the other team's sticks and one of its white bones. If it guesses wrong by picking the black-striped bones, it loses its own stick and its chance to guess. When a team wins all the other team's sticks, it gives its own sticks to the opposing team. When it wins its own sticks back, a total of ten "won" sticks, the game is over.

The bone-hiding team tries to distract the guessing team by gesticulating wildly with the sticks, singing native songs, shouting, and beating on drums or hollow logs. There usually is one person who winds up being the designated song leader, due to his or her knowledge of the old songs and ability to sing. This person is responsible for changing the beat or tenor of the songs to meet the needs of the game. If a team is on a roll, the songs tend to get faster and louder, the crescendo amplifying the win skein and making the losing team more desperate and more likely to make a mistake in guessing. Conversely, if the game is close or if a team is just hanging on with few sticks, then the songs and beat might be slower and more deliberate.

In traditional hand game Indians would match bets. If one member on one team put up a blanket or a horse, he would seek a member or a supporter of the other team to match that bet. Now it's cash and not goods that are wagered, although it still is on a 1:1 basis. One strategy in the game is to pay close attention to people who have bet the most, theorizing that they might be more vulnerable to "flinching" or indicating where they are hiding the bones if they have more to lose.

Taunting is an important and stylized part of the game. To distract or demoralize the other team, the player having fooled the other team's guesser might open his fists and twist the bones around to the beat of his team's drum and song intimating, "Here are the bones. We fooled you! Don't you wish you had them?" If a team does guess which hands hold the solid white bones, the losing team tries to look "Indian-faced" and condescending, as if the winning guessers were extraordinarily lucky. No one seems to get offended by the taunting. It's part of the game, and everyone appreciates stylized dash. While taunting and deception are called for, cheating is seen as dishonorable, and it never rises above the level of suspicion.

Bill Johnson a Northern Paiute and student of the game, said there never is any strong, permanent team leader in hand game, and that reflects Indian notions of groups.

"Indians are kind of loners," Johnson said. "They make their own bets in handgame, even though they are part of a team." So the game tends to fit the Indian notion of leadership.

The family is the only core unit. Other combinations—clans, tribes, or colonies—are transient creations. Ultimately, each person is on his own.

Saturday night was the blessing ceremony and round dance, the culmination of the Pinenut Festival. At 8 P.M. the Walker River Singers climbed to the bandstand, while the anxious crowd awaited in that magical time of day that is dusk. Serving as the master of ceremonies, the lead singer worked the crowd with a panache of ethnocentrism.

He began by talking about elders who had been coming to the festival for years but who were not with them that night, too sick to attend or passed on "They were great people, but we will have to carry on as best we can without them," he said.

He then talked about the need for new singers, for young people to learn the language and the songs so that there can continue to be a festival. He chided his audience about taping the songs but not doing anything with the tapes, except playing them as background music at home. He suggested that tapes are no good unless you learn from them, and in quintessential Indian self-deprecating humor, he

recalled a difficulty he had using a tape recorder once, while he and some other good old Indian boys were drunk and singing songs. He never got the thing to record, so now he never uses one. "The tape recorder should be between your ears," he said.

Then the moment had come. The head singer said, "It is time for us to form our circle and dance the round dance. We have a lot of pine nuts. It's been a good year. It doesn't matter how you dance. It is important that you be a part of the circle of hands."

By families and as singles, people began to move from the perimeter toward the ceremonial pine tree, forming a series of concentric circles, creating enough circles of increasing size to accommodate all the people who wished to dance. People held hands and faced inward to the pine tree. Young people next to old people; Indians joined with whites. Someone gave me a gentle push in the back to get me going.

The lead singer began to beat his drum and sing. Slowly, the circles began to turn clockwise around the pine tree. The dance steps didn't seem to matter. People simply shuffled their feet in small, measured steps to the beat of the drum. The other movement consisted of rhythmically moving the clasped hands up and down in an elliptical locus in concert with the pulsating flow.

Anita Collins, at that time tribal chairwoman, and George Moose, an appointed elder, slowly walked around the ceremonial tree inside the innermost circle of dancers. Moose would cast pine nuts on the ground, like a farmer spreading seed by hand, and incant a prayer. Collins would periodically touch the tree and pray. The round dancers ritualistically tamped the nuts into the soil as they danced, giving thanks for the harvest, for each other, for the continuing tradition, and offering themselves to the timeless circle.

One time the head singer became political, criticizing the Bureau of Land Management and how it handles pine nut gathering. "The BLM only allows native people to gather fifty pounds of pine nuts, while commercial pine nut gatherers can have three hundred pounds. That's not right. The native people shouldn't be limited to only enough for one month while outsiders have

Tug-o-war
In years past the tug-o-war contest at the Pinenut Festival would be waged between tribes, families, or bands. Now, team membership is open and fluid. It's still a male bastion and winners covet bragging rights.

Indian car contest
In typically wry Indian humor, one of the events at the Pinenut Festival is the tongue-in-cheek Indian Car Parade and Contest. The object is to show off the perfect reservation car. That's typically one whose paint has largely faded, whose door has to be opened with a screwdriver and whose tires are as bald as a baby's head. But a car that is too obviously junk misses the spirit of the contest and is disqualified. The car has to run.

Cradleboard

Indian mothers report that fussy infants become strangely at peace when they are strapped into cradleboards. Beadwork symbolizes both the sex of the child and the origin of the maker. Usually, cradleboards are handed down from one generation to the next. The ones in this photograph are three generations old and of dramatically increasing value because fewer young women are learning the craft.

Rodeo

When asked whether Indians are more or less patriotic, Viola Kennison said, "Probably more patriotic, due to colonization." Perhaps that's one reason why Native Americans are such devoted supporters of that quintessential sport of the cowboys—the rodeo. The All Indian Rodeo at the Pinenut Festival is sanctioned by the Western States Indian Rodeo Association. Purses are $300 per event with a $40 entry fee.

all they need. Those of you who are smarter and more learned than I should write your congressman and tell them about this injustice. If you don't and if the BLM is not stopped, then this pine nut harvest and way of life that we have had for all time might come to an end."

The dance continued.

Then, the lead singer suggested to the men that they lean over and kiss a person on the cheek. "Or, maybe on her ear."

A pause and tittering among the dancers.

"Oh," he continued, "I hear you like that.*"*

At the end of the blessing ceremony and round dance, I had to leave. In spite of being there only four days, I didn't want to leave the circle and the reservation. There had been a feeling of peace for me there. On the road hurtling homeward under a finely etched sky, I felt an odd sadness and longing, then an understanding. The driving and the dancing were but two ends of a continuum, or rather two points opposite each other on a circle. We had celebrated community, life's union and reunion. From that circle we draw the strength to be alone.

Children of the West Desert
The Celebrated Future

There is an ironic tension between past, present, and future that is visited on children. It's a public truism that every community celebrates its future through its kids. School bond elections, for instance, hinge on the argument that if a new school isn't erected or more books purchased, the community will likely falter with the prospects of its children. Yet while we treasure children as vessels carrying hopes for the future, we sometimes erect signboards in the middle of their paths to help them circumvent the present. We try to protect children from experience, because it threatens their innocence. We want them to mature—to develop a history—but we also want to isolate them from the potentially scarring present. To balance this legerdemain, we look to the past.

Communities equate the innocence of children with the perceived innocence of a public past. To protect children, we encourage them to absorb adult memories of the past, regardless of whether those memories are mythic or real. Either way, they become instructional ways of living in the present. That's a primary reason why families are moving from cities to rural communities: to secure their children by investing in the virtue of a landed past.

It might turn out to be a fool's journey, even in the West Desert. The largest population growth rates in the 1990s have been in rural communities. That's partially due to ranch towns becoming bedroom communities as suburban sprawl oozes out, but some folks are trying to escape large cities by leapfrogging into empty space. To an urbanite used to seeing blocks developed overnight, the visual effect might not be noticeable. But to a small town like Baker, four new homes and families are a significant challenge to old ways of doing things.

Right now, a major battle with the legacy of time looms on a plot of land that has become important because it is a remnant of the Old West, when Anglos thought the best way to manage the future of Native Americans was to herd them onto reservations and away from their nomadic pasts. The Skull Valley band of Gosiutes in Utah wants to make its land a temporary storage site for high level nuclear wastes. It would be paid handsomely for that right by a consortium of power companies, a boon for a poor tribe prevented from developing gaming businesses by Utah laws proscribing all gambling. The arrangement has challenged families and created tension between the Skull Valley band

and the Ibapah band of Gosiutes on the west side of the Deep Creek Mountains. Meanwhile, the state of Utah tries to thwart that sovereign decision by legislating control of roads leading to the reservation and throwing up prohibitively expensive bonding requirements.

The stakes are high because the outcome means saddling some land and communities with a future of 10,000 half-lives. It also is a wake-up call to all those who live in the West Desert. We must remember that we are its children.

Kids with tires

The West Desert always has been the road less traveled, and it still is relatively undiscovered. However, small towns are increasingly attractive for urban expatriates because of what seems to be their retained innocence. Consumerism isn't as apparent in an agrarian economy. Accrued wealth is plowed back into the land. Kids can be happy with used tires or a ball and bat without a mitt.

Free lab pups

There is only one intersection in Baker, Nevada, and just like in cities, that's where folks sell their cars or advertise free lab pups, catering to a mobile western community. It's a crucial intersection, too, because it marks the spot where the road takes off from town to Great Basin National Park. That asphalt link is a permanent path to Baker'sfuture.

Stefan Hoffman wearing Superman cape

When I asked Stefan Hoffman of Home Farm what pictures we would take if he had a camera, he replied, "old forgotten photographs." Asked to explain, he said old forgotten photographs are like those photographs of his older sister Alicia taken when she was a baby. "You put those photographs in a book," Hoffman said, "and you forget about them. Then you can pull out the book one day and remember them."

Schurz kids playing basketball

Sports provides common ground in the West Desert, its simple earnestness supplying an uncorrupted lesson that can be preserved only on a schoolyard playground. It brings communities together and reflects the increasing diversity of the West. On the Walker River Paiute Reservation, Indians play basketball with Anglos, boys with girls.

John Paul Hayward at piano

John Paul Hayward is too young to take up the piano. The Eskdale youth will have to wait until third grade for his first lessons. Nevertheless, he knows that music is the pulse of his community, seeing his parents, grandparents, uncles, and aunts play in the orchestra and at Sabbath services. The community hopes he carries on its tradition.

Gold Hill from a distance

This cabin, owned by a casino proprietor in Wendover, is one of only two remaining structures from old Gold Hill, a mining community that once boasted 3,000 people. Now, three people live there full time. The weekend population doubles with people who do a little prospecting and trade tales from mining's halcyon days.

IV

Recapitulation

Levis sign

Always in a rush to catch up with its established siblings to the east, the West lurches into its future. The land is new enough that images from the past have yet to fade away. As the West Desert strives to create a dynamic future, it must resolve its memories of the past—what was real, what has become myth.

When I began this documentary, several questions rooted in my study of American civilization drove my inquiry. A moment approximately 100 years after the official closing of the frontier and a little more than a decade from the millenium seemed a good time to revisit the notion of Jeffersonianism. Did people of the land turn out to be exactly the kind of independent yeomen Thomas Jefferson envisioned? Do people now living on the last frontier in the lower 48 states, the West Desert, practice the kind of democracy that Jefferson believed would serve as the nation's storehouse of republican virtue, maintaining a pure strain of American democratic character that could be used to revitalize the inherent corruption of the cities?

As I started to talk to people, I began to reframe those questions. Instead of narrowly looking at the practice of electoral democracy, I began focusing on a different application of democracy—the creation and maintenance of community. While the workings of elected government are perhaps the most visible symbol of democracy in action, they are becoming increasingly foreign to many Americans. For most of us, democracy is more accessible and understandable in the ways that we interact with others to make our communities.

Issues regarding community have been a large part of the previous photographs and text. People of the West Desert have ably offered their perceptions of how their communities work. Their insights and critical self-appraisals offer points of discussion. Some of them will be explored in this recapitulation, although most remain embedded in the previous chapters. In this personal reflection I ask what, then, does community look like on a vestige of the last frontier called the West Desert? Can it provide any lessons for the greater American community?

1

Creation of Community

Land as the Shaper of Community

The West Desert is a psychically raw place that lacks the glossy veneer of red rock or deep powder snows. To an urban eye transfixed on a distant horizon on Interstate 80, the Great Basin landscape only appears on the periphery of perception. But to the people who live there, the land represents a kind of "belonging," as both Elveda Martinez of the Walker River Paiutes and JoAnne Garrett of Baker said. To draw strength from the land, one must be grounded in a sense of that place. To be out of land is to be out of place.

There still is the promise of space in the West Desert. Plots of land can be purchased at reasonable cost where a family can dig its heels into the alkaline soil—providing they can find water.

There are those occasional atomistic spots of isolated community, fragile specks that one sometimes sees on the horizon, before the edge of the earth disappears into space. A machine-made rectangularity is the only clue that they are buildings. Seeing them only with a certain amount of squinting and strain, one first guesses that they must be abandoned, vestiges of the first attempts to build community in the high desert 150 years ago. Not every human touching the earth turned the desert into a garden. Indeed, many of those distant buildings are abandoned and crumbling, but not all. Sometimes, there still is a rutted, rocky dirt road that even West Desert counties neglect to re-grade in the spring that leads to an occupied settlement. That community represents the ultimate in organiza-

tion. That person or family is totally alone, and they must make it largely on their own. There is no community of companionship or support. While they likely aren't totally self-sufficient and must make occasional forays into town for supplies, the world would little note nor ever remember their being or passing.

Most communities in the West Desert are larger than that. These larger clusters of social protoplasm conform to the mineral, soil, or riparian opportunities that the land provides or grow up around major highways. Wherever they live, however, there is a psychological resonance individuals strike with the land. Each resident of the West Desert seems to have a perpetual awe of the land and its resolute hardness. By bearing under that hardness, a person becomes part of that essential materialism that constitutes land. So, while each person might physically bond to the land in a different way, rancher versus miner versus tourist guide, each intuitively understands the other's psychological attachment.

For Ed Alder, the principal of West Desert School and a farmer, it's the land and the changing seasons that speak to his soul. He said, "If I chose any other area to live, I could have farmed a lot easier than I do here. The ground would be a bit better. The water would be more plentiful. But it's these mountains, I think. You sit down there in the evenings and watch the sun set, and just watch a show *every* night, and a sunrise *every* morning. And the storms rolling in from the south, seasonally when they come through. I'll miss that when I have to leave. I really will. And to be able to walk in any direction for miles and come across just treasures in the desert. A little coolie. A little draw with a little community in there that hasn't changed for thousands of years."

Alder likens his community to that kind of climatic permanence. He trusts that it will always be there, and there is strength in the simple survival of a community on a parcel of land that doesn't offer an easy resting place.

"I guess I'm most proud of my [community's] stubbornness," Alder said. "Their survivability. It's like a windstorm whipped through here economically and emotionally. But they're still here. When the wind dies down, they're still here."

When I asked Talmage Weis, co-founder of The Fraternity of Preparation, what would happen to the group if not everyone wanted to move to Montana after losing their land, he said that a community must be defined by physical proximity. Should some of the fraternity choose to stay in Utah, the group wouldn't attempt to maintain a common treasury and united order. Each would go its separate way and become autonomous. Each person has the right to choose to which community he or she belongs. Weis also maintains that a community needs to own property. Otherwise, it can't be self-governing.

While it's been elevated to the status of noble cliché, if not myth, land and property do offer promise for many West Desert citizens. Next to their families, land is the most real element in their lives. It's tied to human hope and personal aspirations, even long after the supposed closing of the frontier.

Ed Alder put it this way: "It's like I've wondered, 'Why do I like to farm? It's hard work. There's very little money in it.' I think it's because, and I may have a crop wiped out with cows or wiped out with drought or whatever, but every spring . . . And I think that happens for all the people out here. You start in February and the first warm day hits and you're perpetually planning ahead, you're perpetually saying," and Alder lapsed into a kind of incantation as he said, "'This year. This year I'll do it right. This year it'll happen. This year the grain will get this high. This year my calves will all make it. They won't die.' It's just perpetual optimism."

Alder likes the living with other people on the land that gives rise to their mutual optimism. "We all get together and we lie through our teeth to each other about how bad things are. And then we go off and plow another forty and put the ground in, put up another fence, and gamble. I guess we're gamblers," Alder said. Ironically, the only gambling promoted in Utah—gambling on the future. Nevadans can only laugh.

Communities Forming as a Response to a Threat From the Outside

Cecil Garland, the Callao rancher and peace activist, paraphrased Robert Ardrey in *African Genesis* when he said, "The greater the hazard, the more the people will cohesively join together, when there's an external hazard. And then Ardrey poses a question. 'What happens when you have almost complete security? Do people fall apart?' And I think they do."

Garland continued. "There's almost a total lack of cohesiveness in the United States

today. None. It's nonexistent. And that's because there are almost no external hazards. I call it 'toxicity in victory.' We were poisoned by our victory in World War II. We're still suffering from it, the toxicity of it."

"But this community functions pretty well when it recognizes an external hazard. Like in the MX." Certainly, MX was a prominent factor in the recent history of community formation in the West Desert. More than any other outside threat in the past, it brought disparate people together. Ranchers joined with environmentalists in uneasy truces to fight the common enemy, constantly being sure not to assume too much from the alliance with strange bedfellows.

Ranchers, for the first time, saw themselves in opposition to their government's wishes. They had a better knowledge of what the land could provide and tolerate. When their personal experiences began to conflict with their government's plans, they were ready for change.

A new kind of community began to be formed in the West Desert. People began to pay more attention to each other. They recognized their strength in each other. They learned what they could do as a community of interests rather than as separate communities.

Some in the West Desert still see the federal government as a threat. While MX would have done real damage, there is irony in the anti-government stance because probably no other institution has had a greater hand in developing community in the West Desert than the federal government. It's provided electricity. It instigated the creation of a telephone system. It offered incentives for water development. It chained lands claimed by descending junipers and reseeded them for grazing. It offered the land's mineral wealth for a song, with the promise of local jobs the primary compensation.

The federal government is like the rich uncle living elsewhere that nieces and nephews will deride in his absence for his profligacy and foolishness but who, nevertheless, expect his favors. The relatives want the money he offers, but want it without strings attached. Nor do they want to claim him as kin. Similarly, people of the West Desert wrestle with that conundrum. While they welcome the benevolent paternalism of Uncle Sam, they dislike the regulations that come with him. They like the deep pockets and the willingness of Uncle Sam to dole it out, but they don't like having to go before him fawningly and seek approval so that they can get the cash. Their strain of fierce, ascetic independence is threatened with the seductive allure of federal largesse, and they find the situation emotionally awkward.

Great Basin National Park feels that tension, even while it has been a prime mover in the creation of community in the West Desert. In some ways it is a community apart, since it is the physical manifestation on the ground of that distrusted, distant bureaucracy in Washington. There is some turnover in personnel, too, that adds some instability in the Baker community. Young, single people sometimes find it hard to work at a national park surrounded by disproportionately more land than people. Nevertheless, many of the park staff are integral members of the community. In fact, many park staffers are longtime residents who later made their careers at the park.

Nevertheless, in the sense that Lehman Caves National Monument/Great Basin National Park and the adjacent Humboldt National Forest have been an outsider, that Interior and Agriculture presence has figured into the creation of community in southern Snake Valley. The ranchers and miners, especially, have been leery of its powers and long arms. They fought against the formation of the national park, some wanting it to be designated as wilderness instead, fearing that a park, and more visitors, would mean eventual loss of grazing permits to urban folks who complained about stepping on cow pies. Others like the late Joe Griggs felt that a national park would spur the growth of gaming interests in the area, and for him those were loathesome creatures many steps below the level of ranchers on the ladder of human worth.

When they fought against the park, the ranchers were put in an awkward position. While they might have characterized the fight in their own minds as a battle against a distant bureacracy out of touch with life in the West, it wasn't that simple. Townsfolk in Baker like Bill Rountree who made their living off tourism wanted a national park. It could have been civil war.

But discussion was guided by a public civility and an understanding that it wasn't as simple as us versus them. For instance, Daisy Gonder, part of the longest ranching lineage in Snake Valley, worked at the national monument during the deliberations over whether there should be a national park. When she left Baker, at her going away party, she publically thanked all members of the community for not asking her to take sides. They recognized her awkward position and they respected her neutrality. The formation of the national park never became a battle of ideology in Baker. It always was about practicalities, like grazing and mining, and life on the ground.

The establishment of a national park by a decree of all the people of the United States, led by the congressional initiative of then-Representative and now Senator Harry Reid (D-Nevada), did have long-reaching effects on the community of Baker. While Baker still is unincorporated, the town did organize itself when it looked like the park was going to become a reality. The town council was formed as a way for the community to have a concerted voice in development of the park, especially its boundaries and the grandfathering of certain local privileges.

While the land around Baker with its meadows and springs has always been there, the Baker Ranch has changed hands, grown, and shrunk due to the effects of speculation based on outside rumors. While the current Bakers have owned the land the longest, it has been large and small due to mismanagement and misplaced dreams. At times, people have bought the land, not as a cattle ranch, but due to speculative schemes from the outside. Once there was supposed to be a large hydropower project for the area, and that would make the land more valuable as recreational property. Then there was going to be a dude ranch. Only cattle ranching by people running the ranch with a keen eye for business has ever gleaned a profit from the southern Snake Valley bottoms land.

Gold Hill is another community that has lived and died on outside influences, especially international geopolitics. Whether the public need was for arsenic or tungsten to fuel the engines of progress or war, Gold Hill was the site for exploration and extraction. The town prospered when conflicts waged on the outside needed its wares and the government ran a railroad line to get it. It began to die when the metals no longer were strategic and the rails were taken back for scrap.

Then, there is the ultimate community formation due to the threat from the outside— the Fraternity of Preparation. Members of the fraternity, first meeting in Salt Lake City, began worrying that the end of society seemed near. The society that they saw in the city where they lived seemed alien to them. Their beliefs made them separate. Government encroachment on personal liberties, drug and alcohol addictions and crimes, moral decay, coupled with a fundamental reading of scripture, led them to believe that the Second Coming must be close and that they should prepare themselves with a community. Recognizing that they couldn't build the type of community they wanted in the city, due to the seductive allures of the devil's dominion represented in government, they chose to strike out the farthest they could get from civilization, where they could build their own cloistered community answerable only to God.

Communities as Refuge

More than one person variously described their community as a refuge. In fact, it has been the rule more than the exception, and the description spans a wide variety of people. When people of the West Desert talk about their communities as refuge, it's the only time when their voices reflect a hint of urgency, when the pitch increases or the cadence quickens.

"Refuge" and "time running out" seem to reverberate from the same chord.

Jay and Frances Banta at Fish Springs National Wildlife Refuge love the "insulation" of their isolated community, arguably the smallest in the West Desert. Still, they don't consider themselves living on the frontier because all their needs are met on the refuge and they are electronically hooked to the rest of the world by satellite, fax, and modem. Nevertheless, they dread the thought of ever leaving Fish Springs. It's the ultimate family cocoon. For them, Fish Springs is a refuge they purposely and willingly *went* to, rather than a place they *ran away* to.

Ed Alder thinks that one day the Deep Creek Range, like all proposed BLM wilderness areas, will be seen as a refuge from the cities. He is thankful to live in an area like that, and would like to see the mountains above his farm receive the official consecration they already deserve. Similarly, he sees his home in Trout Creek as a refuge for his kids. It's like it's the end of the line. There's no better place to go to escape what he sees as the threat of random, senseless violence in the cities. While he fears the slow advance of irrationality, he still trusts Trout Creek as an island of rational cause and effect. While there is violence there, it is acceptable, like a farming accident or a fight at school. At least there is reason in that kind of threat to the family, and for him, that is the definition of a refuge.

Annette Garland, a teacher at the Callao School and Cecil's wife, sees Callao as a "sanctuary." She and her daughter Bertha go to Salt Lake City only when they have to and stay only as long as necessary. They run back to Callao at the earliest possible time. Even the mall doesn't attract Bertha. "Heaven's no," Annette said. "I mean, we walk in the mall. We do the mother-daughter thing, but it doesn't take us long to head back to the sanctuary. Where it's quiet. It's where we don't see weird people, even though we must look weird to people from Salt Lake. We feel safe, and time slows down a little bit."

Garland continued. "You get on those freeways and it's terrifying. And being in town in the mall is terrifying. So I don't think of it [the West Desert] as a frontier. It's a way to escape what's over there."

2

Maintenance of Community

The spark that creates a community is the same spark that must remain in order to maintain the community. That energy lies in the willingness of people to make community and in the constructive interrelationships that townsfolk court and sustain. The impulse for gestation, birth, and development must reside in the people or public institutions who see themselves, and their institution, as necessary parts of the community. Community is formed and maintained through human will and activism. Community is not a given, nor is it some Deist notion that once created it goes on tickin' by its own spontaneous kinesis. Community is an ongoing process. A community of competing interests isn't likely to be as functional as one whose public interactions are less coercive and damaging to the ego—of the person and, by transferral, the community.

There is a pragmatic simplicity in the way that this latter community works. Simply put, persons recognize other persons. People rub elbows often enough that they know one another. They also know when another member of the community has a particular need. Annette Garland put it this way when she referred to how Cecil treats others. While she claims that she tends to have a more liberal world view, allowing for governmental paternalism toward its fallen souls, she is more judgemental when it comes to dealing with individual people. Cecil, on the other hand, like many conservatives

speaking on a macro level, says personal problems are due to individual failure. But face-to-face, Annette says he would be one of the first to offer a helping hand. While everyone in the West Desert would agree that, ultimately, each person is responsible for his or her own life, those same people see each other as individuals with faces and peculiar histories. It's either a denial of ideology, human pragmatism, or simple altruism that leads folks to care for each other on a one-to-one level.

This kind of community expression assumes the individual as the foundation of community. Individuals are expected to take individual action and pragmatically interact with other individuals on the same level. Persons assume personal responsibility for their lives and their community. Of course, there still is a hierarchy of prestige and respect in the community, one that often is a function of time spent there, but in terms of gathering voices, all must be welcomed and not patronized. A foundation that rests on the individual makes practical sense, too, because it acknowledges the place of history and self-perception in community formation. Supposedly, the West was settled by rugged individuals, revisionists aside, so individual interaction is a logical place for community maintenance in the West Desert.

Community is maintained through sharing, both in an interpersonal sense and an economic sense. Sharing actually is institutionalized in united order communities. No one owns any property. Rather, all share equally in the wealth that the public creates for itself. That notion of selflessly giving, sacrificing, and sharing becomes a powerful bond that unites the community into a cohesive organization, one that can think and act with concert. Decisions are made through pure democracy, with each individual expected to understand the issues and voice his or her feelings. While all votes won't be unanimous, there is unity of purpose once the decision is made. In a united order community, the individual gives up an egocentric world view because he or she believes that the needs of the community are greater. Moreover, that person also firmly understands that ultimately the individual is strengthened by being part of that community and drawing upon its collective reserve of strength, energy, and will.

While not as strong a unifying force for sustaining community as a mechanistic united order plan, places like Home Farm maintain a cohesiveness through sharing too. That sharing comes on two levels. There still are community chores to be done if the community is to survive, and each week residents come together to divvy up those duties, usually by self-selection based on interest and through a logic stemming from publically acknowledged expertise. There is the sharing that comes from each person taking the responsibility once a week of preparing the community food at dinner.

Sharing takes place, too, in a spiritual sense at Home Farm. That kind of interaction between individuals that builds a sense of community comes in the biweekly study meetings when students of the wisdom teachings of Vitvan come together and talk about what the philosophies mean and how each person interprets them and tries to implement them in his or her life. But not all residents of Home Farm are as closely tied to the teachings of Vitvan. For some, their venue of instruction and script for spiritual guidance is the land itself. Not just the land in and around Home Farm. Rather, there is a notion that the earth is the common bond that we share, and proper caring for that land necessarily creates and maintains community in people who must live on that land together and share its resources.

Val Taylor said that giving people freedom to be as they are and who they are is fundamental to Home Farm. "That's another thing about living out here. At the school we focus on, 'If I want the freedom to become who I am, then I need to give that freedom to everyone else to be who they are.' Part of our challenge here is to grant that freedom to people. We have to set limits for them if they can't set their own.

"People who live out here in Baker, who are not involved with the school, who don't understand the school, basically have that same philosophy," Taylor continued. "'I live out here because I don't want to be in a big city with city regulations. I don't want to have to put my dog on a leash. I don't want to be told I can't have twenty-five rabbits and chickens in my back yard.'

"Now, they might have a few beers at the Outlaw and start talking about how weird this guy is and how different he is. But there's a tolerance built into the life out here because we're interdependent."

People self-select themselves for community maintenance chores and simply do it. As another example Taylor cites the volunteer fire department. "If I sit here and see smoke coming from someplace," and Taylor snapped her fingers, "everybody is out. Nobody has to say, 'Are you sure that's a dangerous fire?' It doesn't matter. If I see smoke over towards Silver Creek, everyone's there. It just happens."

While only funerals are public in Ibapah and Callao, with weddings being private, all events in Baker are public. When there is a wedding in Baker, everyone in the town is invited to the celebration. Invitations are sent to everyone, and if someone inadvertently doesn't get a personal invitation, one is posted on the wall in the post office. Bakerites come together in sorrow and happiness. They share all.

Sharing in an economic sense comes through trading services. This is not the retail, storefront, incorporated trading of utility. Rather, business seems to grow less formally and tactically in the West Desert. Bill Rountree purchased a used backhoe because he noted that no one had one in Baker and several projects could have used one. Dean Baker saw that the growth of

Great Basin National Park meant there would have to be more housing, so he built a few apartment units; or he guessed that there will be some new construction, so he stockpiled sand and aggregate for making concrete foundations.

In turn, the federal government through Great Basin National Park and the Humboldt National Forest office in Baker provides cash flow for the community. More important, park salaries are more substantial than ranch hand wages and more reliable. Many ranching families need the steady infusion of money from a second job to supplement the vagaries of a business tied to the whims of nature and global economics. Families in the area are more stable because of the economic support of park jobs.

Eskdale is unique in that it is an entire community perceiving itself as trading services to the rest of the community. Being a united order plan in an area of sparse population, it has to be creative in how it pulls in cash flow in order to sustain itself. Not all its foodstuffs, material goods, and construction can be generated from scratch. So Eskdale sells its services. It has a large shop and garage that provide machining and automotive services to the larger Snake Valley community. When a hapless tourist's car breaks down in the vicinity, he or she often will go to Eskdale to get it fixed at the garage.

This sharing of services has a salutory effect on the maintenance of community beyond its economic sustenance. Often, the service a person or community provides the rest of the community is the only service like that in the community. Of course, that means that there is no competition, with possible attendant monopolistic problems, but rarely does sharing of services in the West Desert work in such a predatory manner. Rather, people are happy that someone can provide that service now, as it didn't exist before. It means that life in the West Desert will become a little easier, and the community is made more whole and self-sufficient. There is less need to venture out.

Trading services brings people together. While there is an economic incentive, of course, business sometimes is perceived as a kind of giving, because often the businesses grow from the spark of contribution, like Bill Rountree buying a backhoe because he knew the community needed one or Eskdale repairing a car. In the case of a community like Eskdale, which could tend to be isolated due to cloistering and a united order plan, providing services integrates it more into the community. There is less suspicion, more acceptance of diversity, more interdependence. A community becomes a gestalt.

Recognizing the Individual

Along with sharing comes tolerance and respect for the individual. All the people I interviewed claimed there is genuine regard in southern Snake Valley for each other that gets manifested in a public civility. Listening has as important a role in maintaining that civility as speaking one's mind. Listening does not mean one group making its case then either leaving or turning a deaf ear to the opposition, with the understanding that some larger body of decision makers, like an elected commission, will sift through the competing claims and grant power or compromise. When community works in the West Desert, it's because people face and deal with each other.

Al Hendricks, the former superintendent of Great Basin National Park, says that the compromises Baker has made generally have been sound ones. "By and large, the directions the community has taken have been fairly well debated and discussed. While in certain cases I may have disagreed with them, they were well thought out and appropriate for the moment when the decision was made."

As an example, Hendricks gave the park's size. He would have wanted it larger, but it was not anything he had any control over. He felt it is large enough that the vital resource can be protected, although he wished some of the actual basin had been included in the park.

Ed Alder, principal of the West Desert, agrees with Hendricks. He believes that as an individual, he is listened to in northern Snake Valley. More importantly, he feels like he can have an effect on his community as an individual. Perhaps that's because he shares the community's values, or it's simply because the community knows him as a multidimensional person rather than as a label. Alder wonders if the emotional strength that comes from that realization really is possible in cities, with so many people and so many isolated special interests who don't know each other and therefore have no reason to respect and listen to one another.

"I could practice it in Salt Lake just as well, but would I make as big an impact on what really affects me?" he asked. "No. Out here, when I stand for one thing or another, it makes an impact in my life. And on others. I have a little more control over that."

Diversity, Critical Mass, and Community Maintenance

It seems that any community needs a certain critical mass for both community formation and maintenance. The size of that mass is indeterminate. It's really measured by more than simple numbers of people. It has more to do with community energy and people identifying with their community. There has to be diversity, too, within that critical mass. Communities lack cohesion when either critical mass or diversity are missing. Moreover, it seems that communities are sustainable and more adaptable to the future when they have this combination. Then they don't have to rely upon a growth mentality to define themselves as a community.

So much of the self-perception of the West has relied on growth and expansion. Thomas Jefferson purchased the Louisiana Purchase, partly because he cannily understood the international geopolitics of the time that created the possibility of purchase. He acted quickly and then politicized the situation to the point that Louisiana became a deal that no one in nascent America could refuse. But it wasn't just the addition of raw land and resource that motivated Jefferson and the generally broad congressional constituency to make the leap and buy the land. Jefferson's notion of the yeoman farmer—his inherent goodness, and his beneficial effect on democracy if he were allowed to pursue his natural inclination to build and grow—and James Madison's belief that land was needed as a safety valve to relieve the pressure of population in big cities that might lead to uncontrolled antagonism due to physical concentration, easily aligned themselves into an argument for the purchase of Louisiana. Ultimately, both their arguments and visions were grounded in the mechanistic vision that the West would be the primordial, continuing factory for growth and development, either providing raw resources or population stress reduction, and ultimately the eternal flame for democracy. Growth, expansion, and the West became synonymous. That legacy now has become the burden of the West.

The immediate future will surely test the presence of critical mass and diversity in Baker. The community has notoriously avoided master planning and zoning. It never seemed especially important, as growth was always slow and minimal. Now, faced with expansion because of the new water and sewer system, there is more a sense of community urgency. The willingness to grapple with the issue, in spite of a deep-seated, historical reluctance to do so, seems to be a mark of community health, a sign of a functional community. How is that possible?

First, Baker has a critical mass of people to make the community functional. While the town itself has only about 50 people, there are another 200 in the "municipal," voting district area who are perceived as being part of the town and community. It's important to look at that number qualitatively. Two hundred fifty people might be too many or not enough under different circumstances.

For instance, it's important for a community to have a visible link with its past as a way of generating critical mass. That could be present in monuments or historical buildings like the old Baker School. Usually, though, families provide a community's most effective umbilical cord to its history, and that's the case with Baker.

Very often in the West Desert, families have been associated with the land. In the first days of settlement in the 1800s, one could refer to a spread as the Baker spread or the Gonder Ranch or the Dearden place. On the open range, branding carried the family imprimatur onto wherever the cattle or sheep might wander. Later, when barbed wire was introduced and the BLM institutionalized grazing allotments, the ground and the family name became indelible. The old families and their ranches were locked into place, as long as the family held onto the title, or onto itself.

Ranch families themselves became more attached to the land when that land beneath their feet began sheltering the bones of ancestors. It's one thing to have your antecedents' graves somewhere in some ancient graveyard in New England that is now overgrown with underbrush, lost and forgotten to anything but time. It's another to have a daily reminder of your family's roots when you arise, and the first thing you see is the family graveyard etched onto the top of a knoll 100 yards away.

It's even more important to have that history imbedded in people who walk along the streets, who people can see and talk to. In Baker, the Gonders, the Eldridges, and the Bakers provide that symbol of origination and continuity through time. It's as if critical mass for a community follows the quantum notion that past, present, and future are more than intertwined. They are the same relative concept, existing coincidentally and seamlessly.

Bill Rountree talked about the generational interplay in Baker and how townsfolk respect and cultivate generational differences. All age groups are expected to be a functioning part of the community. Old people are treated with the same respect that one would offer to a newcomer or child. Eighty-something Virginia Eldridge tells the story of an incident with a child from the outside who brought with her some of her community's dysfunctional attitudes regarding the aged.

"I was over here in the post office and one day I was walking home and there was this little girl, you know, probably nine or ten. She'd come in from hinter out. The kids were all playing on the store porch. When I started to come over, they all started, 'Hi. How are you Virginia?'

"'How are you kids?' I said. Then I said [to the newcomer], 'How are you? What's your name?'

"And she got smart. She said something about, 'Old woman. None of your business.'

"Well, I never had to do a thing about it. All the other children jumped onto her. 'That is no old woman. That is Virginia and you don't talk to her that way.' Boy, I'll tell you, she got it from her peers right now. And that's the type of children we have, and of course, they've got to have pretty good parents or they don't come out with that kind of kids."

Critical mass also means that people choose to live in the community. Most people live in Baker by choice, not because they have to. In fact, people often must sacrifice to live in the West Desert. Bill Rountree runs a motel seven months a year, hustles occasional backhoe jobs, and does welding for both love and money. None make him rich.

When a person chooses to live in a community like Rountree, he is necessarily more bound to it. Sacrificing to live in that community creates a kind of spiritual bond that is stronger than a material link. In giving self to the community, a person receives acceptance and the community adds to its critical mass.

Critical mass also means a group of people with a diverse set of experiences. Those experiences might be education, as in the case of many of the people of the School of the Natural Order, or ranchers who graduated from college, like Dean Baker and Owen Gonder, emphasizing range science or business management from a consumptive perspective, or federal land managers like Great Basin National Park superintendent Becky Mills, whose graduate degree is in social welfare. Denys Baker majored in history at the University of Utah. JoAnne Garrett focused on the arts at Berkley.

Or those experiences might be life experiences, like Bill Rountree's struggle to find a home after the anomie he faced in Los Angeles and the mayhem he witnessed in Vietnam. Home Farm's Rex Harvey, a contractor, and John Shepherd, a carpenter, know construction and can tell when a contractor is purposely cutting corners, like in the construction of the new Baker School. From behind her bar, Denys Baker has listened to the stories of the denizens of the asphalt, either motorists just passing through, migrant Mexican laborers staying a bit longer, or Eskdale women foraying out of the community into the larger world. She sees how pieces fit together in the community. JoAnne Garrett's experiences with activism, community organization, and ties to movers and shakers in other areas become a community resource and help build and sustain the critical mass. Critical mass, however, means not just having those community resources. It means the community recognizing and respecting those talents and conscientiously and purposely incorporating them into the community fabric whenever possible and appropriate. It means those individuals offering their expertise to the community.

A community must be willing to accept diversity into its critical mass too. There have to be differences in the stock of the community. It's almost like a cultural gene pool. For a community to be healthy and adaptable, like a species it needs raw genetic material that provides the building blocks and capacity for resiliency when faced with random change; and change is inevitable in the life of any community, even in small communities the size of those in the West Desert. Equally important, that cultural gene pool needs constant reinvigoration of new genes coming in from the outside. Otherwise, like a species it runs the risk of becoming inbred and culturally sick. Most importantly, a community must protect the smallest, rarest portions of its cultural gene pool. The majority needs the minority more than vice versa. Socially accepted diversity, then, means a community welcoming new people with their probable new outlooks and different ways of thinking and looking at problems and opportunities.

Probably, no other subgroup in Baker has contributed to bringing in new people and new cultural genes more than the School of the Natural Order. Moreover, the very essence of being a student, the mental set of inquiry and embracing of change, the seeking out of new ideas and experiences, the processing and linking of those ideas and experiences, and the sheer delight in the new and the possible, makes folks at the School of the Natural Order a reservoir of diversity and potential change for Baker.

Eskdale mirrors the successful functioning of Baker in the same ways. There is a critical mass of people and a kind of socially accepted diversity in spite of the regime and authoritarian nature of a patriarchal united order.

The 20 families now living at Eskdale provide most of the talents that the community needs to exist, including teaching. There are those in the community like John Conrad, the veterinarian, and Dean Hayward, the accountant, who also can generate enough cash flow to pay the living wages of those, like the teachers, whose labors for the community don't bring in money. Equally important, residents' skills run the gamut from hands-on expertise like Bruce Weight's mechanical and organizational genius, John Hansen's farming prowess, Mitch Cole's printing and machining background, and Eunice Cole's dairy management to largely intellectual gifts like Kathleen Hayward's adeptness at literature and Joe Beeson's former professional work as a nuclear physicist at Idaho National Engineering Laboratory. Of course, everyone is an accomplished musician. Moreover, everyone is encouraged to stretch himself or herself. Mitch Cole prepares a lesson for sabbath school based on his reading of the Bible, even though a facility with words and oral delivery might not be his best skills. There is the understanding that individual development, besides providing a more fulfilled life for the person, also adds to the energy of the critical mass of community.

Eskdale practices the same sort of generational respect as Baker as well. But there is a difference. At Eskdale families are more a visual unit of social construction. Ranch families often are separated by their lands. The next ranching family might live five miles down the dusty dirt road. At Eskdale families live together and work the land together.

Every person at Eskdale is given a responsibility in the maintenance of the community, including the children and the aged. The youngest children take recess from school to come over to the dining hall to lay out the silverware and tableware for meals. The elderly assume those community responsbilities that fit their interests and physical abilities, although once a person has reached a certain senior age, and after decades of supporting the community, the community feels that that person has earned the right to pick and choose what he or she wants to do, if anything. That's Eskdale's notion of "retirement." Yet even the elderly choose to help out, because serving the community and each other is the foundation of the society and it is learned, socially ingrained, and supported by all. The assignment and rotation of chores at Eskdale, people self-selecting themselves for responsibility, provide the cement for community.

There is respect for diversity at Eskdale too. Doug Childs relates the story of one of his boys, who is a kind of prodigal son, who left the church and now lives in Las Vegas making custom furniture. Doug still loves him deeply and respects his decision, knowing that "he still is a good person."

The community holds a warm spot for those who choose to leave. The community understands that the individual should be allowed to explore his or her own gifts, and that is why Eskdale puts so much stress on education in everyone's life. The education at the Shiloah Valley School is provided within a fundamental Christian framework. Nevertheless, there is the unwritten understanding that education will naturally lead to cultural diversity as people experience new ideas. The community knows that most residents will leave Eskdale at some time to follow other opportunities. The group trusts they will carry the community with them, because they share a faith in themselves and each other. Should people want to return, they are welcomed, space permitting, because Eskdale has decided to accept the other. It believes cultivated experiences enrich the community by bringing in new cultural genes that help the community grow.

There is a dichotomy added to the concepts of critical mass and socially accepted diversity—the degree of homogeneity. Any community will be made up of subgroups, and there needs to be enough of them to provide cultural resource. Yet, those subgroups need to be able to talk to one another and have a feeling that each shares the others' goals and values—a critical mass of homogeneity. Too much heterogeneity can prevent that from happening, just as too much homogeneity and a lack of diversity can.

In southern Snake Valley, the different communities—ranching, hospitality, national park, School of the Natural Order, Eskdale—are each large enough to claim a stake in the society. Moreover, by claiming and maintaining a stake, they are perceived by the others as players in the community that have to be recognized and accommodated. With enough communities of functioning size, there seems to be more interplay and mutual respect. This leads to community cohesion.

So, a community needs to be large enough, diverse enough, and have a shared, inclusive history to establish lines of communication and to foster community enfranchisement. In urban communities that can be carried to extremes, with too many communities, too much diversity, and separate, exclusive histories, which leads to more associationism and special interest mentalities.

Community as a Response to Communication Systems

While settlement in the West originally might have been caused by proximity to water or natural resources, or a few years later by attachment to transportation routes, communication systems are more important to the maintenance of community after the initial settlement period. Communication systems are what make the atomistic West a community of interests. Sometimes those systems are nothing more than physical proximity and interpersonal interaction. Other times, they are technologically based.

The mail always has had a hallowed place in the hearts of westerners. Mail service quickly followed settlement, whether it was the grand year of the Pony Express in 1860, to consecrate the transcontinental breadth of the nation, or the more prosaic hauling of mail by stagecoach or train shortly thereafter.

There was a mystique and childlike faith in the nation's mail service in the pioneer period of the American West. When Wayne Gonder's Grandfather Baker, later to be patriarch of Baker, Nevada, decided to emigrate west, he sold the family's hogs in the Midwest. He worried about carrying all the money and the family's future on his person, so he blithely sent the money to himself in care of the "Post Office, Alta, Utah." He anticipated arriving there some months in the future with his mules to haul ore. But he gave no thought to the possibility that the U.S. Post Office in a booming mining town only a few years old might be unreliable and that his family fortune would get waylaid. His blind optimism was rewarded, as the money was awaiting him when he arrived.

Mail service in the 1800s was as regular as Mother Nature and banditry would allow. People excused irregularities as the price of living on the edge of the frontier. So with that West long tamed and even the West Desert laced with graded roads, albeit mostly dirt, one would expect the U.S. Postal Service to be regular. It is regular, but it only comes two days a week by Star Route mail carrier. Ironically, the service that used to bring letters, foodstuffs, or mail order brides has been supplanted by a private mail delivery service. UPS is a more fundamental part of the lives of residents of the West Desert now. It runs a daily schedule. If a person needs a particular part to repair a piece of farm machinery, if it's stocked in Salt Lake or Delta, it can be in the mailbox the following day. The U.S. Postal Service plays backup, although it still is the sole provider of missives that warm the heart or chill the soul.

Sometimes the U.S. Postal Service will deliver the mail to a mailbox by the side of the road, like in northern Snake Valley, where there is no U.S. Post Office. When there is a small post office in a community, like Baker, or when the post office is part of another business, like the Pony Express Stop in Ibapah, residents must go to the post office to pick up their mail.

Don Conway, former postmaster in Ibapah, said, "Having the post office in a rural community like this is kind of like having a milk cow. You can't leave home. Mail comes in Tuesdays and Fridays and you have to be there to sort it and put it out. Then, your post office has to be open six days a week."

The telephone is a johnny-come-lately to West Desert communities in Utah. For most of the history of the area, there have been no phones. The first technology that linked the area with the outside world was the radio telephone. There was one at Ibapah at the Pony Express Stop and one at Eskdale. The reception was barely intelligible, went down during bad weather, and the unwritten understanding within the communities was that it was to be used for emergencies only.

Nevada Bell laid telephone lines to Baker, Nevada, earlier, but the connection didn't cross the state line. Garrison, Utah, only five miles from Baker, would wait almost 50 more years. Wayne Gonder in Garrison talks about the mechanics of using the telephones in the Baker store on the Baker Ranch as a child. "When we left here," Wayne said, "you'd never know whether or not the phone was useable. If it wasn't, you'd have to go clear to Ely." Ely is about 70 miles and close to two hours' drive from Garrison.

Over the past five years, the last few outpost ranches in Utah have gotten telephones—at least those who wanted them, and most hungrily awaited them—even though it means more cash outflow from meager monthly budgets. That would not be happening either if it were not for two forces: the federal government and a dogged entrepreneur, Art Brothers. The federal government probably was guilty of hubris, laying telephone lines into the area from Wendover before MX was a done deal. It felt that it would have no problem convincing the super-patriotic populace of the security and economic advantages of having MX in its backyard. Brothers had tried to get the Utah Public Service Commission to grant him the right to bring telephones to the Utah portion of the West Desert as early as 1964. But with opposition from Mountain Bell, who wanted the rights but really didn't want to do the work, he continually was turned down. When the federal government began constructing the telecommunication infrastructure for MX, that coincided with Mountain Bell's decision to relinquish its right to telephone service it finally determined would be unprofitable.

Once the first tendrils of telecommunication for MX had been partially laid, Art Brothers of Beehive Telephone saw an opportunity for connecting the rest of the northern West Desert, from Grouse Creek in northern Utah to Eskdale. He knew that there was a deep longing for telephones. In spite of a sparse, decentralized population, Brothers felt that a one-man operation like his would be able to bring telephone service to the West Desert.

He began stringing cable and communities started negotiations. At first, Brothers literally strung the cable on the most available supports, not wanting to take the time or spend the money to dig underground conduits. Instead, he looped the telephone cable on top of fence posts and barbed wire. Now most telephone cable is underground.

Gold Hill was one of the first stops, being only 35 miles due south of Wendover. Brothers told Gold Hill that he would bring telephones to them if he could get five people to sign up and pay the connection charges. In Gold Hill that meant the whole town had to agree. Joe Murphy really didn't want a telephone and had decided to decline. His neighbors began putting the emotional squeeze on him and he relented.

Murphy isn't convinced that the telephone has made much difference in his life. "We got by just as good without the telephone as we do with it. It makes no difference. I don't use it. I've just got it there in case someone wants to call me. Oh, your relations and stuff. And everybody worries about ya. That's the only reason I put one in. I didn't want one."

One the other hand, Molly Gonder in Garrison cherishes her telephone. While her husband Wayne believes that the arrival of highline power was more important to the community than telephones, Molly isn't so sure. At first, there were 17 on one party line in Garrison. The telephone was something you used only for business or medical emergencies. It wasn't for idle chatter. It was seen as a shared community resource. Neighbors' needs were taken into consideration. Few people abused it. Telephone service was so long in coming that they recognized its importance and treated it like something of physical value, like a mineral or stand of old growth that shouldn't be squandered. Now, everyone in Garrison has a private line, and Molly Gonder likes to chat.

The community of Eskdale has its own telephone exchange, supported by a phalanx of heavy duty batteries in case the power ever should go out. Whether conscious or not, Eskdale's decision to go high tech with its telephone system coincides with its parallel decision of the past 20 years to break out of its isolation and extend itself and its good works to the rest of the world.

The world of the information superhighway is starting to reshape communities of the West

Desert. Ron Webber ranches in Ibapah most of his time yet maintains his structural engineering business by telecommuting. Mike Schneider can afford to leave New York City three months a year because he can bring his computer and his writing with him to Home Farm.

Dean Hayward, an accountant and the business manager of Eskdale, services national accounts from Eskdale. While some of his clients are concerned that living in a desert outpost will make him inaccessible to their problems when they arise, Hayward points out that they assume that they could immediately have his time if he still maintained his office in Salt Lake City. They had to make an appointment then, and they'd still have to. Hayward assures them that modem and fax ensures his proximity. A bigger challenge for him is maintaining an appropriate fee schedule. He reports that there is the tendency on the part of some potential clients to argue that he doesn't warrant the going rate for an accountant handling national accounts because he lives in the desert, where there's nothing to spend one's money on, and that since he lives in a united order community, which is socialistic, he doesn't need money anyway.

Ed Alder foresees a time when northern Snake Valley will be a community of telecommuters. "I see in a hundred years a lot more people living here. With computers, people can do what they had to run to town to do for business. Now, you can do it at home. I see people saying, 'I've got to get out of Salt Lake. I've got to get out of the gangs that are running around shooting at doors.'"

Of course, Alder's West Desert School is critically tied to new technology and communication systems. That's partly why the Tintic School District spends much more per pupil, $6,800, to educate kids at the West Desert School than the approximately $3,100 that is spent in an urban school district.

Communication systems are more than telecommunication or digital technology. Roads fill that role, and they probably have been more fundamental in the creation and maintenance of communities in the West Desert than any other technology. Because West Desert communities increasingly are tied to the economies and the extended families of the Wasatch Front, the ability to get back and forth is of increasing importance. Yet the mostly dirt roads are a testament to the reality that towns in the West Desert are not that far away from the old frontier. If a road is paved, it usually hasn't been paved for long. The old Lincoln Highway, which U.S. 6/50 supplanted, was a dirt road. The road to Garrison from U.S. 6/50 has been hardtop only since 1982. So, while county road crews periodically scrape the dirt and gravel roads, the absence of wagon wheel ruts is about the only difference in West Desert roads from 100 years ago; that and the fact that it is now cars and trucks that course those wider, but still dusty, roads rather than buckboards.

In fact, itinerant county road crews are an important part of the social infrastructure of the West Desert. They are an actual subgroup in the culture. Annette Garland relates how the town of Callao looks forward to the road crews coming out to stay periodically, as they work on the local roads every four months. Because of the distance from their home base, county road crews stay in the community for a week, living in the old school. But it's not the commercial trade with the road crews that is important for the community. After all, there are no businesses in Callao to claim some of the workers' disposable income. Rather, the community thrives on the social intercourse. The crews bring new stories and new viewpoints.

Roads became important communication systems in the West Desert partly because telephones came to the region so late. Ironically, roads also forced face-to-face communication, a community-reinforcing interaction that is lost in telephone conversations or e-mail. Ed Alder talks about the days before telephones in northern Snake Valley when the roads provided the channel of communication.

"Without the phones and mail twice a week, when you met somebody [on the road], it was kind of like you dumped. You had all these things stored up. You did all your coordinating with them in the middle of the road. For a week. Because you weren't going to see them again. You made all the alternative plans if things didn't work out before you left, because you could never go back and say, 'Oh, hey, I forgot.' You were a lot more organized that way.

"Today," Alder continued, "you say hello, visit and leave, because you know if you forget something, you're going to get a phone. Maybe we're a more shallow organization."

For as much as he travels, Ed would love to see paved roads come to the West Desert, but he doubts that it will happen in his lifetime because the roads now are county roads, and counties simply don't have that kind of money. He says that the funding would likely have to come from the state. Ironically, if a paved road comes to northern Snake Valley, Alder thinks it likely will be due to the Deep Creek Mountains becoming a BLM wilderness area. Urban visitors might create the demand for that kind of access.

Sometimes, communities try to maintain themselves in a restrictive manner through their roads. It's a kind of "Katie, bar the door" mentality. That was the case with the spur to Ibapah branching off U.S. 93, the Ely-Wendover highway. Originally, Anglos in Deep Creek Valley opposed a hardtop road leading to their town in order to protect their community. Instead, it was the Gosiute Indians who were more responsible for the road being paved. As Don Conway, former owner of the Pony Express Stop in Ibapah, related, "The paved road started on the reservation and came north, instead of going the other way. You'd think it would come from U.S. 93 out here. But the only reason that road is paved is because of the Indians. The area people out here didn't want it paved because it brought in a lot more people and traffic. Then it brought in electricity and telephones. Now, everbody in the valley almost has satellite dishes. The oldtimers in the valley really don't like that. They still oppose it."

If hardtop roads are a long time coming, will airplanes serve instead? They already are present in the West Desert. Dean Hayward is considering Eskdale buying an airplane for the community to take care of any emergencies. Since there is an airstrip in back of the compound, most of the expense would be in the cost of the plane. Ranchers in Callao and Baker already use them to get in and out of the West Desert quickly. Usually, they purchase them to facilitate business rather than recreation, but they also are available for the communities during an emergency. As airplanes provide quick physical access to other communities, they become a communication system for the West Desert.

It might be stretching it to call highline power a communication system, but no development has done more to change the lives of people in the West Desert than the arrival of electricity. In the sense that electrical power brought convenience and saved time, that new time became available for more social interaction.

Highline power was a long time coming. While the Rural Electrification Administration was formed by Roosevelt during the Great Depression, wiring of rural America didn't happen overnight. Snake Valley waited until 1978 for highline power. Before that, residents used diesel generators to provide minimum power for pumping water for culinary purposes and some refrigeration. Irrigation from wells, however, where the water level is 200 feet below the surface, wasn't possible until more electrical power came to the valley.

When Virginia Eldridge, now in her 80s, was a child, her family used a washing board. Then, they obtained two crank washers. Wash day for the family would take most of the morning. Every kid had to run a machine. "One went this way and one went that way," Eldridge said. "I tell you, with a big family, wash day was something else again. You carried the gol damn water and heated it on a cookstove with wood. In summer, you were dying with the heat. In winter time, it wasn't very nice out there."

As much as she values her telephone, Virginia still thinks electrical power is the most important utility to come to southern Snake Valley. "I've spent too many damn years," Virginia said, "trying to crank an old Maytag washer, and before that, you had one of these that you had to push with your arm. I tell ya, they wear you out. So, that power. Oh boy. I thought I'd never live to the day when I could shove something into the wall and it'd work."

Right now, power from the Western Power Administration, which supplies Mt. Wheeler Power and Snake Valley, is a little cheaper than private generators, as is most electricity from government reclamation projects. That price likely will be going up, however, when the WPA begins decreasing water surges out of Glen Canyon Dam in order to protect riparian habitat.

Building a community is an itch that humans have to scratch. Long ago, our species learned that we could do things together that none of us could do alone. Even those "back to basics" folks, those who try to learn to do with less and create as much as they can for themselves, those types of people who sometimes wind up in the West Desert, still seek the counsel and support of like-minded people. There are no more hermits in the West Desert than in Reno, Las Vegas, or Salt Lake City.

Sharing resources and labor was one reason why communities formed in the West Desert. Then, there was another factor. Faced with the overwhelming power and presence of the western frontier, humans built communities partly as a defense. Roads brought commerce, yet they also facilitated communication and respite from isolation. Mails brought commercial information and stages brought packages, but they also brought ideas and human interaction. Each new addition to the infrastructure of community took away some of the power of the frontier over the lives of its transgressors. There was counterpoised power not only in numbers, but in the aggregate of interactions between people who made up those numbers.

As the frontier ebbed, community grew. There was a herky-jerky equilibrium that linked the two. One could grow or take back only at the expense of the other. While, of course, the frontier did not need communities for definition, communities did need a frontier to define what they were. A community offered an antidote to the numbing loneliness of the frontier. A community meant that one need not face the white depth of isolation. For a community to survive, it needed to meet the frontier head on and weigh against it with all the strength of humans working against a common foe.

Although its communities are exceedingly small and not far removed from the old frontier in absolute numbers or density, the West Desert no longer is a real frontier. Communities have leavened it, although the myth of the frontier still is a sacred icon for those communities. It's become part of the self-perception of people, especially older residents. The frontier is gone but not forgotten. Its memory sculpts character.

If someone is isolated, it is usually by design. Moreover, it is a state that must be assiduously tended to. Otherwise, community tends to spread inexorably. Now the West Desert is inextricably linked to everyone and everyplace else. No stitch of millenial technology is missing from the fabric of the West Desert. Radio predated television in the West Desert, and not just because it has been around longer. Radios could work on batteries, while televisions really needed that highline power. Now each are omnipresent, with radio probably having a larger audience due to historical use patterns, lack of many TV channels, and perhaps, due to more discriminating tastes. Small food stores, a barber shop, or any of the few commercial places where people congregate are offering videos for the growing numbers of VCRs. Satellite dishes begin to dot the sparse landscape, like mushrooms only blooming once a millenium, when the conditions are just right.

The West Desert is a cluster of communities now, and while they strive to retain some of what they perceive to be their primordial virtue, the imprint of the frontier, it is difficult for them. The same construction that carved them out of the wilderness cannot be turned off. Community maintenance means recognizing that communities change. A community is a process, and once created and set in motion, it is dynamic. It cannot be created and then crystallized. Once hardened by amber, it cannot function.

3

Extensions of Community

Like every other place where two or more groups take up residence, the West Desert is made up of communit*ies*. There is a plurality of different subgroups, some of which integrate better than others. Degree of interaction between communities, however, is not the same thing as extension of community. Communities can interact on the most basic of levels, perhaps in the utility exchange of goods and services, but still not extend themselves to each other. The former situation is a kind of reciprocal exchange of value; the latter is an offering of community self. One is pragmatic, the other altruistic. In between is the line that separates the individual from community or communities from each other.

Once created by the concerted effort of its members, a community tends to undergo a process of measurement and evaluation of the area outside the community. It classifies the parts of the community and its range. What is outside the range becomes the boundary of another community. Community perceptions grow and are nurtured by this process of comparison. Community, then, is a form of centering, a mix of ethno- and geocentrism. Whether or not a community chooses to extend itself depends upon how rigid the ethno- and geocentrism become.

Ethnocentrism first has an effect on a community's perception of itself. At some point a community begins to look at its history with selective perception, usually because it is more gratifying to see itself in a certain light, to remember some things and choose to forget others. History tends to become myth. Looking at it another way, myth is history drawn by a caricaturist. The prominent features are exaggerated and complexity is reduced. Nevertheless, myth is a more powerful force for organizing the community. It becomes the active agent in the process of culturization of new members to that community.

As a person becomes interweaved into the fabric of the community, that community's ethnocentrism then begins to shape the person's self-definition and self-perception. In seeking acceptance, a person often must assume the *a priori* shared perceptions that the community has of itself and that it expects of its members. To the degree that a person shares something in common with another member of the community, that person is a part of the community. When a person declares himself or herself as being in opposition to the major community and shares nothing in common with the community, even with a recognized minority subgroup, then that person is placed outside the geometry of the community.

Once tied to a community through acceptance and drawing strength from that alliance, an individual adopts the values of that community. The ethnocentrism of the community can then become an ethnocentrism of morality. The practices of maintaining the community, like annual pioneer reunions, are consecrated as ritual. The community becomes sacrosanct, as individuals reify the legitimacy of the community. Moreover, the community and its accepted members can become infused with "rightness." This is the right way to live, and this community is the physical manifestation of the right way to live. Myth becomes a moral force. No longer is the community just a pragmatic alliance. It tends to become a symbol of the inherent goodness of the members. What is not like the community, what is outside the community can be perceived as suspect, as alien and fallen from the grace that is shared by the declared community. It can become "them" versus "us," and we represent what is good and fundamental, because our community is grounded. Such self-perceptions make the extension of community difficult.

Last, there is the obvious geocentrism of place, the origin of all things in the West Desert. People put down roots in a community that rests upon dirt, that is surrounded and defined by mountains that allow entrance and egress only through passes that are discovered through them and become known to the people in the community. Both land and people are bounded by physical perimeters. A single valley or trickle of stream coursing from the mountains becomes the locus of community. The land provides the substance and reason for living upon it, or it takes it away with drought and erosion.

People in a community share a common ground. For people of the West Desert, land is the reason they are there, either historically through family settlement or because of individual attraction to it. Land is the one thing that they have in common, both pragmatically and emotionally. In that sense it is the first cause of both individual and community. It proscribes definition and boundaries. Moreover, it is that common ground that Daniel Kemmis says in *Community and the Politics of Place* must be the eventual political and economic wellspring of western communities. It is both their source of will as well as their reservoir of confidence that permits them to extend themselves to others.

There was a poster on a wall in the community kitchen of the Fraternity of Preparation at Vance Spring that talked about "agape love." Agape love is selfless love. It is the love of giving to another for the pure sake of the act, not for any expectation of in-kind giving. Agape love means extending oneself wholly and without favor or accounting.

Being a united order community, the fraternity is built upon a foundation of agape love, with a slight twist. Instead of giving directly to another, the person selflessly gives to the community, which in turn selflessly gives to the person as need arises. But that extension to each other that the fraternity practices internally is difficult to effect outside the community due to ethnocentrism. Two things tend to prevent it. First, the fraternity seeks to be totally self-sufficient. That makes even the basic exchange of utility uncommon. So the relationships that could grow out of the commerce never get a chance to flower. Second, the fraternity's *raison d'etre* is grounded in an ironclad notion of popular sovereignty. The fraternity firmly believes that the U.S. Constitution and common law give members the first right of creating their own community that owes no allegiance to anyone or anything other than God. While the fraternity recognizes it must coexist with other communities and follow the criminal and civil laws of men that they have created in order to honor the Ten Commandments and protect the social fabric, it will not accept any entity as being greater or more powerful than its own sovereignty. All rights not specifically granted to the federal government by the Constitution are retained by the people. To the fraternity "people" means duly constituted communities.

This notion of sovereignty in the West often makes it difficult for communities to extend themselves. To do so could imply that a community is giving up some of its fundamental rights. The community fears that, once gone, those rights can't be retrieved. Then the community would have lost its fundamental strength. The Fraternity of Preparation isn't purposely cold to its neighbors nor is it hostile to them. When people wandered into the fraternity compound, in spite of its warning signs to keep moving and the eye-level barbed wire, they still were welcomed. As Talmage Weis said, "They are only strangers once."

While the fraternity didn't have much informal, gracious interaction with citizens of Beaver County, Utah, due to physical separation from the few towns and a drive to go it alone, the fraternity did want to be accepted by its neighbors. It honestly did want to get into court and be judged by a jury of its neighbors and peers. It would have liked the people of Beaver County to look at the Constitution and say "yea" or "nay" as to whether or not the fraternity has a fundamental right to build its own community ultimately answerable only to God's laws, as long as it does nothing wrong nor interferes with its neighbors' rights. The fraternity likely will seek that same kind of acceptance through the courts from its neighboring communities in Montana.

Of course, there is a problem in that stance. The fraternity wanted the people of Beaver County to accept them, but it denied the rights of that duly constituted community to question whether the lands were being used for religious purposes, and therefore exempt from taxation under federal code. The fraternity couldn't accept powers of oversight and assessment to Beaver County that the county claimed as its sovereign right. The fraternity wanted an extension of community, the protection of the social compact and sovereignty grounded in the Constitution, but it also wanted to be left alone and didn't want to have many dealings with the outside. Sovereignty rigidly applied, then, might help an individual community to coalesce and maintain itself, but it does set up obstacles to that community interacting in constructive ways with other communities.

Few other West Desert communities have to wrestle with that teleological concern. They don't have an ethnocentrism that makes it difficult to interact in the broadest and fullest sense. For most West Desert communities, it is easy to extend themselves, even though they may have different ideas as to who actually is part of the "official" community. For instance, Val Taylor, the deputy voting registrar in Baker, notes that "true" Bakerites are a bit persnickety about the size of the town. As registrar, Taylor gets data from the state taxation board indicating that there are 200 people living in the Baker area.

"Now the people who live in the township get very upset when I tell them about going to JP meetings and telling those people that I live in a town of two hundred," Taylor said. "They say, 'No you're not. You're from a town of only twenty or thirty.' They see their little geographical limit of Baker as being Baker. All the folks who live up the hill, and the park service people, they're not counted by the oldtimers. Yet when I go to a JP meeting in Las Vegas and tell them I'm from a town of two hundred, that's still a very tiny town to them."

All the people I interviewed report that they are deeply concerned with everyone in the community, and an attack on one, or a misfortune to befall one, is an attack or misfortune to which all will react. The southern Snake Valley community, to Taylor and others, is more than just Baker, Nevada. For instance, when there was a bad fire in Garrison, Utah, a short time ago, the Baker fire department went there to help. Local people raised money and collected clothes, toys, and games for the kids. Doug Childs reports that Eskdale initiated a drive in its community to come up with extra blankets and clothes for the stricken Garrison family. Ironically, too, the new fire station and county shop in Garrison, Utah, was built, in part, by an honor farm of felons from Nevada supervised by the Nevada Division of Forestry.

West Desert Extensions to the Wasatch Front

It's safe to say that no one in the West Desert has any love or respect for the cities. At least people wouldn't say that to your face, even if they do harbor a hidden thrill of visiting Sodom every once in a while. Fortunately, their communities have been far enough away from most urban centers in Utah and Nevada that they haven't been impacted by urban sprawl.

Baker, Nevada, is approximately 300 miles from Reno-Carson City, 240 miles from Las Vegas, and 200 miles from Salt Lake City. In spite of being Nevadans, however, many people in Baker frowned when I asked their opinions of Reno and Las Vegas. The gaming industry is seen as a tawdry business, one beneath those who make their living from the land. They'd rather keep that southern Nevada city at arm's length, although its growing-like-Topsy dynamic is making that more difficult, as Las Vegas is trying to claim all unused and unappropriated underground water rights in White Pine County. Few from Baker ever drive to Las Vegas or Reno if they're headed to "the city." When people in Baker and the rest of the West Desert think of the most immediate city, it is Salt Lake City and the Wasatch Front. While they don't extend themselves or their community to cities in Nevada, even the relatively close Ely, they do have tenuous ties to the Wasatch Front.

People of the West Desert have a love-hate relationship with the Wasatch Front. On the love side, communities that have sizeable numbers of Mormons, like Garrison, Callao, and Ibapah, are emotionally tied to Salt Lake City through their church. Also on the affective side, most people in the West Desert have relatives who live along the Wasatch Front. Joe and Virginia Eldridge periodically visit them. Annette Garland comes from Bountiful, a bedroom community of Salt Lake City. The polygamist prophet Owen Allred lives in Salt Lake County but his Associated United Brethren Church has several clusters of church members in the West Desert. Ed Alder considers himself just an extension of that part of his family that lives in Salt Lake City, many of whom lived in Snake Valley at one time.

People of the West Desert also have friends who live along the Wasatch Front, and they will occasionally visit them, although the overwhelming movement is friends from the Wasatch Front coming west to visit folks in the West Desert. George and Veronica Douglass used to live in the avenues of Salt Lake City, and they still visit friends in town. So does their son, Buck. Jay and Frances Banta at Fish Springs make periodic forays into Salt Lake City to stay with friends and savor the urban culture.

Bill and Kathy Rountree have a yearly ritual. During the depths of winter, when Bill's motel in Baker is closed for the season and Kathy's graphic design business slows down, the couple escapes to Salt Lake City for a weekend of movie binging. They'll watch seven movies in three days. Bill says that they "hole up and eat popcorn, mainly." He loves to stay at a hotel and let others serve him for a change.

Consumption of Wasatch Front media flows in the other direction. All the television and radio signals available in the West Desert come from the Wasatch Front, unless a family has a satellite dish. Usually, they are scratchy and not all channels come through. There are no daily newspapers. Only Baker gets a twice-weekly Ely newspaper. In this sense the Wasatch Front and the West Desert are bound to each other.

Ed Alder looks at the penetration of electronic communication systems in the West Desert and sees an indelible change in the community of northern Snake Valley. "We're more involved now with the Wasatch Front because of the phones and the road systems and the power. The media's been out here many times. I think we depend upon each other more than our fellows in Salt Lake, but I don't think it's as much as we used to, because we have all our other resources to draw from, just by the fact that we're a lot closer. The phones, the television, the radio. We're just around the mountain, basically, where we used to be around the world."

Right now, the hottest television station in Utah is the channel that carries Utah Jazz basketball games. KJZZ is frantically trying to build a network of transmitters to bring the signal to distant areas like the West Desert. The demand is coming from the ground up. An absorption with professional basketball might turn out to be the common interest that ultimately will link urban and rural areas, in spite of the regional politics of division.

Public television and radio, too, play a major role in the West Desert. Besides providing some of the stronger signals, they also deliver a more sophisticated level of information and entertainment that many West Desert residents prefer. Annie Douglass watches children's programs on PBS, while her grandparents George and Veronica will watch KUED at night, mostly for the news and "green" programs. Cecil Garland won't watch TV, although the Garlands do have one in the house so that they can view videos. KUER public radio is on in the background every night while Cecil reads. JoAnne Garrett in Baker is especially thankful for KUER. It brings her the news commentaries, classical music, and jazz that are her media staples.

The Wasatch Front is important for recreation. John Woodyard at Home Farm tries to make an occasional skiing foray to the Front, although writing poetry and doing odd jobs doesn't provide a lot of cash for lift tickets. Now he finds himself taking his mountain bike to Salt Lake City every once in a while to ride some mountain trails. Boys from Eskdale periodically drive to Salt Lake City to watch their heroes, the Utah Jazz. Two season tickets were given to Eskdale by a benefactor, and they have become the most valuable, shared property in the united order.

The Wasatch Front is critical to people of the West Desert for its shopping facilities. While he often can get most farm parts from Delta, Buck Douglass has to make periodic trips to Salt Lake to get parts that he needs or upon which he can apply his engineering genius to change them into something else that he really needs. Joe and Virginia Eldridge say that the Wasatch Front no longer just means Salt Lake City. They report that the new Wal-Mart and Kmart in Cedar City draw most of their shopping dollars. As Virginia said, "Now the Wasatch Front is no longer just up there by Salt Lake. It's clear down the country."

No one, though, likes to stay long in the Wasatch Front. To a person, no matter what subgroup they belong to in the West Desert, they say that they tire of the urban pace very quickly. No one can wait to return to the West Desert, and when they do return, to a person they also say they give thanks that they live where they do and not in Salt Lake City. The Wasatch Front is the alien, and it grows more grotesque, frightening, mystifying, and threatening to people of the West Desert all the time. If they could, people of the West Desert would build a wall between themselves and urban Utah. Since they can't, they draw a line in the sand instead.

George Douglass listens to the traffic reports on Salt Lake radio when he gets up in the morning. Each day it's the same. Congestion. "It's sheer madness," he said, and he vows that he'll never live in that city again, no matter what the reason. Cecil Garland says he gets a disturbing feeling every time he has to drive to Salt Lake City.

"Living in Callao," Garland said, "I'm one of the freest people left in the United States. There are more laws here concerning what we do with cattle than there are what we do with people. And so, every mile that I travel toward Salt Lake, I have the feeling that I'm giving up correspondingly that much freedom. And when I get right in Salt Lake, it isn't correspondingly. It's exponential.

"It's simply too bad that people don't realize that with congestion comes regimentation and loss of freedom," Garland continued. "If they could ever realize that, they'd take all the past governors they've had here, except for the possible exception of Scott Matheson, and lynch 'em. Because these governors swim a river of fresh cow shit every morning to bring in a new business and a new group of people to the state of Utah, which turns around and exacerbates the whole spectrum of problems—more flush toilets, more dirty automobiles, more school systems, more crime, more drugs, more et cetera, more et cetera. And yet we seem absolutely and totally incapable of managing our affairs except in terms of a burgeoning human population, with all the corresponding problems that occur. We don't know how to deal with it. We cannot deal with it."

Ed Alder is less alarmed as he reflects on his own world in Trout Creek. He notices a slight change. Life in the West Desert is becoming faster and more like the Wasatch Front. "We get caught up in the gas-and-groceries run like everyone else," Alder said.

When asked whether they think it's possible to transplant small town values into urban Utah, Cecil and Annette Garland grow sad. "The tragedy is that we . . . ," and then Cecil switched to, "*You* aren't being reinvigorated by the intrinsic values of the countryside. Just the reverse is taking place."

Annette then said, "Yeah, we're becoming contaminated."

People live in the West Desert by choice. The Wasatch Front might be a lure to some, but it's a necessay evil to many more. Home and community are west of the Wasatch Front.

4

Threats to Community

The West Desert is not Eden. Urban Utahns and Nevadans who have had the last mote of the Old West leave them drive along Interstate 80 and look across the desolate stretches of basin and range topography and probably perceive it as the closest thing to hell on Earth. Nor is the West Desert a perfectly functioning community. It is not like a watch that a distant supreme being constructed to run effortlessly and continuously, never needing intervention. Because the West Desert is composed of human beings, because it does not lie inside a bell jar, it is in flux, and change necessarily means dislocation.

There are threats to community in the West Desert. Some of those threats are internal, and others are forces working from outside the West Desert. Westerners, as Richard White notes in *It's Your Misfortune and None of My Own: A New History of the American West*, can see themselves as victims. They place the epicenter of their travails and pain outside their communities, and therefore, outside their control. Last century, they saw themselves as the powerless pawns of eastern bankers, industrialists, and railroad barons. Now the antagonist most likely will be pictured as "urban interests," "environmentalists," or "government bureaucrats." That's an unfortunate mental set because often the real problems lie inside communities, and by refusing to look within, communities in the West Desert deprive themselves of the ability to control their own lives and destinies.

One of the internal threats to community in the West Desert, already alluded to, is centered in the dynamics of ranching. Simply put, ranching families tend to outgrow their land and therefore their operations. Education complicates the threat. Because ranchers know that their ranches have to be run like businesses in order to survive, they encourage their children to go to college. When they return, the ranching enterprise is invigorated, and the perspective of the community is broadened, but that's only if they return. Education can lead people in new, unforseen directions.

When families leave, either due to seeking a nearby high school or breaking up of the ranch, that creates dislocation in communities. The established social order must be reconstituted, either by doing with fewer community resources or by adapting to new families coming onto the land to build another ranch and family dream. When the size of the communities are so small, as are so many in the West Desert, the effects of that dislocation and realignment are necessarily more pronounced.

JoAnne Garrett talks about the "embattled" personality of westerners and refers to the damaged psyches of those whose extractive industry practices harm the land. As ranchers and miners have had to battle mounting environmental forces that focus attention on those practices, some of their vulnerabilities have become apparent. One of them is "the way grandpappy used to do it" syndrome. While some accept change graciously and realistically, others have not, preferring to draw lines in the sand, as if refighting a range war from the distant past. Those embattled resource extractors refuse to compromise. To do so would be an affront to the legacy of "grandpappy," who supposedly fought so hard for the rights, and privileges, of ranchers and miners. Any less militancy and grandpappy would look at his offspring as weak.

Ranchers and miners were the first Anglos on the West Desert. Correspondingly, institutions have evolved to protect their "first in line" position. Prior appropriation of water rights is just one example. They want those privileges locked in place, sometimes monumentalizing themselves as original families as a rationale for warranting them. Some extractive users of the land refuse to acknowledge the mistakes of the past or realistically accept that the dynamics of the New West have changed, that other users of the land demand, and deserve, to be equal partners at the negotiating table. Others like Dave Eldridge search for common ground, while arguing for fair rights.

But the old ways die hard, as Jay Banta says. George Douglass adds that ranchers have been born into a legacy and they refuse to change. In that refusal to change, there is an internal threat to community in the West Desert because ultimately power is spreading out, along with the West.

Ranchers and miners don't want more regulation, but they also have not been good at policing themselves. Miners have a history of leaving their rusty refuse cluttering the ground when common sense says they should have cleaned up after themselves, frustrating prospectors like Jack Shaffer. Some ranchers turn a blind eye when they see another rancher damaging the resource with callous disregard—for instance, running more cattle on the range than his AUM permit allows. They are reluctant to get involved for several reasons. First, ranchers often have to strike delicate balances between themselves, for instance, allowing one to move cattle across another's land, due to the checkerboard nature of land ownership in the West. Second,

ranchers and miners are a historical vestige of what could be called the tyranny of rugged individualism. While the initial period of eking out an existence from the frontier warranted tough-minded people, that narrow focus on self-interest and the coronation of individual rights is a legacy of Jeffersonianism that is ill-suited for community building in the 21st century.

The West always has been plagued by its legacy of atomism. In the drive to settle the frontier, the first impulse, of course, had to be self-sufficiency. The individual and nuclear family had to sustain themselves before community formed. But self-sufficiency is a barrier to interdependence. As rugged individualism becomes mythologized, as self-sufficiency becomes righteous and insular, community becomes threatened.

Sometimes, people withdraw into themselves. That isn't as critical to the overall needs of community as whole groups seceding from the social contract, but often the walling off by an individual can have broad community effects. Take the controversy of the Callao School. When there were enough younger children in Callao to reopen the grade school in 1994, rather than busing them to West Desert School, the community proposed that the old, one-room Callao School building be traded to the county and the school move into the larger, vacant Mormon wardhouse. Seemingly, all the local folks were behind the idea—except for one. Partly because he didn't like the rest of the community, partly because he had his own, personal designs on the old wardhouse, partly because he never really became part of the community, sending his kids away to school rather than having them go to the local school, he secretly put in a bid for the old wardhouse. Then he told the county that he'd withdraw his bid if they would promise to make a bid and use the old wardhouse for county road crews.

Ultimately, the community rallied and overcame the machinations of the rancher. Had he been successful in his socially disrupting plan, however, the community would have been at greater risk. Not only would residents have lost the opportunity to have a better school building for their children, they would have lost a sense of power over their ability to control their destiny as a community. Individual hegemony and self-interest would have been seen as preeminent. Communities, then, can become embattled and deformed when people place themselves outside the commonwealth. When the sizes of communities are small, the good or bad will of individual personalities takes on greater ramifications. When a community is small like Callao, those "mutual animosities" that Cecil Garland refers to are less diluted and, therefore, more poisonous.

Polygamy is becoming a divisive wedge in parts of the West Desert, partly because of engrained reactions to it. Some believe it's a pestilence. They argue women are treated as chattels and children are abused. Women are trapped into the system, pledged to older men when they still are in puberty. Young boys can grow up hating their fathers because his infidelity dishonors their mothers. Children cannot inherit property in a usual sense. It only comes through the father, the prophet, if there is enough to go around. Children support the prophet, usually through a united order, and can accrue their own wealth only if they start a new church with themselves as the center.

Another attitude toward polygamy is benign. This view is a libertarian concept that is grounded in the respect of privacy rights. If three consenting adults agree to the arrangement, then that ought to be their right. Virtue and good works aren't precluded in polygamous relationships. These are strong, close families. The only right that the state might have in controlling the practice would be to ensure that the children of any of those unions aren't abused, that they are not coerced into the practice, and that their basic rights to education and legal protection are maintained. Moreover, "abuse" is a fine line, one that the state ought to approach carefully, and in this view, much power would be granted to polygamous parents to raise their children as they see fit.

Of course, polygamy has been a force in Utah since territorial days. Then it was both a tenet of religion and a social structure. Daniel Gonder, the grandfather of Wayne Gonder and one of the first two men settling in the Garrison area, married one of two sisters from a polygamist family who had moved there from Fillmore. Gonder's partner, Bill Gregory, married the other sister. Then, as more men moved to Garrison to ranch and farm, they married daughters from that same polygamous family. Polygamy became a settling factor in Utah. By having large families and maximizing the birthing capacity of childbearing women on the frontier, polygamy allowed communities to grow faster than normal.

Polygamy can be a cash flow generator for the ranches and farms run by polygamous families because of government nutrition and welfare policies. Because they can't be legally married, "sister wives" sometimes can qualify for single-parent welfare payments. Although welfare fraud is illegal and sometimes investigated, counties are reluctant to plumb the social arrangements of people living together. Through the federal Women, Infants, and Children program, the more children a woman has, the larger her individual nutrition entitlement checks. One polygamous prophet once remarked to Talmage Weis that the government actually was helping them build their community with these payments, and he encouraged the fraternity to follow the same path. The fraternity has steadfastly refused to enter that kind of relationship with government, no matter how alluring. While new workfare rules and budget cutbacks are lessening the possibility of abuse, some people of the West Desert resent their taxes going to support a life-style they abhor.

While neither Ed Alder nor Annette Garland feel polygamy is a problem within northern Snake Valley schools, some families, both Mormon and Gentile, show concern. Poverty can be a breeding ground for dysfunction, and polygamous families can be exceedingly poor. Cecil Garland says the community at Pleasant Valley "lives in abject squalor." People hear stories of more misbehavior at the West Desert School and wonder if it has something to do with polygamy. Rumors fly that there is more drug and alcohol abuse, and they attribute those behavior problems to children from polygamous families. Regardless of whether the rumors are true, the perception is real, and that becomes a threat to community in the West Desert.

In spite of the internal threats to community in the West Desert, many West Desert denizens would characterize the threats to their community as coming from the outside. Part of that is due to the traditional "victimization" complex of westerners. Part of that characterization is due to the fact that communities always find it easier to define the other as scapegoat. It's more difficult to look at oneself and one's community of friends and peers as the source of weakness as well as strength.

Certainly, there is heightened tension between urban and rural interests in the West. To what degree that polarity is actual or contrived is a matter of argument, however. Too often, political power interests thrive on mistrust and division between people. Then the media can simplify arguments in the rush to publish, and fairness and objectivity in a report of a public issue can mean finding the two most strident voices on the issue, voices who are the furthest apart on the continuum, and allow them to define the issues and set the agendas. So groups like the "wise use" movement in the West, which wants to "reclaim" lands from the "foreign" government in Washington, or environmental groups that scream "Cow free!" have come to represent the two sides in the West Desert. It is in the groups' best self-interests to promote that public annointment. Actually, most residents of the West Desert probably lie somewhere in between these two extremes, people of the West Desert included.

For instance, most ranchers interviewed feel that the BLM grazing fee could be increased to between $3 and $4 per Animal Unit Month without doing much harm to their balanced operations. They just want guaranteed access to that public land for grazing. They also want to retain water rights and be credited for work they do on public land. So it would appear that an appropriate increase and compromise would be possible. Instead, the AUM fee in 1998 is $1.35, the minimum set by Congress, down from $1.97 in 1994, a period during which interest rates and oil prices, primary costs in raising cattle, actually fell. Yet the fee supposedly is based on real costs of raising beef balanced against current cattle prices. At the same time cattlemen lobbyists and elected senators and representatives from the Old West, mostly Republican, went on attack. In their partisan jousting with secretary of the interior Bruce Babbitt, and in the larger fight against a Democratic president for the votes of constituents, they argue that any change in the AUM would destroy the West. They stridently maintain that it's just one more example of the "foreign" national government misunderstanding the needs of the West and trying to take away its ability to control its own destiny. Ironically, they don't represent the level-headedness of their commodity-based constituents, but they do represent its old myths. Is the AUM a real fee, then, or a political fee?

Rural westerners do feel legitimately threatened by that new westerner in the cities, who used to be nothing more than a harmless buffoon that cowboys could make fun of in bars at night after the real work was done. Now, however, that city dweller seems to be taking an active interest in how things are run in the West Desert, and there is resentment and a fear that misunderstanding and misinformation, multiplied by greater urban numbers, will wrest power to control the destinies of people who feel they live closer to the land in the West Desert.

People of the West Desert resent the elitist attitude of some environmental groups, most headquartered in cities, with lobbying presences in Washington, D.C. They also feel baffled by what they perceive as environmentalist stances that imply human beings are aliens on the land. It appears like self-loathing. JoAnne Garrett relates a story that dramatizes the gap.

"I remember a hike up Wheeler Peak with a guy from the Reno Sierra Club who looked down from way up on top of Wheeler Peak at the few ranches in Spring Valley. There was a little oasis down there, and he was enjoying this rarified atmosphere on Wheeler and looked down and said, 'Eeww!'" and Garrett wrinkled her nose to mimic his disdain. "That kind of pureness is a little offensive, especially if you know the perfectly good people who sweat over that place and call the beauty of it. I always remember that moment as being part of that polarization that simply won't do."

Urban dwellers feel they too live in the West Desert. They aren't just a cancer on its outskirts.

They resent the characterization that they don't know enough about how the land has been used historically and should be used to make intelligent decisions about current uses of public land. To urban dwellers that looks like the old interests trying to protect their privileges when everyone else is having to change. Urban westerners understand that there is a New West in which they have a stake. This new consciousness with its new values might just be the last best "chance to create a society to match its scenery," as Wallace Stegner said in *The Sound of Mountain Water.* So urban people of the West Desert look warily at rural people of the West Desert and are caught between the desire to support their neighbors and to weed out those who refuse to recognize their antiquated or unfair special privileges.

Ultimately, the tension between rural and urban interests is based on a mutual feeling of accelerating change. Bill Rountree fears "thrust fault change," the kind of cataclysmic, often bureaucratic change that kicks the foundation out from under people. Whether living in a city or a rural area, people sense an anxious feeling of gross metamorphosis. There are people too who would seek to exploit those inherent fears toward change to further their personal goals of attaining power.

Certainly, people of the West Desert are aware of the signs. Something is in the wind, and it doesn't smell good. Before, they've been a kind of end-of-the-line, a place that people never really paid much attention to because of its isolation and perceived barrenness. Now, outside interests are beginning to notice the West Desert, and the locals are nervous about the giant waking up. Suddenly, control over change seems to lie in someone else's hands, in Washington, on the Wasatch Front, or in Las Vegas and Reno-Carson City. The giant is beginning to demand things, and his power is frightening. Suddenly, there are new alphabetic powers to be reckoned with. While it used to be just the BLM, FS, FWS, and REA, now it's SUWA (Southern Utah Wilderness Alliance) and EPA. While people of the West Desert eventually took effective control over the first agencies, they fear they won't be able to bend the newer organizations to their will. Moreover, the federal land management agencies

no longer seem to behave like trained animals. So change seems even more likely, and the rate of change could accelerate.

Bill Rountree regrets that Baker didn't apply pressure to help convert the telecommunication link from Ely to Reno from analog to digital when the opportunity arose. Perry Steadman, an AT&T design engineer who also lives in Baker, pressed the issue with Rountree on citizens of Baker. It was just too tough a sell. Rountree says it died because of a "lack of support and understanding in Baker." Bakerites had just recently moved to digital dialing, and that seemed good enough. Rountree thinks it's a dead issue because he doesn't see anyone adversely impacted by it. Everyone can do what they want to do. "We have, by and large, pretty good phone service," Rountree said, "and that's good enough. Nobody's trying to put in a branch of TRW where you really need that kind of thing."

Rountree and Steadman were looking toward the future, anticipating a time when Baker and other small West Desert communities might become the mecca of telecommuting entrepreneurs who choose to live in small hamlets while doing on-line business with the rest of the world. In that world you can't afford to allow your communications infrastructure to be limited in what it can handle for the future. While the time might not be ripe, Rountree and Steadman feel that Baker must be futuristic. But it's hard to persuade a community to change when its primary economy and mental set still is grounded in commodities and extractive use of the land.

Sometimes people of the West Desert identify the wrong institutions as the source of forced change. David Livermore, director of the Great Basin Field Office of the Nature Conservancy, says that he finds it ironic that some rural people lump the Nature Conservancy with all "radical environmental" groups when in fact there is as much pluralism within the environmental movement as there is in the West Desert. Livermore says he often hears ranchers and farmers complaining that it's groups like the Nature Conservancy and other land trusts that are closing family farms and ranches. Livermore responds by saying that the overwhelming causes of closure of family farms and conversion of land from extractive production is growth of the cities, converting farmland to suburbs, and equally important, global competition. Livermore adds that the goal of the Nature Conservancy is actually to keep land in production, by buying conservation easements and keeping small family farms and ranches economically viable so that they don't have to be sold to developers.

The primary competitive threat to ranching and farming is from overseas producers. Moreover, many of the large-scale mining companies now working in Nevada using heap leaching techniques to extract gold from old ore dumps or from lower yield properties are owned by foreign companies. Bruce Babbitt was forced to sell gold mining claims patented under the unchanged Mining Act of 1872 to American Barrick Resources of Canada for a little over $10,000. The gold reserves in those claims are estimated to be over $10 billion, and no royalties need be paid to U.S. citizens under that antiquated law, although some mining companies are now offering small royalties to avoid public relations disasters.

So the agents of competition and change often lie elsewhere for people of the West Desert. But those antagonists are hard to recognize. They don't have a presence like the Nature Conservancy or other environmental organizations. Often, they don't have a name. It's easier to beat on the straw man offered to you by enterprising politicians than it is to wrestle with the real cause of your problems and forced change.

To sustain their communities, people of the West Desert must somehow diversify their economies. Faced with global competition for their old, extraction-based commodities and tighter environmental restraints imposed by an increasingly urban West—and by themselves—people of the West Desert no longer can do things "the way grandpappy used to do it," even if they wish to. That inevitable result would be decay and death. There is a need for mining because we still need to make things. Ranching is important because we still need to eat and clothe our bodies, but it is likely to become more of that landed aristocracy that Ron Webber describes. Ranching has been and must remain an integral part of the community of the West Desert, if for no other reason than to retain the strength of that cultural gene pool.

Fortunately for the West Desert, there are other marketable qualities. There is tourism. Great Basin National Park will continue to draw more people once it is discovered, and the Deep Creek Mountains likely will be one of the most popular wilderness areas. There probaby will be some new tourist facilities built to take care of the destination visitors who would enjoy those bits of the West Desert.

But tourism in the West Desert is likely to be something different than industrial tourism, as the land of the West Desert doesn't lend itself to that kind of development. In this sense tourism won't be a great economic boon to the West Desert. The richest resource of the land of the West Desert is its solitude, something that can't be mined by industrial tourism developers. While some might try, there is a logical impossibility in that quest. Solitude is fragile and elusive and not found outside of the self. It is not something that one can go to on a three-day weekend and find packaged for ease and efficiency. Solitude is inimical to packaging, and gross tourism would destroy what it seeks to exploit in quick fashion, faster than the slowly eroding resources in the national parks. Solitude will continue to be something individuals discover in the West Desert, something they find out about themselves through the land. The experience is equivalent to "Eureka!" but it isn't something that can be shared, or discovered, in a tour group looking at a natural wonder.

Finally, perhaps, the old frontier will realize one of the possibilities that James Madison and developers of the nation envisioned in the early 1800s. The West will become the safety valve of the cities. The West Desert, raw and still untamed, with sparse vegetation and no services, offers peace and restoration of the soul. It is the last best place in the sense that it has no readily perceived value, other than its hardy existence. There is the danger that the West Desert could become a tin town of communities of old trailers strewn over the landscape. Folks without much often are attracted to the West Desert because it seems so much like them. But lack of available water, private land, and the basics of economic infrastructure probably will make it unlikely that those types of communities will form to exploit the solitude. It also probably will never become 20-acre ranchettes for snowbirds or summer swallows who would lock up the land for themselves. One of the safeguards of the West Desert against private exploitation is that it is largely public land. The private or state land that could be coerced for sale from the Utah Public Trust Lands Administration wouldn't be attractive to neo-squires who need more amenities when roughing it. Most private land, too, is in the hands of ranchers and miners. Protection of their livelihoods means protection of open space.

So, tourism in the West Desert likely won't make people of the West Desert rich. Ultimately, people of the West Desert will have to mine their greatest resource—themselves—if they want to maintain their communities into the next century. They are a rich resource. They are bright, tough, self-reliant, industrious, and ingenious. Their minds and their willingness to work are their most valuable resources. They also have a wealth of energy in their communities. If they can decide upon a common vision and overcome their sometimes sacrosanct independence, they should be able to devise ways to make it. A beehive of active intellects offering products of the mind over the information superhighway might turn out to be the final realization of the promise of the frontier and the West Desert.

The key is to think small. Community is more easily formed and managed when it is less complex, and especially when people willingly rub elbows. The irony with cities is that population density encourages the notion of gross mass not critical mass: mass media, mass marketing, mass corporatism. It's efficient for business but it's lousy for community. The richest resource of the West Desert is size. In the Great Basin and elsewhere, thinking small is a sustainable resource.

Selected Bibliography

Altman, I., & Ginat, J. (1996). *Polygamous families in contemporary society.* Cambridge: Cambridge University Press.

Bateman, R. R. (1984). *Deep Creek reflections: 125 years of settlement at Ibapah, Utah, 1859-1984.* Salt Lake City: Author.

Beeston, B. W. (1966). *Purified as gold and silver.* Idaho Falls, ID: Author.

Carter, T., & Fleischauer, C. (1988). *The Grouse Creek cultural survey.* Washington, DC: Library of Congress.

Coles, Robert. (1997). *Doing documentary work.* New York: Oxford University Press.

Collier, J., Jr., & Collier, M. (1986). *Visual anthropology: Photography as a research method.* Albuquerque: University of New Mexico Press.

Ferguson, D., & Ferguson, N. (1983). *Sacred cows at the public trough.* Bend, OR: Maverick Publications.

Fiero, B. (1986). *Geology of the Great Basin.* Reno: University of Nevada Press.

Griggs, J. (1974). *Let there be light: A rural electrification documentary.* Forest Grove, OR: Times Litho Print.

Gross, L., Katz, J. S., & Ruby, J. (Eds.). (1988). *Image ethics: The moral rights of subjects in photographs, film, and television.* New York: Oxford University Press.

Houghton, S. G. (1976). *A trace of desert waters: The Great Basin story.* Glendale, CA: Arthur H. Clark.

Johnson, E. C. (1975). *Walker River Paiutes: A tribal history.* Schurz, NV: Walker River Paiute Tribe.

Kemmis, D. (1990). *Community and the politics of place.* Norman: University of Oklahoma Press.

Larson, P. (1977). *The deserts of the Southwest.* San Francisco: Sierra Club Books.

Limerick, P. N. (1987). *The legacy of conquest: The unbroken past of the American West.* New York: W. W. Norton.

McPhee, J. (1981). *Basin and range.* New York: Farrar, Straus, Giroux.

Morgan, D. L. (1947). *The Great Salt Lake.* Albuquerque: University of New Mexico Press.

Rogers, G. F. (1982). *Then and now: A photographic history of vegetation change in the central Great Basin desert.* Salt Lake City: University of Utah Press.

Smith, H. N. (1950). *Virgin land: The American West as symbol and myth.* New York: Vintage Books.

Thompson, G. A. (1982). *Some dreams die: Utah's ghost towns and lost treasures.* Salt Lake City: Dream Garden Press.

Trimble, S. (1989). *The sagebrush ocean: A natural history of the Great Basin.* Reno: University of Nevada Press.

Vitvan. (1984). *The christos: Teachings for the new age.* Baker, NV: School of the Natural Order.

Water in the West: A collection of reprints. (1997). Paonia, CO: High Country News.

Wheat, M. (1967). *Survival arts of the primitive Paiutes.* Reno: University of Nevada Press.

White, R. (1991). *It's your misfortune and none of my own: A new history of the American West.* Norman: University of Oklahoma Press.

Wilkinson, C. F. (1992). *The eagle bird: Mapping a new West.* New York: Pantheon Books.

Index